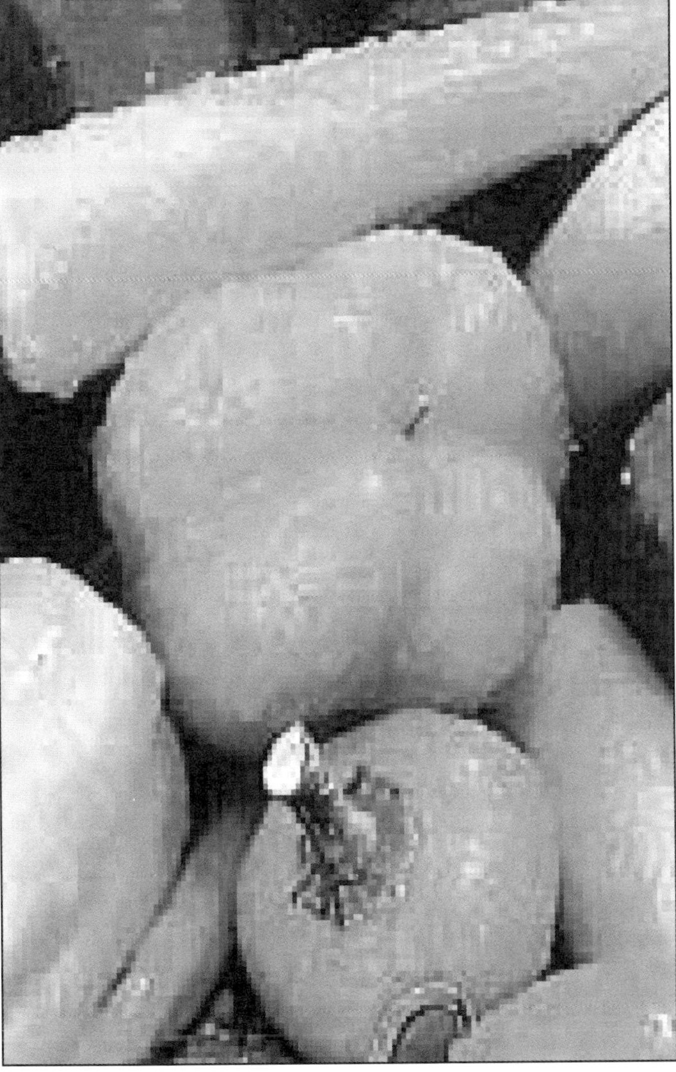

The Mittleider Gardening Course

By

Dr. Jacob R. Mittleider

Edited & Revised by James B. Kennard

Published by

Food For Everyone Foundation

(888) 548-4449 – www.growfood.com

We express gratitude for editing assistance for this edition by David & Sue Gillmore.

Contents

How to Use This Course

The purpose of *The Mittleider Gardening Course* is to help you take advantage of Dr. Jacob R. Mittleider's 55 years of gardening experience so you too can be a successful gardener—a *Garden Genius* in your own right. Dr. Mittleider strongly believes the best way to become an expert gardener is by *doing*. So this course is designed to help you do just that.

Here is the suggested way of using the four major parts of this course.

Part I: Introduction

Start by going through this section to get an overview of the Mittleider Method and to decide which type of Mittleider garden you would like to implement: soil-beds, grow-boxes, or both.

Part II: Soil-Bed Basics

Go through the lessons in this section if you decide you would like to use soil-beds.

Part III: Grow-Box Basics

Go through the lessons in this section if you decide you would like to use grow-boxes.

Part IV: Mittleider Advanced Topics

Refer to these lessons, as needed, to learn more about advanced gardening topics.

NOTE: Some of the information in the *Soil-Bed Basics* lessons will be the same as that found in *Grow-Box Basics*. So if you decide to go through both sets of lessons, you can skip topics you are already familiar with.

How to Get the Most Out of Each Lesson

The most productive way to go through these lessons is to ***plan your own garden*** as you proceed. If this is not practical or possible, then use these lessons to plan a hypothetical garden.

Remember, your mind will be most "fertile" for learning and remembering when you actually need to use the information you are learning about.

Follow these steps as you go through each lesson:

Step 1: Think About Each Question

What do I already know?
What did I just learn?

The topics in each lesson are organized as a set of commonly asked questions. The first time you read each question, ask yourself: "What do I think the answer to this question will be?" Then read the information provided and ask: "Did this section teach me something I didn't already know?" Jot down any "ahas" in the margins provided or put an asterisk next to significant information that is new to you.

Step 2: Notice the Tips

Notice the special tips provided in the lessons and put an asterisk next to ones you want to make sure and use as you plan and create your garden.

Step 3: Refer to the Reference Tables to Make Decisions

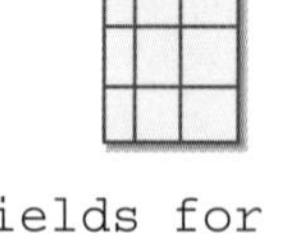

Yields for Common Garden Crops

As you go through the lessons, watch for the reference table icon in the margins. These icons will remind you that additional information is available in *Appendix C* to help you make informed decisions about planning your garden. Refer to these tables, as needed, to make your gardening decisions.

Step 4: Consider Related Topics

Glance at the *Learn More* headings and topics that appear in the margins. Consider whether or not any of these advanced topics might be useful to learn more about. Mark the ones you want to look up. Some *Learn More* references will refer you to other parts or lessons in this gardening course. These references are shown in ***bold type***. Other references will suggest you look at additional information provided in other books written by Dr. Mittleider. These other reference book titles are *underlined*. Refer to *Appendix E* to learn more about Dr. Mittleider's other books and how to order them.

Learn More

- Soil-Beds vs. Grow-boxes
  *See **Part I : Introduction***
- Dr. Jacob R. Mittleider
  Food for Everyone

Step 5: Complete the Garden Genius Activities

Whenever you see the *Garden Genius* heading and icon in the margin, you will be given a suggestion for implementing what you have just learned. The Garden Genius activities will help you complete actual tasks for planning or preparing for your garden. Use the forms provided in *Appendix A: Soil-Bed Garden Genius Planning Forms* or *Appendix B: Grow-Box Garden Genius Planning Forms* to complete these activities.

Garden Genius

Part I: Introduction

What is the Mittleider Method?

The Mittleider Method combines the best features of soil gardening and hydroponic* gardening, but without hydroponic expense! It's a complete, easy-to-follow plan that eliminates guesswork and ensures success anywhere—an apartment patio, a city yard, a country lot, a farm.

The method is based on maximum utilization of space, time, and resources. Crops are large because plants are close together, nourished by supplemental feedings of natural mineral nutrients (as in hydroponics), but with no special equipment.

Also, unlike hydroponics, the Mittleider Method gives plants access to the natural soil for nutrients as yet unknown or that, while not essential to plant growth, are useful in human nutrition. You can use the Mittleider Method by raising crops in either soil-beds or grow-boxes.

* hydroponics: A method of growing plants in which the roots are suspended in nutrient-laden liquid. It requires very expensive buildings and equipment.

Why use this method?

The Mittleider Method has proven to be an effective, easy-to-use way of improving garden productivity in over 40 different countries. Here's what people around the world are saying about the Mittleider Method…

"In the middle of Monument Valley's desert area, lush vegetation is flourishing. Dr. Jacob Mittleider, an expert on gardening. . . has shown that food can be produced in the world's worst soils."

Marsha Keele, Monument Valley, Utah

"Everyone in the Agriculture Department has been amazed at the results obtained. I didn't think we could do it, but you have shown that it could be done in this country."

Bob Ackeroid, Papua, New Guinea

"Dr. Mittleider has demonstrated that despite extremely unfavorable soil conditions, an abundance of vegetable crops can be produced by using his procedures. And this method has given hope to discouraged farmers throughout the Island."

General James P. Lampert, Okinawa, Japan

"I came prepared to be critical as we are often inundated with programs that are neither practical nor sound. I left completely converted by the simplicity and soundness of the system and results."

C.D. Promnitz, Zimbabwe, Africa

". . . his garden looks like a work of art. The neighboring collective farm field is full of weeds, but here where the land is the same, you won't see a single weed."

IZVESTYIA (newspaper), Moscow, Russia

Who developed this method?

Dr. Jacob R. Mittleider

Dr. Jacob R. Mittleider, world-renowned international agricultural consultant, developed this method of gardening while conducting family garden-size agricultural training and program development in 27 different countries. The Mittleider Method is based on 55 years of study and gardening experience.

After 20 years of growing flowers and vegetables commercially, Dr. Mittleider embarked on a program of sharing his expertise with gardeners and would-be gardeners around the world. In 1964 he was asked by Loma Linda University in California to take an extended trip to study the diets of the people in developing countries. He traveled through the Middle East, Africa, India, Australia, Southeast Asia, and the South Pacific.

He found that the diseases, insects, and nutritional deficiencies were similar in all countries visited and that the agricultural problems closely resembled those in the United States. He concluded that the solution to their food problems simply required carrying out the recommendations of experts in plant nutrition and following scientific agricultural practices.

Thus he developed the Mittleider Method of gardening—an easy-to-use method that allows gardeners to raise an abundance of vegetables and other crops on almost any soil, in practically any season, in almost any climate, and virtually at any elevation.

Dr. Mittleider has authored numerous books as well as audio tapes and videos on gardening. To see descriptions of Dr. Mittleider's other books, refer to *Appendix E*.

How is this method different?

Here are some differences between traditional gardening methods and Mittleider Gardening Methods.

	Traditional Method	Mittleider Method
Overall	High yields are hard to get. Each of the gardening tasks require so much skill and understanding that few beginners can raise a productive garden.	With step by step instructions - like a recipe - even beginners can raise highly-productive gardens.
The Gardener	To grow a garden, the gardener must have skill, experience, good soil, the cooperation of nature and a green thumb.	Following this success recipe anyone can grow any vegetable in any soil, in any climate with minimal water and effort per unit of produce.
The Soil	A good garden begins with good soil. The richness of the soil is the single most important factor in gardening success.	Although good soils are desirable, highly productive gardens can be grown in any soil. Custom soils for grow-boxes can be made if necessary with minimal cost.
Garden Layout	Organize the garden using regularly spaced rows designed to accommodate the wheel spacings of a tractor.	Organize the garden using soil-beds or grow-boxes, using row and aisle spacings based on most efficient use of resources.
Plant Spacing	Use traditional spacings between plants to accommodate the horizontal growth plants use to seek the light.	Use narrower spacings and increase accuracy with special markers. Train plants to grow vertically for maximum light and to conserve water, nutrients, and space.
The Seed	Plant in the spring when the soil is warm. Because germination is always imperfect, expect some losses and weak plants.	Get a head start by planting earlier in a Mittleider seed house. Increase the head start by transplanting only strong and healthy plants.

	Traditional Method	Mittleider Method
Feeding Plants	Use soil testing to determine which nutrients are needed.	Only the plant can tell you what nutrients it needs. Many nutrients found in the soil are unavailable to the plant.
	Use manure, rotation, and composting to condition and build up the soil.	Although soil conditioning is good, accurate placement of properly balanced mineral fertilizers is more efficient.
	Use traditional fertilizers in their traditional Nitrogen-Phosphorus-Potassium combinations.	Most commercial fertilizers must be properly balanced, adding all of the secondary and micro-nutrients for complete balanced nutrition.
	To reduce expense, apply as little commercial fertilizer as possible.	Apply fertilizer before you plant and several times thereafter.
Watering	Use furrows, sprinklers, and flood irrigation to thoroughly water the land. To distribute the water evenly is very difficult.	Irrigate only the root zones to conserve water and control weeds. If you level the soil water and nutrients will be distributed easily and evenly.
Weeding	Because weed seeds are everywhere, laborious weeding is a necessary evil which cannot be avoided.	Weed control can be easy. Plant promptly after soil preparation. Sprout surface weeds and cut them off as they emerge. Don't water aisles.
Pruning	Pruning is something done to fruit trees, but it is never done to vegetables.	Careful pruning of certain plants can dramatically increase yields. Raise yields by removing leaves that do not support the plant or its fruit.
	Let vine crops like tomatoes, squash, and melons grow horizontally, often occupying 10-30 square feet.	Garden in 3-D! Use stakes, strings, and T-frames to grow plants upward instead of outward, thus conserving space.
Harvesting	Harvest one crop per year.	Harvest two or three crops

	Traditional Method	Mittleider Method
	At the end of the season, plow the old crop under to decompose and build up the soil during the winter.	per year. Increase yields by using seedlings, balanced fertilizers, precision watering, and pruning.
Crop Rotation	Each crop depletes the land. Rotate crops regularly to restore and rebuild the land.	Crop rotation is good, but the use of balanced natural mineral fertilizer is a faster and more. efficient way to replenish the soil. .
Summary	A vast body of traditional knowledge, practices, and prescriptions which beginning gardeners often find daunting.	A RECIPE of time-tested procedures which any gardener can use to grow any vegetable, in any soil, in any climate, with a minimum of water and work.

Is the Mittleider Method for me?

Ask yourself the following questions to decide if the Mittleider Method is for you.

Do I want to:

- produce a large quantity of food in a small area of land?
- minimize gardening time and effort?
- garden with only simple gardening tools (so I won't need to invest in expensive equipment)?
- conserve water?
- achieve uniform plant growth and raise healthy, attractive plants?
- minimize weeding time?
- make sure my plants are getting the nutrients they need for optimum growth (no matter what my soil is like)?
- harvest two or three crops each year?
- grow any vegetable, in any climate, with minimal water and effort per unit of produce?

If you answered "Yes" to any of these questions, the Mittleider Method is for you.

Should I use soil-beds or grow-boxes?

When planning a Mittleider Garden, you must first decide if you want to use soil-beds or grow-boxes.

Soil-Beds (sometimes called grow-beds) are narrow strips of ground prepared for high-yield vegetable production. Soil-beds are usually 18 inches wide and up to 30 feet long. Their length can vary depending on the size of your garden. The width of the soil-beds should always be 18 inches.

Grow-Boxes are bottomless frames used to enclose small plots of soil. They are usually made of wood and are leveled in place. Grow-boxes can be any length or width, but most people use either "mini" grow-boxes, 18 inches wide, or "standard" grow-boxes 4 feet wide.

Grow-Boxes are filled with inexpensive"custom-made soil," a mixture of sawdust and sand, or other inert and organic materials together with a supply of balanced fertilizers. The custom-made soil in the grow-box frame is used year after year. It is never changed nor discarded.

Both options, soil-beds and grow-boxes, will yield very successful results using the Mittleider Method. You can choose to use either or both methods in your garden.

Here are the relative advantages of each method:

Advantages of Soil-Beds

- Require less up-front work.

- Mean less initial expense.

- Are easier for beginners.

- Can use any kind of soil, with no soil amendments.

Advantages of Grow-Boxes

- Can be built almost anywhere.

- Keep the hard subsoil damp and soft, allowing roots to penetrate subsoil.

- Are not dependent on condition of local soils (less need to know about nutrient deficiencies or methods for improving problem soils).

- Provide perfect drainage and aeration for roots and balanced feeding of plants.

- Extend the growing season, since inexpensive custom-made soils warm up quickly in springtime, boosting growth.

- Act as a temperature regulator, since custom-made soils keep roots cool in the summer.

- Take up less space than regular soil - 1 1/2" boards vs 6" ridges.

- Greatly reduce or eliminate weeds.

Part II: Soil-Bed Basics

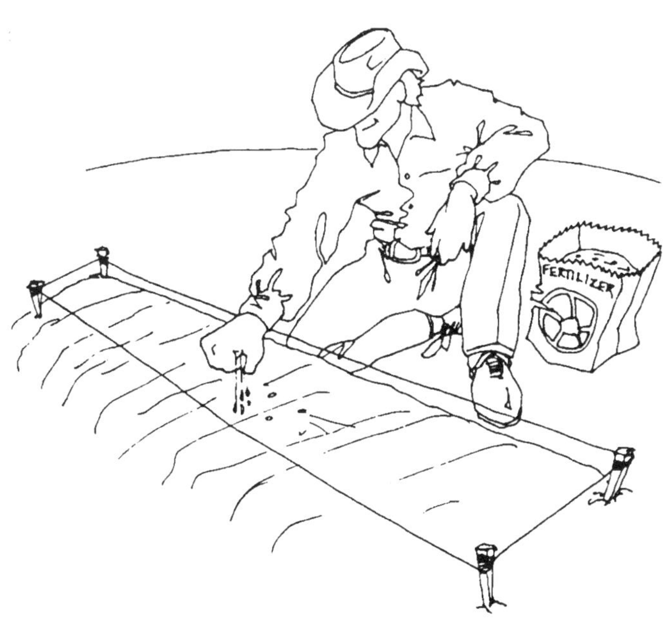

Lesson 1: Planning

In this lesson, you will learn how to answer these questions:

Where should I locate my garden?
What size should I make my soil-beds?
How should I arrange my soil-beds?
What should I plant?
When should I plant?
What tools will I need?
How much time will it take?

Where should I locate my garden?

- Choose a sunny location that gets 6-8 hours of sunshine from mid-morning throughout the afternoon (first law of plant growth).
- Choose a level area. If you choose an area that is reasonably level, there will be less work. An area with a slight southern slope is ideal.
- Plant on the contour if using steeper slopes. Just level the soil-beds themselves.
- Avoid slopes facing north, because they have more shadows, diffuse the sun's rays, and are often too cold.
- Stay away from low spots where drainage is poor. Plants die for lack of oxygen where standing water accumulates.
- Avoid large trees and tall hedges, unless they are north of the grow-bed area. Crops growing in shade do poorly. Tree roots also compete for water and food.
- Make sure water is available close by.

Learn More

- Terracing Soil-Beds
  6 Steps to Successful Gardening (p. 19)
- The Erosion Problem
  Food for Everyone (p. 122)

- Avoid open areas where strong winds blow, or else build windbreaks. Winds can quickly destroy the fragile, but very important plant leaves, reducing your crop yield.

- Protect the area from animals or unwanted visitors. If necessary, construct a chain-link fence 6' to 8' tall.

Garden Genius

On the *Garden Plot Plan* found in *Appendix A: Soil-Bed Garden Genius Planning Forms,* briefly describe where you plan to locate your garden. Does your location meet the criteria listed above?

What size should I make my soil-beds?

The standard size soil-bed used throughout this book is 30-feet long. Each bed holds two rows of plants at the base of two ridges of soil. The ridges are 18 inches apart. Aisles between beds are 3 1/2 feet with 5 feet at the ends of the soil-beds.

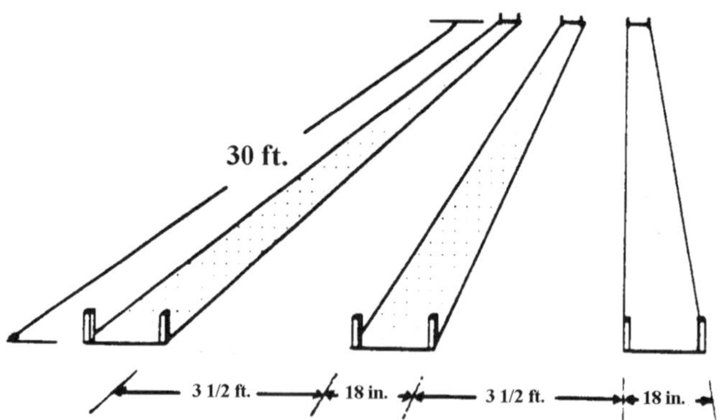

Why 30 feet long?

Since many gardens can readily accommodate 30-foot soil beds, the specific measurements for applying the optimum amount of fertilizer throughout this book are based on this length.

> Tip For smaller gardens, adjust your soil-beds to any length that works for you; then adjust the fertilizer measurements in like manner.

Why 18 inches wide with ridges?

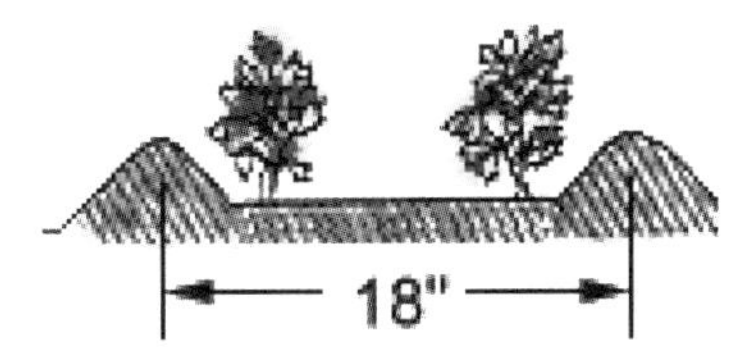

A 12" wide flat area between the ridges allows growing space between the two rows of plants.

The ridges help you to determine where the seedlings or seeds are to be placed (to be explained in Soil-Bed Basics/ *Lesson 3: Planting*).

The flattened center area is designed to carry water and fertilizer to the plant (to be explained in Soil-Bed Basics/ *Lesson 4: Watering* and *Lesson 5: Fertilizing*).

The ridges take the chore out of controlling weeds (to be explained in Soil-Bed Basics/*Lesson 6: Weeding*).

Why such wide spacing—18-inch beds, 3½-foot aisles, and 5-foot end spaces?

"Conventional" gardening places one row of plants every 30 inches—thus two rows of plants take 5 feet. Dr. Mittleider puts the two rows of plants closer together to reduce watering, feeding, and weeding by 50%.

If the space in the aisles between beds is restricted, the result will be poor inspection of the crops. This sets the stage for problems with weed control, adequate watering, disease and insect problems, harvesting on time, etc.

With adequate space, leaves and vines have sufficient room to spread in the aisles for maximum light, essential for best growth.

Wide aisles also prevent foot traffic from damaging plants.

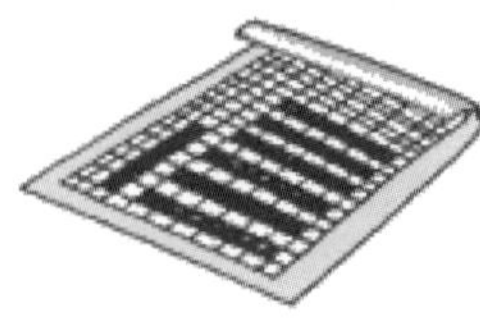

How should I arrange my soil-beds?

Plan in advance the number and placement of your soil-beds by creating a "blueprint" of your garden area.

Facing soil-beds any direction will work. Just plant tall plants to the north or east of short plants.

To create a garden plot plan or "blueprint," first show the outer dimensions of your garden on a grid.

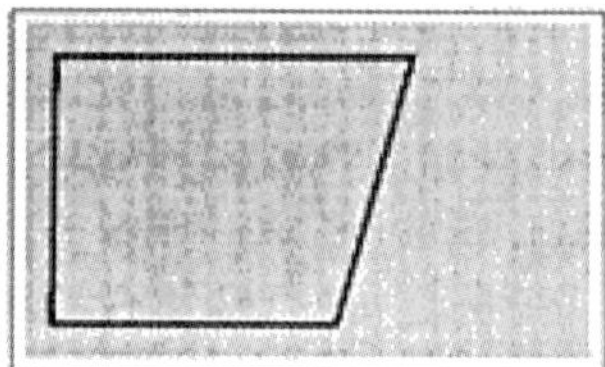

Second, show where you plan to place the soil-beds.

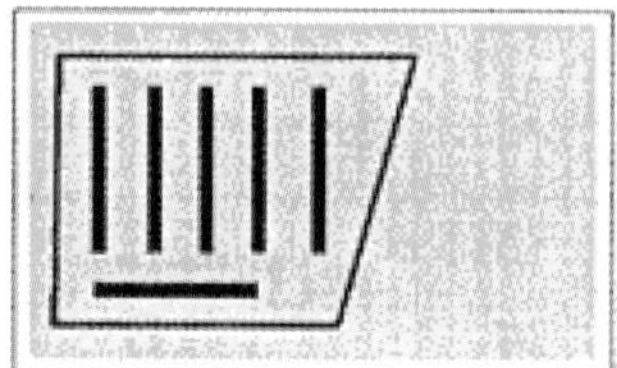

> Tip Remember, if you cannot create soil-beds 30-feet long, create them in simple divisions of 30 feet—1/2 (15 feet) or 1/3 (10 feet). Doing so will help you be more accurate when planting seeds or transplants and applying fertilizer.

Garden Genius

Create a "garden blueprint" for your garden, by following the directions on the *Garden Plot Plan* found in *Appendix A: Soil-Bed Garden Genius Planning Forms.*

What should I plant?

To decide what and how much you should plant ask yourself:

- What will my family eat?
- How much will my family eat?
- How much can I comfortably care for?

Plant only what your family will eat and what you can care for. Here is Dr. Mittleider's suggested garden for a family of four to live on, consisting of only .044 acre.

Sample Garden Plan

What to Plant	How Many Plants	Yield
1 bed potatoes	92 plants	145 pounds
1 bed beans (bush)	180 plants	68 pounds
1 bed peas (bush)	362 plants	90 pounds
½ bed broccoli	26 plants	14 pounds
½ bed cauliflower	26 plants	75 pounds
½ bed lettuce (head)	26 plants	56 pounds
½ bed cabbage	26 plants	70 pounds
1 bed sweet corn	92 plants	92 ears
1 bed zucchini	20 plants	120 pounds
1 bed banana squash	20 plants	120 pounds
1 bed cantaloupes	26 plants	182 pounds
1 bed watermelons	20 plants	182 pounds
1 bed tomatoes	26 plants	156 pounds

Learn MOre

- Growing Crops Vertically
  See ***Lesson 15: Caring for Climbing Plants***
  Let's Grow Tomatoes
  (pp. 64-69)
- Soil-Bed Yields & Costs
  Grow-Bed Gardening
  (pp. 15-18)
- Growing Tomatoes
  Let's Grow Tomatoes
  (p. 122)
- *Garden Planting Details*
  (Appendix C)

Here's what can be planted later in the fall for a second harvest.

What to Plant	How Many Plants	Yield
1 bed potatoes	92 plants	145 pounds
1 bed beans (bush)	180 plants	68 pounds
1 bed peas (bush)	362 plants	90 pounds
½ bed broccoli	26 plants	14 pounds
½ bed cauliflower	26 plants	75 pounds
½ bed lettuce (head)	26 plants	56 pounds
½ bed cabbage	26 plants	70 pounds
1 bed sweet corn	92 plants	92 ears

To harvest two crops with the assortment of foods listed above in one season, it is important to transplant well-grown potted plants in the beds. Lesson 22 will teach you how.

Yields for Common Garden Crops

To help plan your garden, refer to *Yields for Common Garden Crops and the Garden Planting Details* found in *Appendix C:* This table will help you decide what and how much to plant in your garden to meet your family's needs.

As you decide what you will plant, you may need to modify how you arrange your soil-beds in your garden plot plan.

> Tip Place short plants south or west of tall varieties. In this way, the shadows from tall plants will not interfere with the light needed by short plants.

When should I plant?

Because temperature is the second law of plant growth, the proper time to plant partly depends on the climate and the growing season where you grow your garden.

The ***growing season*** usually refers to the days between the last frost in the spring (ADLF) and the first frost in the fall (ADFF) These dates give you a general idea as to when certain crops can be planted in your area and what types of crops to plant.

To help you determine when to plant your garden, find out the ***average day of last frost*** for your area.

> Tip If you do not know the average day of last frost for your area, call your state agricultural extension agent to find out what it is, or look for it on-line.

Plant hardiness also partly determines when to plant.

Hardy plants tolerate frost and cold and can be planted 3 to 6 weeks before the average date of last frost.

Moderately-hardy plants handle a certain amount of cold. Plant these 2-3 weeks before the average date of last frost.

Cold- and frost-sensitive plants don't like cold or frost. Plant them on the average day of last frost and protect them against late frost.

Frost-intolerant plants will not survive any frost and must be planted 2-3 weeks after the average day of last frost.

To see a table showing examples of each of these types of plants, refer to *Plant Hardiness and Planting Times* and *the Garden Planting Details in Appendix C: Reference Tables for Planning Your Garden.*

Learn More

- Extending Growing Seasons
  See ***Lesson 22: Seedling Production***
- Building an Inexpensive Seedling Greenhouse
  See ***Appendix D: Building a Seedhouse***
- Cold-Weather Gardening
  See ***Lesson 23: Cold Weather Gardening***
- Grow-Box Gardening
  See ***Part III: Grow Box Basics***
  Mittleider Grow Box Gardens

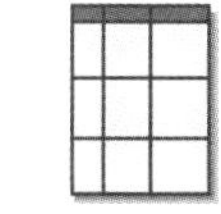

Plant Hardiness and Planting Times

Garden
Genius

Use the *Planting Plan* found in *Appendix A: Soil-Bed Garden Genius Planning Forms* to record when you plan to plant each of your crops. Refer to *Plant Hardiness and Planting Times* in *Appendix C* to make your decisions.

What tools will I need?

You will need the following tools for your soil-bed garden:

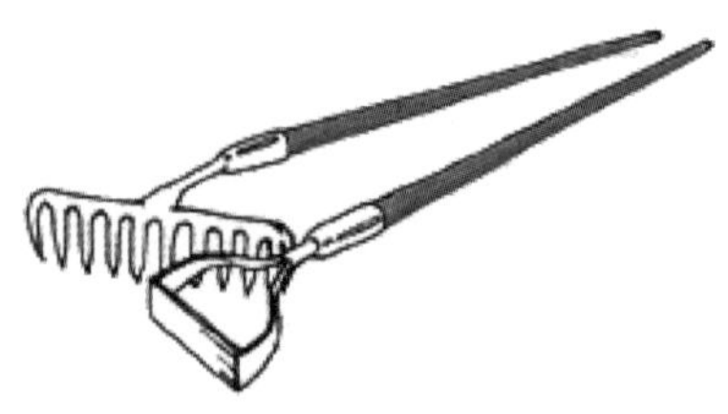

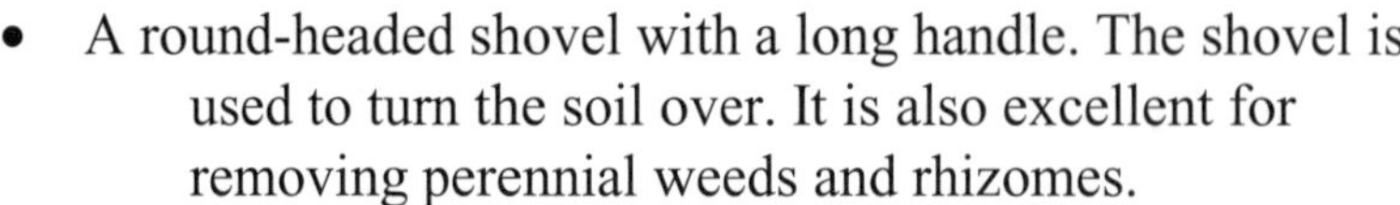

- A round-headed shovel with a long handle. The shovel is used to turn the soil over. It is also excellent for removing perennial weeds and rhizomes.

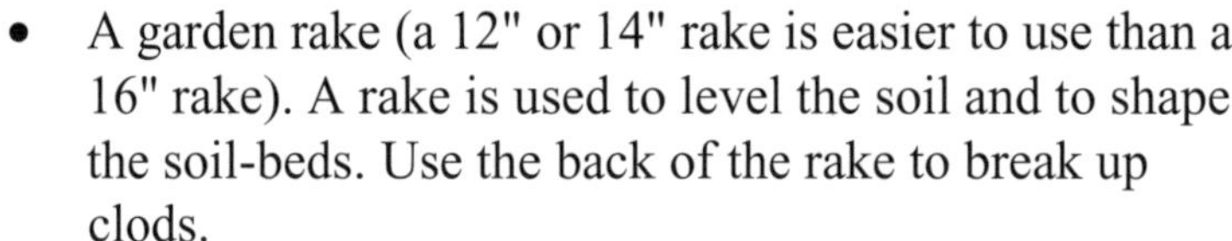

- A garden rake (a 12" or 14" rake is easier to use than a 16" rake). A rake is used to level the soil and to shape the soil-beds. Use the back of the rake to break up clods.

- A straight-blade hoe (also called a scuffle-hoe or two-way hoe) not a curved chopping hoe. Use the 2-way hoe just under the soil surface to remove annual weeds by cutting off below the crowns.

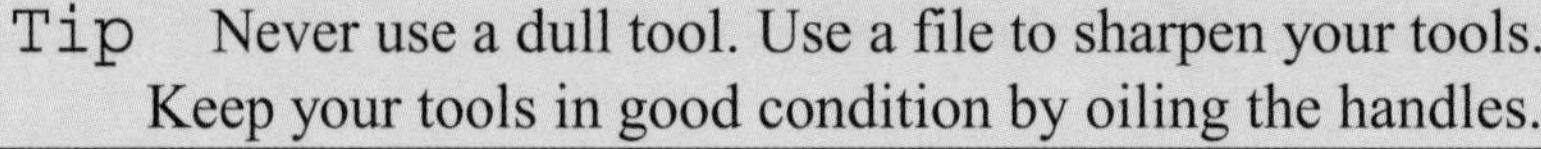

Tip Never use a dull tool. Use a file to sharpen your tools. Keep your tools in good condition by oiling the handles.

- Two five-gallon buckets for fertilizer compounds.

- A garden hose with the end securely wrapped ***several times*** with an18-inch towel extended past the end of the hose. Do not tie the end of the extended cloth. Leave it open.

- The towel around the hose will prevent the water from digging a hole in the soil, and it allows you to turn the water on full volume to water your garden rapidly.

- Home-made fertilizing tool for distributing fertilizer to plants growing in the soil-beds. With this tool, you won't have to bend down or strain your back, and you can quickly fertilize as you walk along the soil-beds.

To make this tool, nail an empty 16-ounce can (open at one end) to the top end of a 1" x 2" x 6' (or longer) strip of wood.

The wood handle will be horizontal to the ground. The can will be perpendicular to the handle with the open end facing the sky.

- You should also use markers to provide proper spacing for plants. Different markers are used for different purposes:

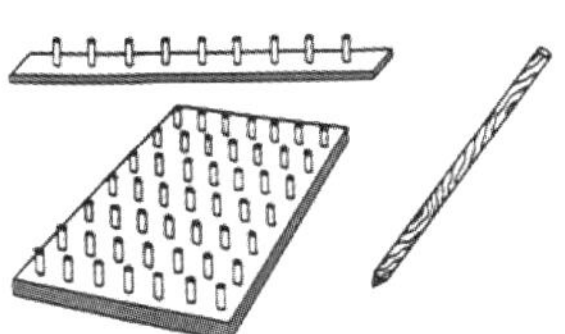

  To mark seed flats
  To press holes uniformly deep
  To space plants in soil-beds or grow-boxes

Here is a summary of the tools you will need for your soil-bed garden. Refer to the *Tools and Materials List* found in *Appendix A: Soil-Bed Garden Genius Planning Forms* to record which tools you will need to get.

- Round-headed shovel
- 12"/ or 14" garden rake
- Straight-edged hoe (two-way hoe)
- Two two-gallon buckets
- Garden hose
- 18" cloth for end of hose
- Home-made fertilizing tool

(You will learn more about markers and how to make them on pages 37 and 38.)

How much time will it take?

The amount of time and work required to build and maintain your Mittleider garden varies according to the size of your project, the condition of the land to be cleared and prepared, and on how you obtain your seedling plants. If you grow your own seedling plants, additional work is involved. (On the other hand, you will save on the cost of buying the seedlings from a nursery AND have them when you want them).

A good sized soil-bed garden to feed a family of 4 consists of a 60' X 40' area, divided into 11 soil-beds 18" wide by 30' long, with 3 1/2' aisles between beds and 5' perimeter aisles.

Learn More

- Home Seedling Production
  See ***Lesson 22: Seedling Production***
- Building an Inexpensive Seedling Greenhouse
  See ***Appendix D: Building a Seedhouse***

The following time estimates are based on a soil-bed garden as described above. Because growing conditions vary widely, these are only approximations.

- To clear your gardening area, construct soil-beds, and make aisles and footpaths, plan on 8 to 16 hours of labor
- To prepare the soil, plant seeds, and transplant seedlings, plan on another 12 to 16 hours.
- To water, feed, inspect, and care for your plants after you have planted them, you should plan to spend 30 minutes per day (preferably in the early morning).
- To harvest your crop may require an additional 1 to 5 minutes per soil-bed, depending on the type of vegetable and the amount to be harvested.

To anticipate your garden work and when it needs to be done, it is helpful to create a ***Gardening Cycle Calendar***—a month-to-month to-do list that reminds you of crucial gardening tasks. Here is an example of a gardening cycle calendar created by Dr. Mittleider for temperate zone 7.

Dr. Mittleider's Gardening Cycle Calendar

Month	Tasks
January	• Plan garden. Will I use soil-beds or grow-boxes? What tools will I need? Where will I locate my garden? • Decide what to plant. What will be started from seed? What will be transplanted? Calculate plant spacing requirements.
February or March	• Plant tomato and pepper seeds in flats indoors or in a seed house or cold frame. Calculate the timing so plants will be 8 to 12 weeks old by the time I set them outdoors.
March	• In the seed house or cold frame, transplant seedling plants (tomatoes and peppers) into larger-size containers to give them more growing room. • In the seed house or cold frame, start cabbage, cauliflower, and broccoli from seed.
April	• When weather permits, plant peas, radishes, and green onions outside. Provide protection from freezing temperatures at night.
May	• Transplant seedling tomatoes, peppers, cabbage, cauliflower, and broccoli. • Plant melons, cucumbers, squash, eggplant, beans, and corn.
June-July	• Care for growing plants. (30 min./day)
July-August	• Harvest first crops. • Start a second planting for second crop.

* This timetable is a typical example of the gardening cycle in Dr. Mittleider's home in Salt Lake City, Utah.

Refer to the *Gardening Cycle Calendar* found in *Appendix A: Soil-Bed Garden Genius Planning Forms* to create your own month-by-month gardening to-do list. You may wish to refer to your *Planting Plan* to note when you need to plant specific crops.

Garden Genius

Lesson 2: Preparing

In this lesson, you will learn how to answer these questions:

How do I prepare my garden?
What about the soil?
How do I construct soil-beds?
How do I level soil-beds?
How do I get soil-beds ready for planting?

How do I prepare my garden?

Clear the Area

- Make your garden beautiful. A clean, neat, and orderly garden is pleasing to the eye, more productive, and has fewer weeds and pests.

- Clear the area by removing all undergrowth and brush, all living and dead shrubs, roots, and top-growth. Remove everything that will interfere with gardening such as trees, stumps, and trash.

Eliminate Weeds

There are two types of weeds: annuals and perennials.

- ***Annuals*** sprout from seed every year. These can be removed with an appropriate tool, or by using a roto-tiller or a tractor to plow them under.

- ***Perennial*** plants keep growing for several years. You must dig perennials up, roots and all, destroying the rhizomes (underground stems) and runners. If perennials are not removed, they will be a continual nuisance throughout the garden, all through the year.

Break up the Soil

The soil should be broken up to a depth of 8 to 10 inches in the bed area and 2-3" in the aisle area (Doing so at this time will speed up the actual shaping of the soil-beds later.)

What about the soil?

Learn More

- Settling the Weed Problem
  See **Lesson 6: Weeding**
  Food For Everyone
  (pp. 313-320)
- Common Soil Problems and Remedies
  See **Lesson 19: Problem Soils**
  6 Steps to Successful Gardening
  (pp. 7-10)
- Soil pH
  See **Lesson 19: Problem Soils**
  Food For Everyone
  (pp. 132-136)
- Testing the Soil
  Food For Everyone
  (pp. 137-141)

Soils are made mostly of basic inorganic elements that include mineral combinations such as potassium, phosphorus, calcium, iron, manganese, magnesium, etc.

Soil serves these five essential functions.

- Provides anchorage and protection for plant roots.
- Holds air and water for plant use (plant growth laws 3 & 4).
- Includes minerals which plants need for food. Soil also holds and stores additional minerals that may need to be applied to it (fifth law of plant growth).
- Acts as a temperature regulator in hot weather (PG law #2).
- Soil affords drainage for plant roots. If soil is too hard and compact, it will not drain (#3 law of plant growth).

Crops fail when one or more of these five essential functions is missing.

Using the recommended Mittleider fertilizing strategy (See Soil-Bed Basics/*Lesson 5: Fertilizing),* will ensure your plants receive adequate minerals that may be lacking or unavailable to plants in your soil.

How do I construct soil-beds?

Step 1: Refer to Your Plan

Refer to your *Garden Plot Plan* to determine where to place your soil-beds.

Step 2: Stake Out Beds

Plot out each soil-bed by placing stakes at each of the four corners (18” by 30’). Tie and stretch string to the stakes to show the placement of the two 30-foot ridges of the soil-bed.

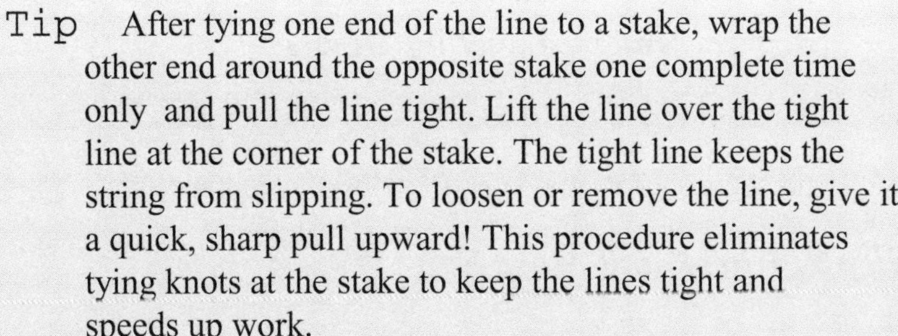

Tip After tying one end of the line to a stake, wrap the other end around the opposite stake one complete time only and pull the line tight. Lift the line over the tight line at the corner of the stake. The tight line keeps the string from slipping. To loosen or remove the line, give it a quick, sharp pull upward! This procedure eliminates tying knots at the stake to keep the lines tight and speeds up work.

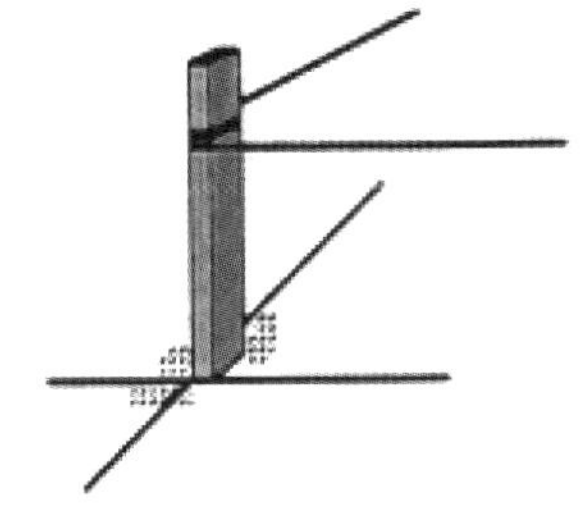

Step 3: Raise the Beds

With a garden rake, pull about 2" of soil from the aisles into the staked-out area. (This will make the soil-beds about 5" higher than the aisles.)

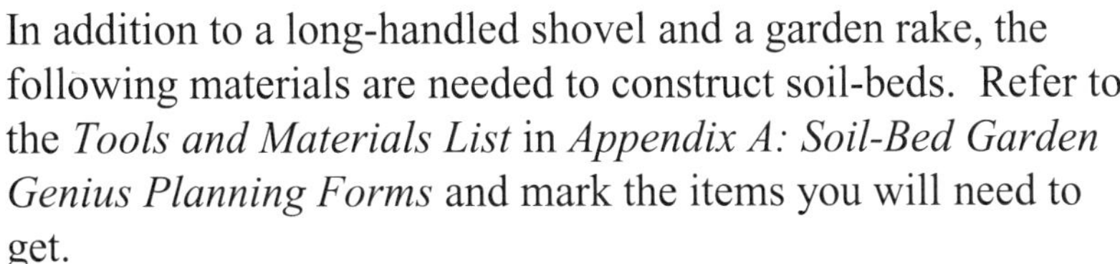

In addition to a long-handled shovel and a garden rake, the following materials are needed to construct soil-beds. Refer to the *Tools and Materials List* in *Appendix A: Soil-Bed Garden Genius Planning Forms* and mark the items you will need to get.

Garden Genius

Tools and materials needed to construct soil-beds:

- 1"x 2" stakes (wooden or metal) 18 inches long, with one end pointed (4 stakes per soil-bed)
- Nylon string or Mason line
- One 2-pound hammer
- Pick-ax for hard soils

How do I level soil-beds?

Leveling is essential, as it facilitates the movement of the water and even distribution of nutrients when irrigating, and makes the process easy and more efficient. A little time spent leveling will save more time later. Here's how to do it.

Step 1: Make a Leveling Device

Lay a straight 8-to-10 foot 2x4 (or 2x3) on edge

and securely fasten a spirit-level to the center of it.

Step 2: Check and Move Soil

Starting at one end of the soil-bed, use the level to check the level of the ground. Move the soil from the high end to the low end so that you create a level area from one end of the soil-bed to the other. Make sure the soil-beds are level with a drop of only 1" in 30', for water to move freely. It is not necessary to level the aisles.

Learn More

~~Terracing~~ Soil-beds *6 Steps to Successful Gardening* (p. 19)

The Erosion Problem Food For Everyone (p. 122)

Step 3: Loosen and Break Up Soil

Moving the soil in this leveling process is a good time to loosen it and break up any clods that were not broken up during the initial ground-preparation stage.

Tip Prepare the soil-beds only as you are ready to plant them. This will give plants an even chance with the weeds.

How do I get soil-beds ready for planting?

Once your soil-beds are formed and leveled, they are ready for the final planting preparations. Here's what you do next.

Step 1: Apply Fertilizers

To each 30' soil-bed, evenly spread **2 pounds** of the Pre-Plant Fertilizer (1 ounce per linear foot for shorter beds) plus **1 pound** of the Weekly-Feed Fertilizer (1/2 oz/foot). You will learn how *to make these fertilizers in Soil-Bed Basics/Lesson5: Fertilizing.*

Step 2: Mix Fertilizers with Soil

Mix the fertilizers and soil together to a depth of 8 to 10 inches with a shovel or tiller. Make sure to keep the beds level.

Step 3: Ridge the Soil-beds

This is one of the most important steps. With the rake tines facing down, pull 2" of soil from the center of the soil-bed to the strings creating a ridge on each side, 4" high on the inside and 6" higher than the aisles.

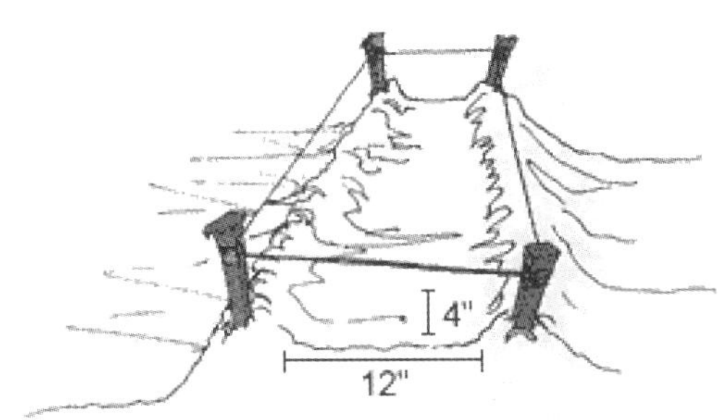

Step 5: Flatten the Center

Next, flatten and re-level the center of the soil-bed, creating an area about 12 inches wide. Make sure it is flat (not rounded). This is where the water will flow during irrigation.

Your soil-bed is now ready for planting!

Lesson 3: Planting

In this lesson, you will learn how to answer these questions:

Should I plant seeds or seedlings?
How should I space my plants?
Can I grow crops vertically
How do I make a marker?
How do I plant seeds in soil-beds?
How do I transplant seedlings?

Should I plant seeds or seedlings?

There are advantages to growing plants from seed ahead of the normal planting season and transplanting them as seedlings in your garden.

Many soils harbor insects and diseases. These frequently kill seeds just as they are sprouting or pushing through toward the light.

Cold soils delay germination. Prolonged germination and retarded growth have a permanent adverse effect on plant growth and yield.

The second law of plant growth requires temperatures between 70 and 85 degrees Fahrenheit for best seed germination, and between 60 and 90 degrees for plants to grow well in the garden.

Healthy seedlings, grown in a protected environment, have the advantage of fast germination and a well-developed root system. When transplanted in the garden, they are better able to resist any antagonistic forces. Thus, yields are better and the crops mature earlier. This lengthens the growing and harvesting period and makes it possible to raise two crops of some vegetable types in the same soil-bed during one growing season.

Learn More

- Home Seedling Production
See ***Lesson 22: Seedling Production***

- Building an Inexpensive Seedling Greenhouse
See ***Appendix D: Building a Seedhouse***

- Importance of the Greenhouse in Disease and Insect Control
See ***Lesson 21: Common Plant Diseases***
Food For Everyone
(pp. 487-540)

In summary, plants transplanted in the garden from seedlings

- are stronger and more vigorous.
- mature earlier.
- produce more uniform and larger yields.
- cut costs on weed and insect control.

You can purchase seedling plants at nurseries or you can grow them yourself in your own inexpensive greenhouse. Most retail nursery stock is not fed and so is nutrient deprived when you buy it. Growing your own assures a healthy beginning.

Dr. Mittleider grows most crops first in the seed house and then transplants to the garden. However, he seeds certain crops directly into the soil.

Transplanting/ Planting Guide

Refer to the *Transplanting/Planting Guide* or Garden Planting Details in Appendix C to learn which plants respond well to transplanting and which are best planted directly from seed.

Use the *Planting Guide* found in *Appendix A* to indicate which of your crops you will plant from seedlings and which you will plant from seed. Refer to the *Transplanting/Planting Guide or Garden Planting Details in Appendix C,* to help you decide.

How should I space my plants?

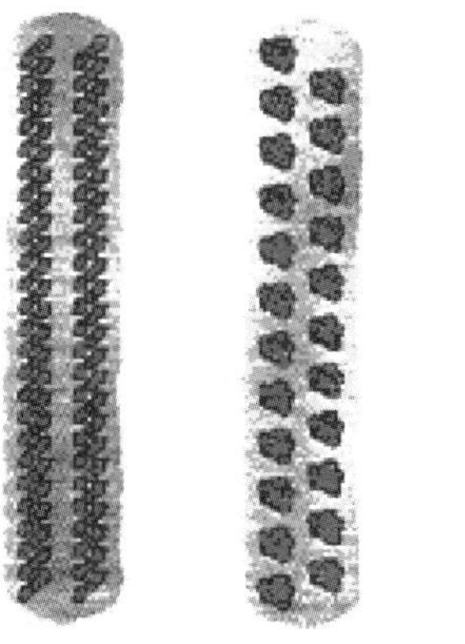

Spacing seedlings (or seeds) uniformly, tailored to their full-grown shape and size, will provide adequate space and light for them to mature. Remembering the first law of plant growth, plenty of light is essential to produce high-yield crops.

Spacing between plants varies according to the type of plant. However, there are three basic patterns for arranging plants in soil-beds.

- ***Double Rows*** are used for plants such as potatoes, corn, radishes, and leaf lettuce.
- ***Double-Alternating Rows*** are used for plants such as head lettuce, cabbage, broccoli and similar-size crops.
- ***Single Rows*** along one side of the soil-bed are used for tomatoes, melons and other large or vertically grown crops.

Refer to the *Transplanting/Planting Guide or Garden Planting* Details in Appendix C to learn about row arrangements and spacing requirements for many common crops.

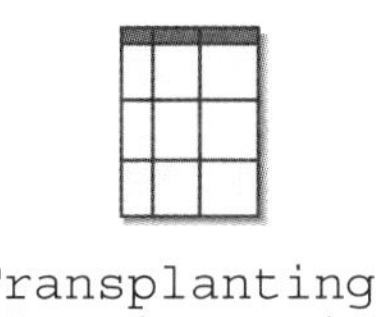

Transplanting/
Planting Guide

Using a marker to mark your soil-beds before you plant is the best way to ensure uniform spacing. You will learn about making a marker in the next section.

Go to the *Planting Guide* found in *Appendix A* and enter the spacing, row arrangements, and depth of planting seeds or seedlings for your crops. Refer to the *Transplanting/Planting Guide or Garden Planting Details* in *Appendix C* as needed.

Garden

Genius

Can I grow crops vertically?

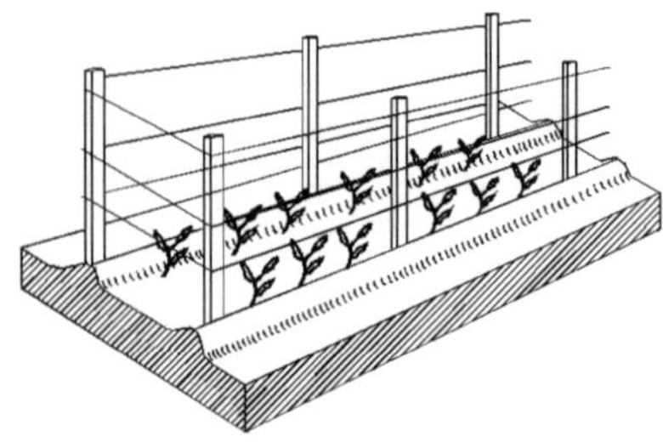

With Mittleider gardening, you can grow plants both horizontally and vertically. Some plants are normal climbers, for example: pole beans, pole peas, and certain squashes. Other crops can be made to grow vertically. These include tomatoes, cucumbers, and melons.

Growing crops vertically has these advantages:

- More plants can be grown in a small area.
- Better quality crops are produced because of the extra light each plant receives.
- Plants are easy to feed, water, prune, and harvest.
- The fruit does not sunburn and the vines and leaves are not damaged during harvesting.
- The fruit does not mildew, get eaten by bugs and animals, or get stepped on.

There are two ways of growing crops vertically. You can use stakes, or you can use T-frame structures (see Lesson 15).

Using Stakes

To grow crops vertically using stakes, you need 2" x 2" x 10' long stakes. These are driven 18 inches into the ground along both ridges. Stakes should be 30 to 36 inches apart on each ridge. Run string or wire between stakes to keep plants confined to the bed area (Appendix F has a good alternative).

> Tip Paint your stakes white before using to improve their appearance and durability.

After the growing season remove the stakes and store them for next year.

Learn More

- Using T-Frames
  See ***Lesson 15: Caring for Climbing Plants***
- Pruning
  See ***Lesson 15: Caring for Climbing Plants***
- Growing Tomatoes Vertically
  See ***Lesson 15: Caring for Climbing Plants***
  Let's Grow Tomatoes (pp. 64-69)

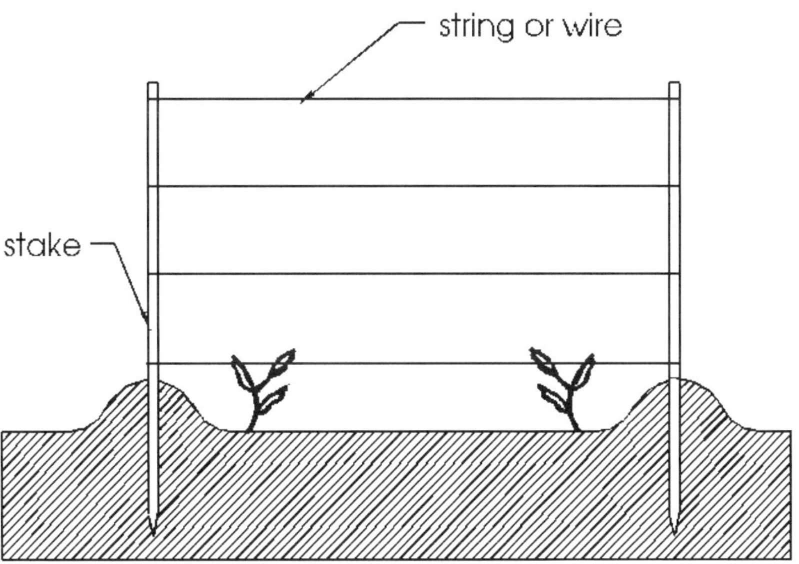

End view of soil-bed showing stakes in ridges.

How do I make and use a marker?

Markers help you mark the soil to ensure uniform spacing between plants.

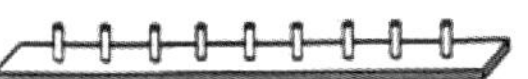

To make a marker for showing the placement of seeds or seedlings at 2-, 3-, 4-, 6-,8-, 12-,18-3½, -,7-,14- or 21-inch intervals, you will need the following materials and tools.

Materials

- several 4 ft. lengths of ½ in. wood doweling
- one 2”x 2”x 8’ wood strip
- glue (preferably water-proof)

Tools

- a saw
- a drill and a ½ in. wood or steel drill bit
- a wood rasp or belt sander
- a tape measure

Procedure

1. Cut the doweling into 2 ½ in. pieces and sharpen one end of each with the wood rasp or belt sander.
2. Starting at 2", drill ½ in. holes in the wood strip at 6 inch intervals on one side, & 7 inch intervals on the opposite side.
3. Glue the pieces of dowel in the holes (pointed ends out).

Using the Marker

- Transplanting in damp soil is preferred, but the same results can be achieved in dry soil if you water immediately!

- With the marker, mark where the planting holes should be by dragging across the soil in the grow-box..

- Make the actual hole just before you set each plant.

- The holes should be large enough to accommodate the root ball without crowding.

Tip The 6 and 7-inch marker is the most useful as a universal marker. Use this marker to make reference points in your soil-beds and then plant with other spacing increments (e.g., 2, 3, 3 ½, 4, and 9 inches) by referring to the reference marks.

Garden Genius

Consider the spacing requirements for the crops you plan to plant. (Refer to your *Planting Guide*, if necessary.) Which markers do you plan to make?

- ***6-inch*** interval marker (between 2 and 12-inch spacing)
- ***7-inch*** interval marker (for 7-, 14-, and 21-inch spacing)

Go to the *Tools and Materials List* in *Appendix A* and indicate which markers you plan to make. Both are recommended.

How do I plant seeds in soil-beds?

If you sow seeds directly into your soil-beds, remember these points:

- Plant at the bases of the ridges, not at the top.
- Use certified seed, whenever possible. (Certified seed is produced under more rigid inspection.)
- Don't plant too early, while the soil is cold!
- Do not cover seeds deep. Use the following guidelines.

Covering Seeds

- Tiny seeds—cover only with sand, sawdust, or peat moss
- Medium seeds—cover ¼" to ½"
- Large seeds—cover ¾" to 1"

> Tip
> Cover seeds 2½ times the thickness of the seed.

Planting Very Small Seeds

The following procedure permits you to plant small seeds evenly and quickly by hand so that thinning later is unnecessary.

Step 1: Mix Seed with Filler

Mix the desired amount of seed with sand. Mix 100 parts of sand with 1 part seed.

Step 2: Make Furrow

Using a pointed garden tool, such as the HANDLE-END of your hoe or rake, scratch a shallow furrow 1/2 inch deep along the inside base of each ridge. The space between the furrows should be at least 10 inches.

Step 3: Spread Seed

Take a small amount of the seed mixture in the hand. With a swinging motion of the hand and arm spread the seed in the furrows along the length of the beds.

> Tip Using a 16 ounce can may increase your accuracy in distributing seeds evenly throughout the length of the soil-bed.

Step 4: Cover Seed

Cover the seed very lightly with sand or special seed-house soil—never with garden soil. Cover with burlap to avoid moving.

Step 5: Water Soil

Water the soil-beds by gently flooding the area between the ridges.

Step 6: Keep Soil Damp

Keep the soil damp but not soaking wet during germination.

Step 7: Remove Burlap

Remove the burlap covering as soon as you see the firstsprouts.

How do I transplant seedlings?

After marking the soil-beds, make holes at each mark. It's best if you make the holes right at the time of transplanting. The holes should be deep enough and large enough to accommodate the root-ball and plant stem without crowding.

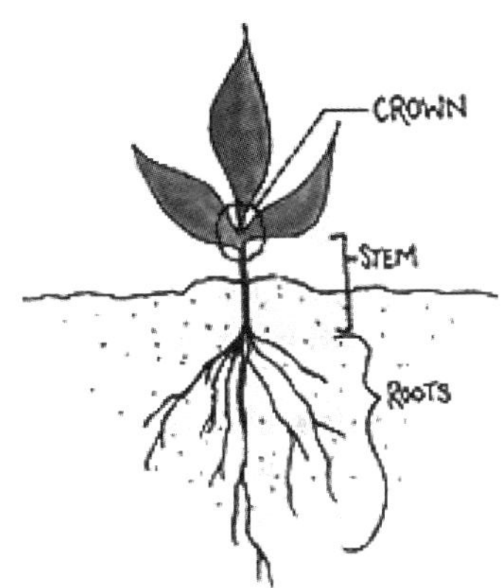

> Tip Water the seedling plants heavily just prior to actual transplanting. Wet soil hydrates the plant and keeps the root ball from falling apart when taken out of the pot.
>
> Transplant seedlings as early in the day as possible to reduce transplant shock.

Transplanting/ Planting Guide

Refer to the *Transplanting/Planting Guide* in *Appendix B* for guidelines on how deep to transplant different crops.

To transplant:

Step 1: Take Plant in Hand

Take a young plant in hand. Slip the plant stem between the index and middle fingers.

Step 2: Turn Pot

Keep the fingers in place and turn the pot upside down. Tap the bottom of the pot with the free hand. If the root ball is wet it slips easily from the pot.

Step 3: Make Hole

Hold the plant by a mark in the soil-bed, and with your free hand make a hole large enough to accommodate the roots.

Step 4: Place Plant in Hole

Turn the plant right side up while lowering the roots into the hole.

Step 5: Position Plant

Set the plant deep, down to the crown (the top part of the plant), but do not plant the crown below the soil level in the soil-bed. Dirt falling on the crown will kill the plant.

Step 6: Fill the Hole

After the plant is set properly in the hole, pull loose soil around the plant to fill the hole. Filling the hole with soil around the plant should take just one movement of the hand. Do not pack the soil around the plant.

Step 7: Repeat Procedure

Repeat the transplanting procedures and plant one plant at each mark.

Step 8: Apply Fertilizer

After a soil-bed is planted, apply 8 ounces (1/4 oz/ft) nitrogen fertilizer in a narrow band between rows, avoiding plant stems.

Step9: Water

Water promptly, thoroughly soaking the soil-bed to dissolve the granular fertilizer and keep the plants from wilting.

Step 10: Start Regular Fertilizing Schedule

Apply the regular application of Weekly-Feed Fertilizer 3 days after transplanting. You will learn how to do this in *Soil-Bed Basics/Lesson 5: Fertilizing.*

Garden Genius

Calculate how much nitrogen fertilizer you will need when transplanting your plants (Allow 8 oz/30' bed - 1/4 oz/ft).

Enter this information on your *Tools and Materials List* in *Appendix A*.

Lesson 4: Watering

In this lesson, you will learn how to answer these questions:

What should I know about plants and water?
How does this method conserve water?
How do I water my soil-beds?

What should I know about plants and water?

- The 4th law of plant growth is water.
- Over 80% of a plant's weight is water. Tender, crisp, flavor-filled vegetables need water often, generally on a daily schedule.
- A continuous "pipe" runs from the tip of the deepest root to the end of the highest leaf in a plant.
- Every time a plant begins to wilt it has already stopped growing.
- In addition to keeping a plant from wilting, water is necessary to carry nutrients from the soil to the plant roots. Dry fertilizer can do nothing until it is dissolved.
- The larger the leaf area of a plant, the more water it requires for transpiration.
- Since soils are not dams for storing water, it is false economy to supply excess water during irrigation. When you see standing water, the soil has reached "field capacity" and can hold no more.

Learn More

Soil Water
*See **Lesson 19: Problem Soils***
Food For Everyone
(pp.106-116)

Is sprinkling a good way to water?

No. Water escapes through the leaves. The droplets you see on plant leaves in the early morning hours are water leaving the plant—this is called transpiration. (A wilting plant is somewhat helped by sprinkling, but usually not enough to support optimum growth.) Sprinkling wastes water and encourages weed growth in the aisles. Sprinkling also promotes fungus diseases such as mildew and mold growth on leaves.

How does this method conserve water?

The Mittleider soil-bed method simplifies watering and conserves water.

- Plants receive water at the roots where they can make the best use of it.
- Water is conserved by minimizing evaporation and over-watering.
- The same water supplies two rows of plants at the same time, thus cutting in half the amount of water used in conventional methods.

How do I water my soil-beds?

Here is the procedure for watering soil-beds.

Step 1: Tie an 18" Towel to the Garden Hose

Wrap the towel **several times** around the hose, and extend the towel 12" past the end of the hose. This will modify the speed of the water coming out of the hose without affecting the water volume.

Step 2: Turn the Water on Full Volume

Water should flood the 12 inch flattened width of the soil-bed and quickly move to the other end of the bed (usually in less than 5 minutes).

Step 3: Allow Water to Reach End of Bed

By the time the water reaches the end, it should have reached the base of each ridge, bringing water to the stems and roots of the plants.

Step 4: Move the Hose to the Next Bed

When you see standing water move the hose to the next bed.

Step 5: Water Daily

If drainage is satisfactory, water the beds daily.

> Tip Less water is lost to evaporation if you water in the cool of the early morning. Water at any time of day if plants show a need for it. Don't wait.

Learn More

- Automating Watering
See ***Lesson 16: Automated Watering***
- Effective Water Systems
Grow-Bed Gardening
(pp. 103-108)

Lesson 5: Fertilizing

In this lesson, you will learn how to answer these questions:

Why do I need to fertilize?
What kind of fertilizers should I use?
How much fertilizer should I use?
How do I mix the Pre-Plant Fertilizer?
How do I mix the Weekly-Feed Fertilizer?
How often should I fertilize?

Why do I need to fertilize?

Plants are like people in that they require balanced nutrition. They get 3 essential nutrients - carbon, oxygen, and hydrogen - from the air, from which they produce carbohydrates. Hence the importance of air as the 3rd law of plant growth.

Plants receive 13 more nutrients essential to healthy growth as water-soluble minerals through their roots, hence the importance of nutrition as the 5th law of plant growth.

The 13 essential natural mineral raw materials from which plants make food have come to be called fertilizers.

These natural mineral nutrients in soil can be compared with a checking account in a bank.

- Every crop reduces the amount of soil nutrients just as writing checks reduces the money in a checking account.
- If the amount of the check is more than the amount in the bank, the bank will not accept the check. Growing crops affect the soil in the same way. Planting a large crop when the supply of fertilizer is too low will result in crop failure.
- Applying fertilizer to growing crops is just like making a deposit to a bank account.

What nutrients do plants need?

There are 16 essential plant nutrients. They include:

- **Airborne Nutrients**

  Carbon (C)
  Oxygen (O)
  Hydrogen (H)

- **Primary Nutrients**

  Nitrogen (N) A component of proteins & chlorophyll. Gives plants their green color, rapid growth, high protein, and yield.

  Phosphorus (P) Plays a vital role in plant reproduction. Affects early vigor, healthy roots, and quality.

  Potassium (K) Vital for plant growth. Produces healthy plants, high-quality seeds and fruit.

- **Secondary Nutrients**

  Calcium (Ca) An integral part of plant cell walls. Promotes early root growth, high vigor, and seed formation.

  Magnesium (Mg) Associated with chlorophyll formation, photosynthesis, and oil and fat formation.

  Sulfur (S) Component of proteins and vitamins. Aids root growth, green color, and seed production.

- **Trace Elements**

  Boron (B) Essential for seed and cell wall formation.

  Copper (Cu) Catalyzes several plant processes.

  Iron (Fe) Is associated with chlorophyll formation which gives plants their green color.

  Manganese (Mn) A part of certain enzyme systems.

  Zinc (Zn) Aids chlorophyll and carbohydrate formation.

Learn More

Hidden Hunger in Plants
*See **Lesson 17: Understanding Fertilizers***
Food For Everyone
(pp. 284-199)

Recognizing Plant Deficiencies
*See **Lesson 18: Nutritional Deficiencies***
The Garden Doctor
(Books 1-3)
Food for Everyone
(pp. 142-254)

Molybdenum (Mo) Plays a vital role in nitrogen fixation by microorganisms and nitrogen processes in plants.

Chlorine (Cl) Essential for plant growth.

No matter how the soil is fertilized, whether by compost, organic matter, or fertilizer from a bag, the elements used by plants are the same. On a molecular level, nitrogen is nitrogen, regardless of its source. What is important is that plants receive an accurate and proper balance of the required nutrients.

The elements used in Dr. Mittleider's fertilizers are obtained from commercial sources. Twelve of the thirteen nutrients plants get from the soil occur naturally in the soil and are mined and then packaged and sold commercially.

Dr. Mittleider recommends the following four-step strategy for applying fertilizers. You will learn how to mix the Mittleider Magic Pre-Plant and Weekly-Feed fertilizers in Lesson 17.

Step 1: Pre-Plant Fertilizing

Before planting, apply fertilizers to the soil-beds and mix with the soil. At this time you should fertilize with the Pre-Plant Fertilizer (1 oz/linear foot) as well as an application of the Weekly-Feed Fertilizer (1/2 oz/ linear foot).

Step 2: Transplant Fertilizing

After transplanting seedlings, apply 1/4 ounce per linear foot of a nitrogen fertilizer in a narrow band between rows in each soil-bed. This will help jump-start the young seedlings.

Step 3: Weekly Fertilizing

After crops are in the soil, wait 3 days and then apply only the Weekly-Feed Fertilizer on a regular basis, every 7 days.

Step 4: Special-Need Fertilizing

Learn More

- Organic vs. Inorganic Gardening
  See ***Lesson 17: Understanding Fertilizers***
  6 Steps to Successful Gardening (pp.44-46)
  Food For Everyone (pp. 258-261)

- How Fertilizers Are Packaged and Sold
  See ***Lesson 17: Understanding Fertilizers***

- Recognizing Plant Deficiencies
  See ***Lesson 18: Nutritional Deficiencies***
  The Garden Doctor (Books 1-3)
  Food for Everyone (pp. 142-254)

- Corrective Treatments
  See ***Lesson 18: Nutritional Deficiencies***
  The Garden Doctor (Books 1-3)

If plants show symptoms of nutritional deficiencies (Lesson 18), apply corrective fertilizing formulas in addition to the Weekly-FeedFertilizer.

How much fertilizer should I use?

Pre-Plant Fertilizing

Before planting, evenly spread the following on each 30-foot soil-bed:

- **2 pounds** of the Pre-Plant Fertilizer (1 oz/linear foot)
- **1 pound** of the Weekly-Feed Fertilizer (1/2 oz/linear foot)

Mix thoroughly with the soil.

Weekly-Feed Fertilizing

Apply **16 ounces (1 pound)** of the Weekly-Feed Fertilizer evenly down the center of each 30-foot soil-bed (1/2 oz/ft). Water after applying fertilizer to dissolve the granules.

Tip

Weigh the amount of fertilizer needed. Pour into can; mark a line on can; fill can to fill line for each feeding

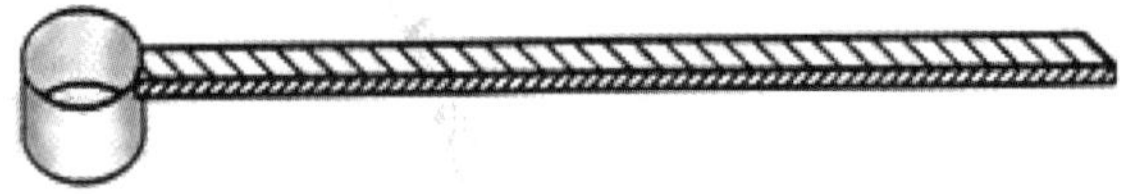

The 16 oz can on your fertilizing tool holds enough fertilizer for an 18” x 30' soil-bed. Hold the tool in your hands at an angle, start at one end, and gently shake the can to distribute the fertilizer. Walk along the soil-bed distributing the fertilizer until you

reach the other end. Refill the can with fertilizer and start on the next row.

Calculate how much of each fertilizer you will need for **one** application on all of the soil-beds in your garden.

Garden Genius

- Pre-Plant Fertilizer
- Weekly-Feed Fertilizer

Enter these amounts on the *Fertilizing Schedule* found in Appendix A.

How do I mix the Pre-Plant Fertilizer?

Pre-Plant Fertilizer is of great importance to healthy plants. It helps seeds to germinate and gives seedlings a healthy start.

> Tip Be accurate in measuring and applying fertilizers to the soil. Overfed plants can produce poor yields just as underfed plants can.

To make ***Pre-Plant Fertilizer***, mix together the following:

- 5 pounds of lime or gypsum *
- 1 ounce boron (20 Mule Team Borax)
- 4 ounces magnesium sulfate (Epsom Salt)

It is easier to mix these ingredients evenly in these smaller amounts. (Doubling this mixture will sufficiently prepare five 30-foot soil-beds.)

> Tip Remember, the most accurate feeding is done by weighing the needed amount and then marking the feeding container. Thereafter always feed that amount.

**Should I use lime or gypsum?*

Lime supplies calcium to crops. Use different sources of calcium depending on whether you have acid or alkaline soils.

Learn More

- What Are Commercial Fertilizers? *See **Lesson 17: Understanding Fertilizers*** Food For Everyone (pp. 255-257)
- Calcium & Magnesium, Macronutrients *See **Lesson 18: Nutritional Deficiencies*** Food For Everyone (pp. 192-200)
- Soil pH—Acidity and Alkalinity *See **Lesson 19: Problem Soils*** Food For Everyone (pp. 132-136)

In areas where the annual rainfall is more than 20 inches, use agricultural or dolomite lime.

In areas where the annual rainfall is less than 18 inches, use gypsum (calcium sulfate).

Where do I get these ingredients?

Garden shops (nurseries), farm supply stores, and chemical shops usually carry packaged fertilizers, including gypsum and/or agricultural lime.

Boron and magnesium sulfate are frequently sold in supermarkets under the following names: *Twenty Mule Team Borax* (a detergent) and *Epsom Salt*—magnesium sulfate (a laxative).

Garden Genius

Based on how much Pre-Plant Fertilizer you will need for your garden, calculate how much of each ingredient you will need.

- lime or gypsum
- boron (*Borax)*
- magnesium sulfate (*Epsom Salt*)

Enter these amounts on *Tools and Materials List* found in *Appendix A*.

How do I mix the Weekly-Feed Fertilizer?

Weekly-Feed Fertilizer provides for the on-going nutritional needs of growing plants.

To make 25 pounds of ***Weekly-Feed Fertilizer***, mix together the following:

Ammonium Nitrate *$AmNO_3$* (34-0-0)	10 pounds 8 ounces
Phosphorus *P* (0-45-0)	4 pounds 8 ounces
Potassium *K (0-0-60)*	6 pounds
Magnesium Sulfate *MgSO4 (Epsom Salt)*	3 pounds 12 ounces
Boron *B* (*Borax*)	3 ounces
Manganese *$MnSO_4$*	2 ounces
Zinc *$ZnSO_4$*	4 ounces
Iron(Fe) Chelate #330	½ ounce
Copper Sulfate *$CuSO_4$*	½ ounce
Molybdenum *Mo*	¼ ounce

Learn More

What Are Commercial Fertilizers?
*See **Lesson 17:** **~~Understanding~~ Fertilizers***
Food For Everyone
(pp. 255-257)

What if I can't find these ingredients?

You can order the Micro-nutrients directly from us at

www.growfood.com/shop. Add 4# of Epsom Salt. And 25# of 16-16-16 will provide the 3 major nutrients (NP&K) needed.

For a short-term substitute to the Weekly-Feed fertilizer, mix together

- 6 pounds fertilizer (16-16-16)
- 1 pound magnesium sulfate (*Epsom Salt*)
- 5 grams boron (*Borax*)

> Tip The simplest way to create the Mittleider Weekly Feed is to purchase a package of Micro-nutrients directly from www.growfood.com/shop and follow the simple directions.

What do the numbers 16-16-16 mean?

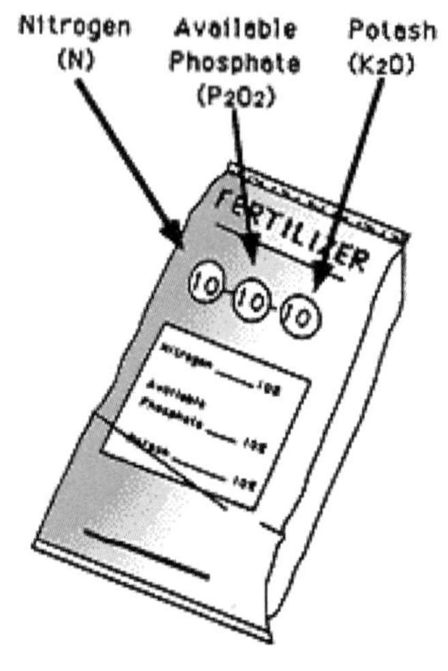

Throughout the world, fertilizer is sold using standard labels. The three numbers show the percent of nitrogen (N), phosphorus (P), and potassium (K) in the fertilizer. For instance, the fertilizer bag shown here contains 10% of each element.

What should I do if I can't find a 16-16-16 fertilizer?

Substitute one of the following mixtures, shown here in order of most acceptable substitute to least acceptable:

- 15-15-15 fertilizer
- 17-17-17 fertilizer
- 20-20-20 fertilizer

Garden Genius

Do you plan to use the standard Weekly-Feed formula listed above or to start by using the short-term-substitute formula?

Refer to the *Tools and Materials List* in *Appendix A* and check off the materials you need to get for the Weekly-Feed formula you have chosen to use.

How often should I fertilize?

Fertilize with the ***Weekly-Feed Fertilizer*** every 7 days, applying down the center of the bed and away from plant stems.

Learn More

Recognizing Plant Deficiencies
See ***Lesson 18: Nutritional Deficiencies***
The Garden Doctor (Books 1-3)
Food for Everyone (pp.142-254)

When to Begin

For transplanted plants, apply the first regular application of the Weekly-Feed Fertilizer 3 days after transplanting and on a weekly basis thereafter.

For crops planted from seed, do not fertilize until the seeds have sprouted.

How Many Applications

To see a table showing how many weekly applications are recommended for various crops, refer to *Suggested Fertilizer Applications and Garden Planting Details* in *Appendix C.*

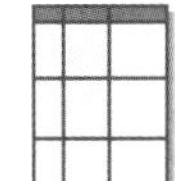

Suggested Fertilizer Applications

Any time plants look like they are hungry, they should be fed. Judge by the visual appearance of the plants

> Tip Fertilizing with Weekly Feed should continue until 3 weeks before harvest for single-crop varieties, and until 8 weeks before the first expected killing frost for ever-bearing plants. If not including lime in the Weekly Feed Mix ever-bearing crops should receive an additional Pre-Plant feeding after 8 weeks.

What are the signs of a hungry plant?

"Plant hunger" is shown by thin, weak looking plants, poor leaf color, blossoms not developing into fruit, and inferior quality of fruit.

Go to the *Fertilizing Schedule* in *Appendix A* and enter the recommended number of Weekly-Feed Fertilizer applications for each of your crops. Use this schedule to record the dates you fertilize each crop.

Lesson 6: Weeding

In this lesson, you will learn how to answer these questions:

When do I start controlling weeds?
How do I control annual weeds?
How can I prevent weeds?

When do I start controlling weeds?

Most of us are used to thinking that we must wait until weeds are big enough to pull up before we worry about getting rid of them. But the best time to start is before they start! Remember, there are two kinds of weeds—perennial and annual.

- ***Perennial*** weeds keep growing year after year from the same rhizomes (underground stems) and runners.
- ***Annual*** weeds start from new seeds every year.

There are two main times to control weeds.

Time One: When Preparing the Soil for Planting

This is the best time to attack perennial weeds. You should try at this time to remove the rhizomes and runners of all perennial plants. Some of the biggest weed nuisances spread through runners. Removing them will save a lot of unnecessary effort later.

Time Two: When the Weeds first Sprout

Usually about 5 to 8 days after planting your crop, annual weeds begin to sprout. This is the time to stop them.

How do I control annual weeds?

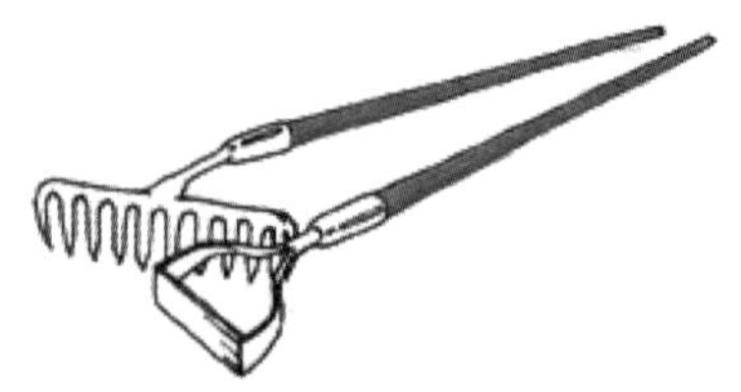

You'll need only two simple tools for Early & Often weeding:

- a garden rake
- a scuffle hoe

Step 1: Pull Soil Away from Ridge

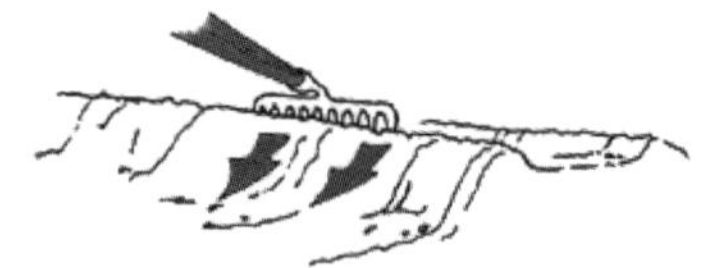

With the 2-way hoe or the rake tines pointing down, pull away the soil from the 4-inch ridge into the aisles, cutting or uprooting all weeds. Caution: Be especially careful—if you have planted seeds—not to disturb the area where you planted them.

Step 2: Pull the Soil Back

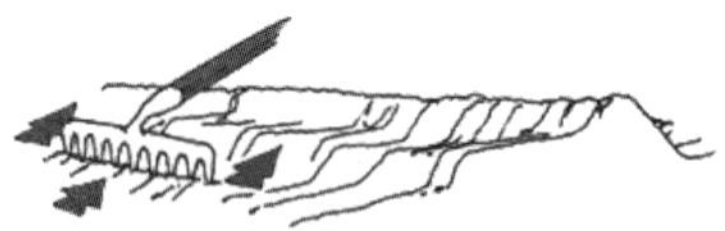

Now turn right around and pull the soil back, rebuilding the ridges, while taking care not to re-plant any weeds!

Step 3: Smother Sprouting Weeds

While reshaping the ridges (those with transplanted seedlings), allow a thin film of dirt to slide around the plant stems. This will smother the weed seeds sprouting among the seedlings.

Step 4: Disturb Area between Rows

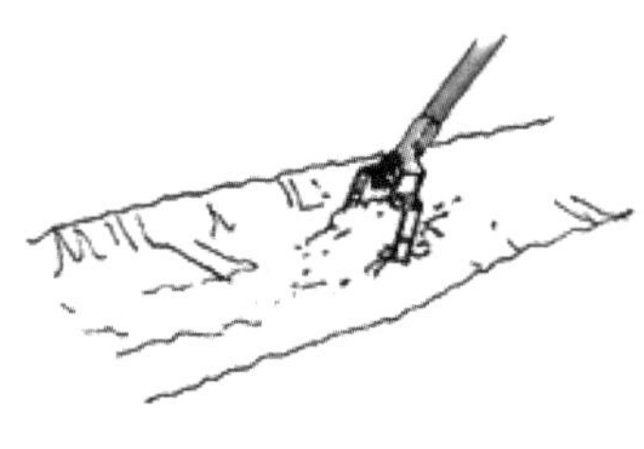

With the rake or scuffle hoe, remove sprouting weeds between the planted rows by disturbing the area between the two rows. Make sure to maintain the flat, level quality of this area (to promote accurate and complete watering).

NOTE: There should be few weeds in the center between the planted rows because the band of fertilizer spread there is strong enough to kill most sprouting weed seeds.

Step 5: Remove Weeds from Aisles

Using the rake or scuffle hoe, remove sprouting weeds from the aisles. Shallow tilling with a small garden tiller is also possible.

Even after you have cleared your garden of annual weeds, it is important to continue using good weed prevention practices.

How can I prevent weeds?

There are several ways to prevent weeds from growing in the first place:

- Irrigate with well water.
- Use a domestic water supply (garden hose connected to water faucet).
- Too lazy to weed? Lay down sheets of black plastic or Weed Cloth. Plant seedlings through small holes cut in it.

  Note: While preventing broad-leaf weed growth, grasses and nut sedges will not be stopped. Weed cloth does allow water to penetrate the soil. Black plastic presents more of a problem.
- Do not put unsterilized manure on your garden. Many weed seeds pass right through the cow.
- Plant seeds or seedlings in custom-made soil (using sawdust, perlite [rock wool], washed sand, coffee hulls, pine needles, ground tree bark, etc.) in grow-boxes. See *Part III: Grow-Box Basics*.

Lesson 7: Harvesting

In this lesson, you will learn how to answer these questions:

> How do I protect my harvest?
> When should I harvest my crops?

How do I protect my harvest?

You can protect and enhance a bountiful harvest by following a few simple rules:

- When the days are hot, harvest vegetables in the cooler morning hours.
- Treat produce gently—avoid bruising.
- Keep freshly-picked produce out of the sunshine and wind. Cool it promptly to keep it from wilting.
- Keep produce clean—consider eye-appeal.
- For the ultimate in health, flavor and eating quality, allow crops to mature and ripen on the plants or vines.

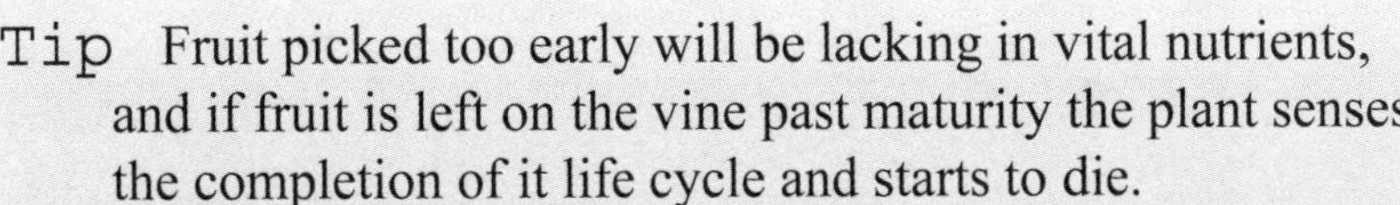

Tip Fruit picked too early will be lacking in vital nutrients, and if fruit is left on the vine past maturity the plant senses the completion of it life cycle and starts to die.

Harvest at peak maturity to assure a long and delicious harvest of healthy fruit.

Learn More

Pruning
*See **Lesson 15: Caring for Climbing Plants***

When should I harvest my crops?

To enjoy vegetables at their prime, you need to pick them at the right time.

Avoid harvesting in the middle of the day.

Do not leave crates of fresh produce in the sun or wind, to wilt and heat up.

Harvest . . .

- ***peas*** when the pods are full - leaves at any time.
- ***broccoli*** and ***cauliflower*** just as the heads loosen and before flowers appear - leaves at any time.
- ***red beets at any size - leaves*** throughout the growing cycle.
- ***red and Swiss chard*** keep outer leaves picked all season.
- ***new potatoes*** while the skins slip easily. (Allow potatoes for winter use to remain until the vines die back.)
- ***tomatoes*** best when red-ripe - to individual taste.
- ***cucumbers*** before seeds develop.
- ***zucchini squash*** at any size, but before seeds develop.
- ***cabbage*** before the heads split - Leaves at any time.
- ***turnips*** while the bulbs are solid and crisp - leaves any time.
- ***sweet corn*** when silk turns brown and kernels are plump.
- ***radishes*** before the bulbs are pithy—they are best in cool weather - leaves at any time.
- ***cantaloupes*** when the fruit separates easily from the stem.

Part III: Grow-Box Basics

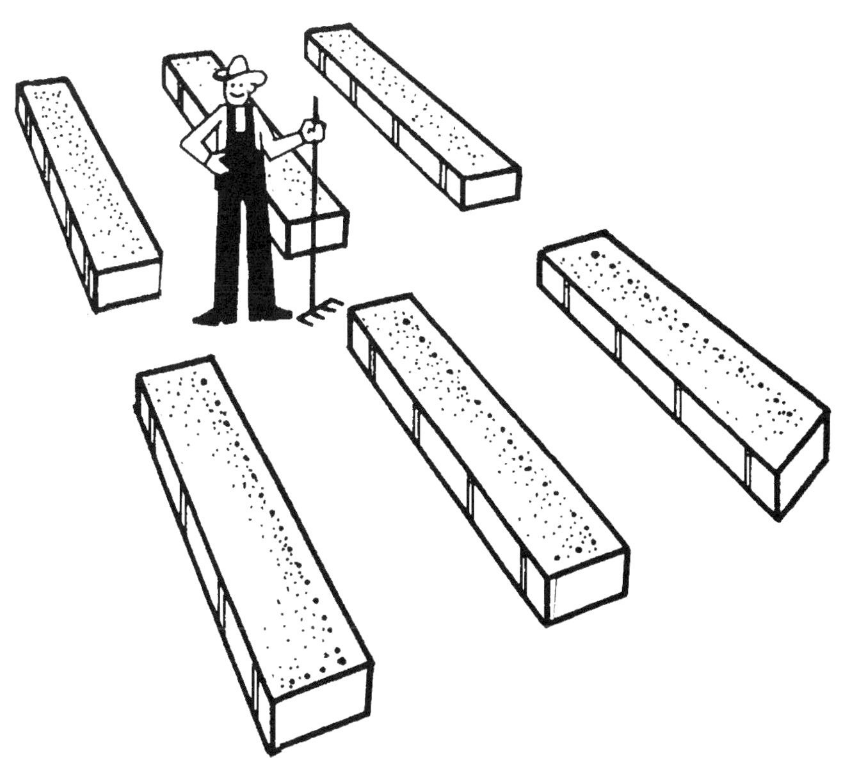

Lesson 8: Planning

In this lesson, you will learn how to answer these questions:

Where should I locate my garden?
What size should I make my grow-boxes?
How should I arrange my grow-boxes?
What should I plant?
When should I plant?
What tools will I need?
How much time will it take?

Where should I locate my garden?

- Choose a sunny location, one that gets 6-8 hours of sunshine from at least mid-morning throughout the afternoon.

- Don't worry about the soil conditions when deciding where to put your grow-boxes. You can build grow-boxes on poor, hillside land, rocky soil, clay, alkali, or asphalt!

- Choose a level area. If you choose an area that is reasonably level, there will be less work.

- Plant on the contour if using steeper slopes. Just level plots the size of the grow-boxes.

- Avoid north slopes (slopes facing north), because they have more shadows, diffuse the sun's rays, and are often too cold.

- Stay away from low spots where drainage is poor. Plants die for lack of oxygen where standing water accumulates.

- Avoid large trees and tall hedges, unless they are north of the grow-box area. Crops growing in shade do poorly Tree roots also compete for water and food.

Learn More

- Terracing Soil-Beds *6 Steps to Successful Gardening* (p. 19)
- The Erosion Problem *Food for Everyone* (p. 122)

- Make sure water is available close by.
- Avoid open areas where strong winds blow, or else construct windbreaks. Winds can quickly destroy the fragile, but very important plant leaves, affecting the result of the crop.
- Protect the area from animals or unwanted visitors. If necessary, construct a chain-link fence 6' to 8' tall.

Garden Genius

On the *Garden Plot Plan* found in *Appendix B: Grow-Box Garden Genius Planning Forms,* briefly describe where you plan to locate your garden. Does your location meet the criteria listed above?

What size should I make my grow-boxes?

Build the number and size of grow-boxes that are needed to fit your plot. Grow-box size can vary to fit unusual boundaries.

If you decide to build several grow-boxes side-to-side, line them up straight for attractiveness and easy working. Provide 3 ½ feet of working space on each side of a box and 5 feet of working space at the ends of the boxes.

The grow-box size described in this lesson & throughout this book is 18 inches wide, 30 feet long (outside dimensions), and 8 inches deep. This size provides easy access to all plants when fertilizing and harvesting . (See 4'-wide boxes in Appendix G.)

NOTE: All fertilizing and plant-spacing recommendations in this lesson will be based on a 18" x 30' x 8" size grow-box.

> Tip If you make your grow-boxes shorter than 30' just remember that the Pre-Plant Mix is applied 1 ounce per linear foot and Weekly Feed is applied 1/2 ounce per linear foot.

Learn More

- Fertilizer Formulas for Special-Size Grow-Boxes
  Mittleider Grow-Box Gardens
  (pp. 180-181)
- Tools and Materials for Building Mini Grow-Boxes
  Gardening by the Foot
  (pp. 37-39)
- Gardening with Grow-Boxes
  Mittleider Grow-Box Gardens

How should I arrange my grow-boxes?

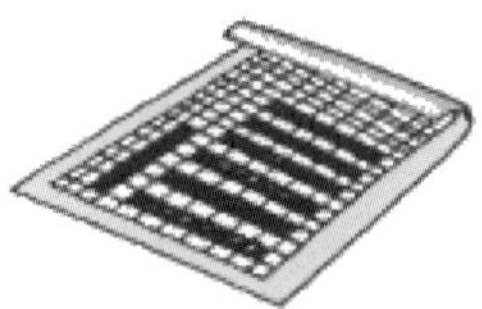

Plan in advance the number and placement of your grow-boxes by creating a "blueprint" of your garden area.

Facing beds any direction will work. Just plant tall plants north or east of short plants.

To create a garden plot plan or "blueprint," first show the outer dimensions of your garden on a grid.

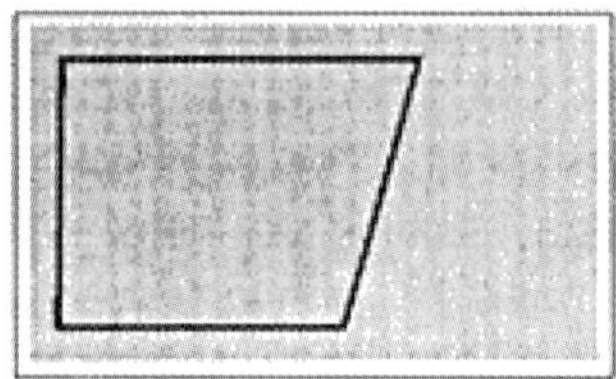

Second, show where you plan to place the grow-boxes.

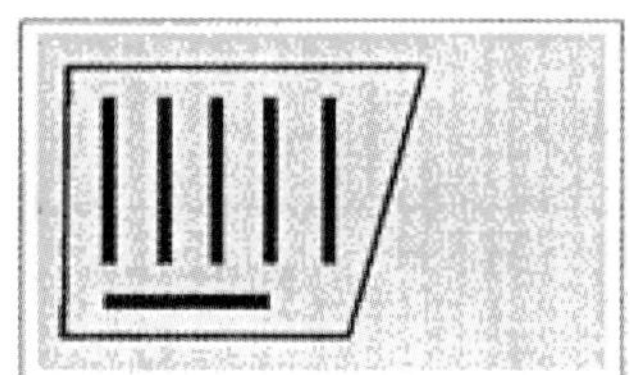

Tip Remember, if you cannot make grow-boxes 30-feet long, create them in simple divisions of 30 feet—1/2 (15 feet) or 1/3 (10 feet). Doing so will help you be more accurate when planting seeds or transplants and applying fertilizer.

Garden Genius

Create a "garden blueprint" for your garden, by following the directions on the *Garden Plot Plan* found in *Appendix B: Grow-Box Garden Genius Planning Forms.*

What should I plant?

To decide what and how much you should plant ask yourself:

- What will my family eat?
- How much will my family eat?
- How much can I comfortably care for?

Plant only what your family will eat and what you can care for. Here is Dr. Mittleider's suggested garden for a family of four to live on, consisting of only .044 acre.

Sample Garden Plan

What to Plant	How Many Plants	Yield
1 bed potatoes	92 plants	145 pounds
1 bed beans (bush)	180 plants	68 pounds
1 bed peas (bush)	362 plants	90 pounds
½ bed broccoli	26 plants	14 pounds
½ bed cauliflower	26 plants	75 pounds
½ bed lettuce (head)	26 plants	56 pounds
½ bed cabbage	26 plants	70 pounds
1 bed sweet corn	92 plants	92 ears
1 bed zucchini	20 plants	120 pounds
1 bed banana squash	20 plants	120 pounds
1 bed cantaloupes	26 plants	182 pounds
1 bed watermelons	20 plants	182 pounds
1 bed tomatoes	26 plants	156 pounds

Learn More

- Growing Crops Vertically
See ***Lesson 15: Caring for Climbing Plants***
Let's Grow Tomatoes (pp. 64-69)
- Using Mini Grow-Boxes
Gardening by the Foot
- Growing Tomatoes
Let's Grow Tomatoes (p. 122)
- Grow-Box yields & costs
Garden Planting Details (Appendix C)

Here's what can be planted later in the fall for a second harvest.

What to Plant	How Many Plants	Yield
1 bed potatoes	92 plants	145 pounds
1 bed beans (bush)	180 plants	68 pounds
1 bed peas (bush)	362 plants	90 pounds
½ bed broccoli	26 plants	14 pounds
½ bed cauliflower	26 plants	75 pounds
½ bed lettuce (head)	26 plants	56 pounds
½ bed cabbage	26 plants	70 pounds
1 bed sweet corn	92 plants	92 ears

To harvest two crops with the assortment of foods listed above in one season, it is important to transplant well-grown potted plants in the beds.

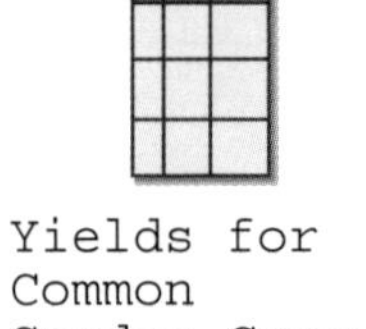

Yields for Common Garden Crops

To help plan your garden, refer to *Yields for Common Garden Crops* found in *Appendix C: Reference Tables for Planning Your Garden*. This table will help you decide what and how much to plant in your garden to meet your family's needs.

As you decide what you will plant, you may need to modify how you arrange your grow-boxes in your garden plot plan.

Tip Place short plants south or west of tall varieties. In this way, the shadows from tall plants will not interfere with the light needed by short plants.

Garden Genius

Use the *Planting Plan* found in *Appendix B: Grow-Box Garden Genius Planning Forms* to record the names of the crops you are going to plant in each grow-box and how many plants you will need to plant in each bed. Refer to and modify your *Garden Plot Plan* as necessary.

When should I plant?

The proper time to plant partly depends on the climate and the growing season where you grow your garden.

The ***growing season*** usually refers to the days between the average last frost date in the spring (ADLF) and the average first frost date in the fall. These dates give you a general idea as to when certain crops can be planted in your area and what types of crops to plant.

To help you determine when to plant your garden, find out the ***average day of last frost*** for your area.

> Tip If you do not know the average day of last frost for your area, call your state extension agent or look for it online.

Learn More

- Extending Growing Seasons *See* ***Lesson 22: Seedling Production***
- Building Greenhouse Sheltered Grow-Boxes Mittleider Grow-Box Gardens (pp. 87-96)
- Making a Simple Greenhouse *See* ***Appendix D: Building a Seedhouse***
- Cold-Weather Gardening *See* ***Lesson 23: Cold-Weather Gardening*** Mittleider Grow-Box Gardens (pp. 123-134)

Plant hardiness also partly determines when to plant.

Hardy plants tolcratc frost and cold and can be planted 3 to 6 weeks before the average date of last frost.

Moderately-hardy plants handle a certain amount of cold. Plant these 2-3 weeks before the average date of last frost.

Cold- and frost-sensitive plants don't like cold or frost. Plant them on the average day of last frost and protect them against late frost.

Frost-intolerant plants will not survive any frost and must be planted 2-3 weeks after the average day of last frost.

To see a table showing examples of each of these types of plants, refer to *Plant Hardiness and Planting Times* and the *Garden Planting Details in Appendix C:*

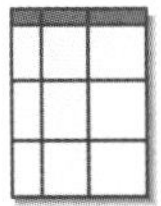

Plant Hardiness and Planting Times

Use the *Planting Plan* found in *Appendix B: Grow-Box Garden Genius Planning Forms* to record when you plan to plant each of your crops. Refer to *Plant Hardiness and Planting Times* in *Appendix C* to make your decisions.

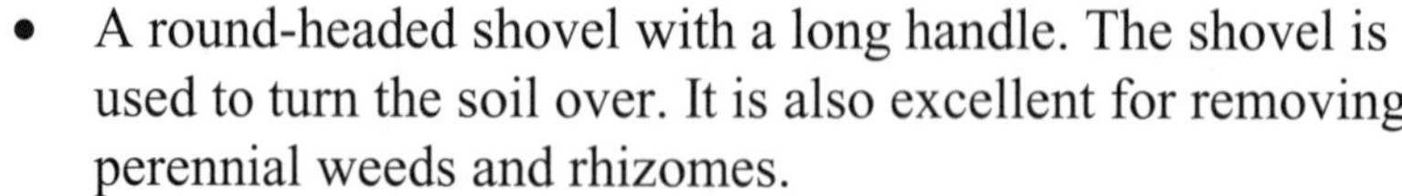

What tools will I need?

You will need the following tools for your grow-box garden:

- A round-headed shovel with a long handle. The shovel is used to turn the soil over. It is also excellent for removing perennial weeds and rhizomes.
- A garden rake (a 12" or 14" rake is easier to use than a 16" rake). A rake is used to level the custom-soil.
- A straight-blade hoe (sometimes called a scuffle-hoe or two-way hoe) not a curved chopping hoe. Use the straight-blade hoe just under the soil surface to eliminate annual weeds by cutting off below the crowns.

> Tip Never use a dull tool. Use a file to sharpen your tools. Keep your tools in good condition by oiling handles.

- Two five-gallon buckets for fertilizer compounds.
- A garden hose with the end securely wrapped ***several times*** with an18-inch towel extended past the end of the hose. Do not tie the end of the extended towel. Leave it open.
- The towel around the hose will prevent the water from digging a hole in the soil, and it allows you to turn the water on full volume to water your garden rapidly.
- Home-made fertilizing tool for distributing fertilizer to plants growing in the grow-boxes. With this tool, you won't have to bend down or strain your back, and you can quickly fertilize as you walk along the grow-boxes.

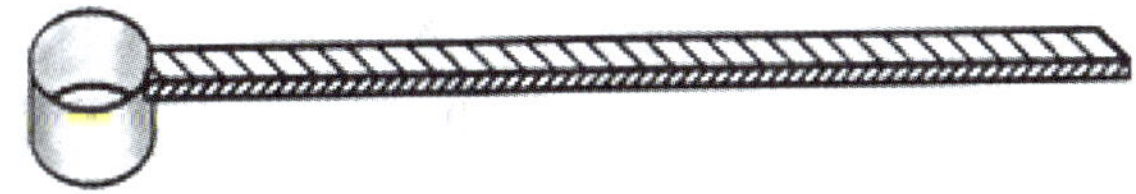

To make this tool, nail an empty 16-ounce can (open at one end) to the top end of a 1" x 2" x 6' (or longer) strip of wood.

The wood handle will be horizontal to the ground. The can will be perpendicular to the handle with the open end facing the sky.

- You should also use markers to provide proper spacing for plants. Different markers are used for different purposes:

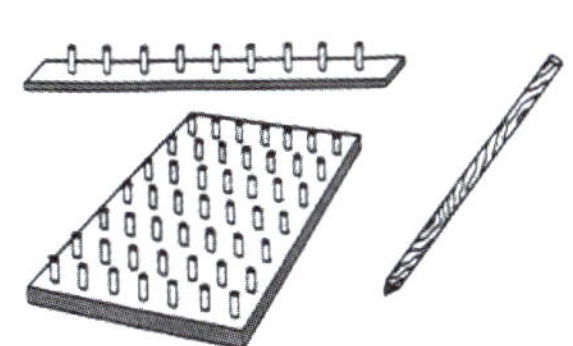

To mark seed flats
To press holes uniformly deep
To space plants in soil-beds or grow-boxes

Here is a summary of the tools you will need for your soil-bed garden. Refer to the *Tools and Materials List* found in *Appendix B: Grow-Box Garden Genius Planning Forms* to record which tools you will need to get.

- Round-headed shovel
- 12" or 14" garden rake
- Straight-edged hoe (two-way hoe)
- Two five-gallon buckets
- Garden hose
- 18" towel for end of hose
- Home-made fertilizing tool

(You will learn more about markers and how to make them on pages 93 and 94.)

How much time will it take?

The amount of time and work required to build and maintain your Mittleider garden varies according to the size of your project, the condition of the land to be cleared and prepared, and on how you obtain your seedling plants. If you grow your own seedling plants, additional work is involved. (On the other hand, you will save on the cost of buying the seedlings from a nursery and have them when you want them.)

A good-sized grow-box garden consists of a 60' x 40' area, divided into 11 plots (grow-boxes) 18" wide x 30' long, with 3 1/2' aisles between boxes and 5' perimeter aisles.

Learn More

- Home Seedling Production
  *See **Lesson 22: Seedling Production***
- Building an Inexpensive Seedling Greenhouse
  *See **Appendix D: Building a Seedhouse***

The following time estimates are based on a typical garden as described above. Because growing conditions vary widely, these estimates are only approximations.

- To clear your gardening area, construct grow-boxes, and make aisles and footpaths, plan on 8 to 16 hours of labor.
- To prepare the custom-soil, plant seeds, and transplant seedlings, plan on another 12 to 16 hours.
- To water, feed, inspect, and care for your plants after you have planted them, you should plan to spend 30 minutes per day (preferably in the early morning).
- To harvest your crop may require an additional 1 to 5 minutes per grow-box, depending on the type of vegetable and the amount to be harvested.

To anticipate your garden work and when it needs to be done, it is helpful to create a ***Gardening Cycle Calendar***—a month-to-month to-do list that reminds you of crucial gardening tasks. Here is an example of a gardening cycle calendar created by Dr. Mittleider for temperate zone 7.

Dr. Mittleider's Gardening Cycle Calendar*

Month	Tasks
January	• Plan garden. Will I use soil-beds or grow-boxes? What tools will I need? Where will I locate my garden? • Decide what to plant. What will be started from seed? What will be transplanted? Calculate plant spacing requirements.
February or March	• Plant tomato and pepper seeds in flats indoors or in a seed house or cold frame. Calculate the timing so plants will be 8 to 12 weeks old by the time I set them outdoors.
March	• In the seed house or cold frame, transplant seedling plants (tomatoes and peppers) into larger-size containers to give them more growing room. • In the seed house or cold frame, start cabbage, cauliflower, and broccoli from seed.
April	• When weather permits, plant peas, radishes, and green onions outside. Provide protection from freezing temperatures at night.
May	• Transplant seedling tomatoes, peppers, cabbage, cauliflower, and broccoli. • Plant melons, cucumbers, squash, eggplant, beans, and corn.
June-July	• Care for growing plants. (30 min./day)
July-August	• Harvest first crops. • Start a second planting for second crop.

* This timetable is a typical example of the gardening cycle in Dr. Mittleider's home in Salt Lake City, Utah.

Refer to the *Gardening Cycle Calendar* found in *Appendix B: Grow-Box Garden Genius Planning Forms* to create your own month-by-month gardening to-do list. You may wish to refer to your *Planting Plan* to note when you need to plant specific crops.

Garden Genius

Lesson 9: Preparing

In this lesson, you will learn how to answer these questions:

How do I prepare my garden?
How do I construct grow-boxes?
Why use custom-made soil?
How do I make custom-made soil?
How do I fill the grow-boxes?
How do I get grow-boxes ready for planting?

How do I prepare my garden?

Clear the Area

- Make your garden beautiful. A clean, neat, and orderly garden is pleasing to the eye, more productive, and has fewer weeds and pests.

- Clear the area by removing all undergrowth and brush, all living and dead shrubs, roots, and top-growth. Remove everything that will interfere with gardening such as trees, stumps, and trash.

Eliminate Weeds

There are two types of weeds: annuals and perennials.

Learn More

- Settling the Weed Problem *Food For Everyone* (pp. 313-320)
- Reasons to eliminate weeds. (Appendix F)

- ***Annuals*** sprout from seed every year. These can be removed with an appropriate tool, or by using a roto-tiller or a tractor to plow them under.
- ***Perennial*** plants keep growing for several years. You must dig perennials up, roots and all, destroying the rhizomes (underground stems) and runners. If perennials are not removed, they will be a continual nuisance throughout the garden, all through the year.

How do I construct grow-boxes?

To build grow-boxes, you can use lumber, cement, bricks, or other suitable building materials. This lesson will illustrate how to construct a lumber grow-box.

Step 1: Level the Ground

Level enough ground for each box area.

Step 2: Stake Out the Dimensions

Establish the location of the corners of the grow-box with cords and stakes. Extend the cords beyond the corners to outline the grow-box dimensions as shown. NOTE: Corners should be square (90°) unless the area is an irregular shape.

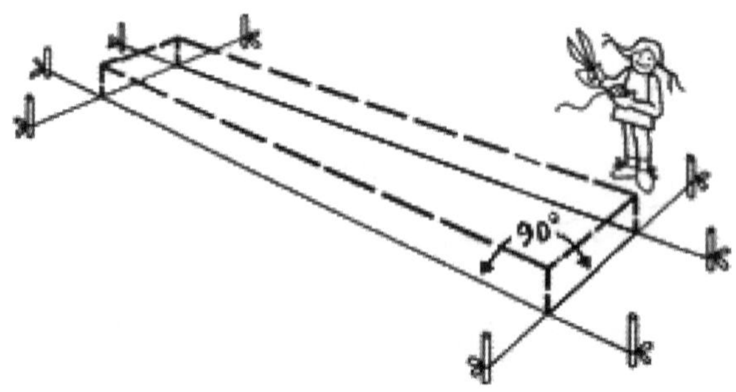

Step 3: Drive Stakes Along One Side

Learn More

- Construction Hints for Building Multiple Grow-Boxes *More Food From Your Garden* (p. 39)
- Tools and Materials for Building Mini Grow-Boxes *Gardening by the Foot* (pp. 37-39)
- Building 5' by 30' Grow-Boxes *More Food From Your Garden*

Nine inches from a corner, along one side, drive the first stake into the ground, to a depth of about nine inches. Always drive stakes on the outside edges of the grow-box, never on the inside edges.

Drive additional stakes about 30 inches apart along the cord line for one side of the box. When nailed or screwed securely to the leveled 2" x 8" boards, the top edges of the boards and stakes should be level (flush).

Step 4: Nail or Screw Side Board to First Stake

Set a side board in place along the cord. Drive the first stake top flush with the top edge of the board. Nail or screw the stake to the board.

Step 5: Attach Additional Stakes

To attach the second stake to the side board, place a level on the top edge of the side board and raise or lower the board to a level position. Then drive the second stake deeper until flush with the leveled board. Nail or screw the stake to the board. Repeat this procedure for each stake until reaching the other end of the box.

Step 6: Splice Side Boards

Side boards require splicing. Here are two kinds of splice: For one kind, take a 12-inch-long 2" x 8" board and nail or screw it across the joint where the side board ends meet.

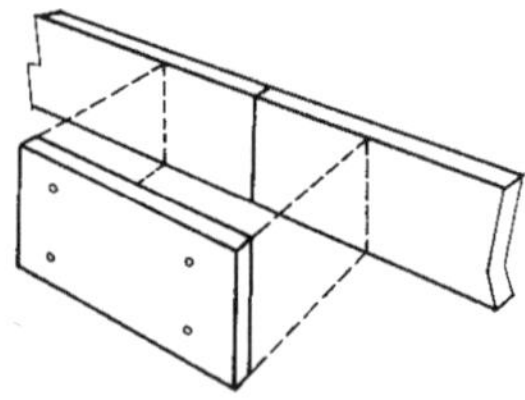

For another kind of splice, drive a 1" x 2" x 18" long stake, centered where the boards butt together. Nail or screw the board ends to the stake.

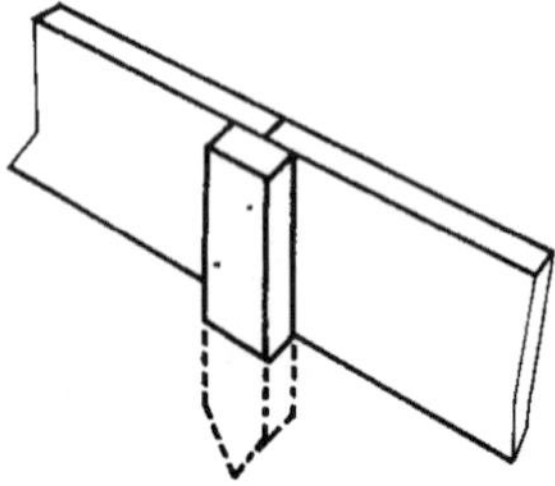

Step 7: Attach End-Pieces

Nail or screw an 18" end-piece to each end of the leveled side.

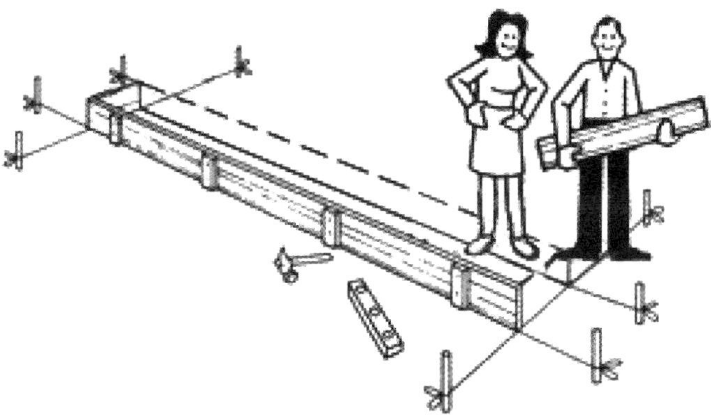

Step 8: Level End-Pieces

Drive a stake near the center of both end-pieces in line with the cord. Place the level like a triangle across the tops of both side- and end-boards. Level the end-board, drive the stake to the proper depth, and nail or screw to the end-piece. Repeat the same procedure for the opposite end of the box.

Step 9: Attach Last Side Board

To level the opposite side board, place the level again like a triangle across the end-piece and the top of the 2"x 8" side board. Level the side board to match the end piece. Drive the stake to the proper depth and nail or screw the board to the stake. Repeat the procedure to attach the board to the other stakes as with the first side board.

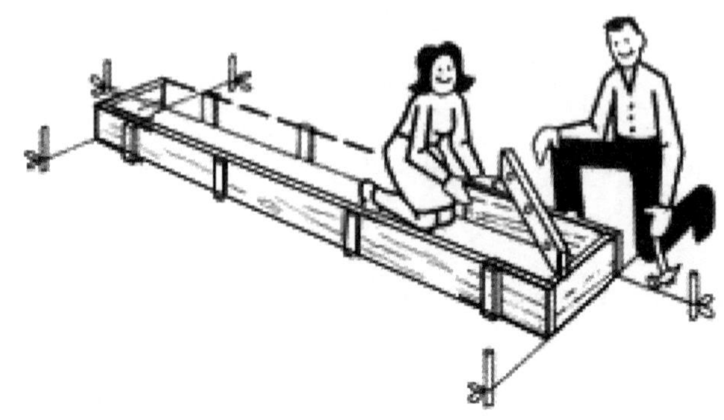

Garden Genius

Here are the tools you will need to construct grow-boxes. Go to the Tools and Materials List found in Appendix B: Grow-Box Garden Genius Planning Forms, and indicate which of these materials you need to get.

- Regular claw hammer
- Three-pound hammer or mallet
- A level at least two feet long
- 100 feet of strong cord

You need the following materials to construct one 18" x 30' x 8" grow-box.

- 63 feet of 2"x 8" treated lumber
- 24—1"x 2"x 18" long pointed wooden stakes

How much lumber (in board feet) will you need to construct your grow-boxes? Calculate this amount and enter it in your *Tools and Materials List* found in *Appendix B*.

Before adding custom-made soil spread 2 pounds of Pre-Plant fertilizer over the inside area of an18" X 30' grow-box (1 ounce per linear foot). Calculate how much Pre-Plant mix you will need to prepare your grow-boxes. Enter this amount in the *Tools and Materials List* in *Appendix B: Grow-Box Garden Genius Planning Forms.*

Why use custom-made soil?

Custom-made soil is a mixture of inert and organic materials such as peat moss, sand, sawdust, etc., to hold the plants and the nutrients plants need to thrive. It performs all of the five functions of an ideal natural soil.

Advantages of Custom-made Soil

Custom-made soil

- provides perfect drainage and aeration for roots, and balanced feeding of plants (3rd & 4th laws of plant growth).
- keeps the hard subsoil damp and soft, allowing roots to penetrate the subsoil.
- extends the growing season, since artificial soils warm up quickly in springtime, boosting growth (2nd law of plant growth).
- acts as a temperature regulator, since artificial soils keep roots cool in the summer (2nd law of plant growth).
- takes up less space than regular soil and increases yields.
- greatly reduces or eliminates weeds (6th "law" of plant growth).
- saves water since water penetrates uniformly, easily, and quickly (4th law of plant growth).

Learn More

- The Soil
  See ***Lesson 19: Problem Soils***
  Food For Everyone (pp. 100-105)
- Soil Water
  Food For Everyone (pp. 106-116)
- Oxygen and Soil Air
  Food For Everyone (pp. 117-121)

How do I make custom-made soil?

Choose any materials such as these and make the combination you like best.

Custom-made soil mixes:

1. 25% Clean concrete sand with 75% Peat Moss
2. 75% Sawdust with 25% Sand
3. 15% Perlite with 50% Peat Moss or Sawdust and 35% Sand
4. 50% Sawdust with 25% Styrofoam Pellets and 25% Sand

Concrete Sand is coarse sand that is used in making concrete, and is available at gravel pits, construction suppliers and nurseries.

Perlite is bits of granite rock "popped" by heat. It is also available at construction suppliers and many nurseries.

Sawdust is safe to use from almost all kinds of wood except walnut. Fresh from the saw or aged—either will work.

> Tip Avoid wood shavings. They are miserable to mix and plant in and tend to flatten into layers and sour.

Remember, the soil under your grow-box can be sand, rock, gravel, good soil, peat, clay or even cement.

Decide which materials you plan to use in your custom-made soil. Enter your choices in the *Tools and Materials List* in *Appendix B: Grow-Box Garden Genius Planning Forms*.

Garden Genius

How do I fill the grow-boxes?

You can mix the custom-made soil by hand, with a cement or mortar mixer, or with a tiller. If you have a large garden, it is best to mix the materials together before putting them in the grow-box frames.

If you have a small garden, you can spread the materials in layers inside the grow-boxes and mix them together using the following procedure:

Step 1: Prepare the Box Bottom

Rake the ground at the bottom of the grow-box. Make it level and even overall with the bottom edge of the frame.

Step 2: Spread Pre-Plant Fertilizer

Spread **2 pounds** of Pre-Plant fertilizer evenly over the inside area of a 18” x 30’ grow-box (1 ounce per linear foot).

NOTE: In arid areas, use gypsum. In areas that get more than 20 inches of rain yearly, use agricultural or dolomite lime.

Learn More

- Soil pH—Acidity and Alkalinity
  See ***Lesson 19: Problem Soils***
  <u>*Food For Everyone*</u>
  (pp. 132-136)

Step 3: Spread Layers and Water

Spread a layer of each custom soil material and water moderately to make a damp mixture. Repeat the process of layering until the frame is full.

Step 4: Mix the Materials Together

Use a rake, shovel, or tiller to mix the materials together.

Step 5: Level the Mixture

After mixing, make sure the frame is level-full only. There should not be a crown in the center. If the frame is not full enough, add more of the soil mixture.

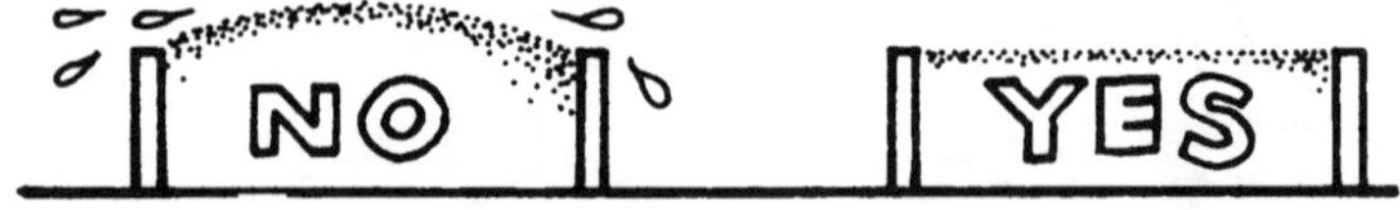

Step 6: Water Moderately

Add enough water to produce a wet medium.

How do I get grow-boxes ready for planting?

The custom-made soil has almost no natural fertility. Therefore, you must supply all the fertilizer the crop needs to produce healthy plants and quality fruit. Here's how you do this:

Step 1: Add Fertilizers

On the custom-made soil in each 18" x 30' grow-box, evenly spread **2 pounds** of the Pre-Plant mixture (1 oz/ft) plus **1 pound** of theWeekly-Feed mixture (1/2 oz/ft). You will learn how to make these mixtures in *Grow-Box Basics/Lesson 7: Fertilizing*.

Step 2: Mix Fertilizers with Soil

Thoroughly mix everything in the grow-box together with a shovel, rake, or small garden tiller. Add enough water to make a wet mixture.

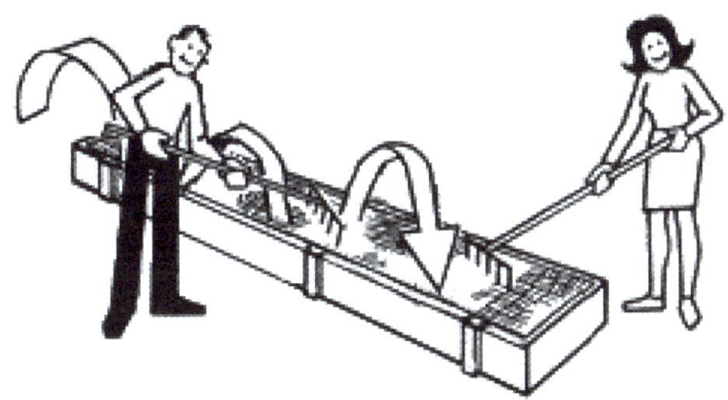

Learn More

- Plant Nutrition
  See ***Lesson 18: Nutritional Deficiencies***
  Food For Everyone
  (pp. 142-254)

- What Are Commercial Fertilizers?
  See ***Lesson 17: Understanding Fertilizers***
  Food For Everyone
  (pp. 255-257)

- Inorganic vs. Organic Fertilizers
  See ***Lesson 17: Understanding Fertilizers***
  Food For Everyone
  (pp. 137-141)

Step 3: Level the Mixture

Level the complete mixture to the top edge of the grow-box. Sprinkle lightly using a fine water spray to keep the soil surface from drying.

Your Grow-Box is now ready for planting!

Lesson 10: Planting

In this lesson, you will learn how to answer these questions:

Should I plant seeds or seedlings?
How should I space my plants?
Can I grow crops vertically?
How do I make a marker?
How do I plant seeds in grow-boxes?
How do I transplant seedlings?

Should I plant seeds or seedlings?

There are advantages to growing plants from seed ahead of the normal planting season and transplanting them as seedlings in your garden.

Many soils harbor insects and diseases. These frequently kill seeds just as they are sprouting or pushing through toward the light.

Cold soils delay germination. Prolonged germination and retarded growth have a permanent adverse effect on plant growth and yield.

The second law of plant growth requires temperatures between 70 and 85 degrees Fahrenheit for best seed germination, and between 60 and 90 for plants to grow well in the garden.

Healthy seedlings, grown in a protected environment, have the advantage of fast germination and a well-developed root system. When transplanted in the garden, they are better able to resist any antagonistic forces. Thus, yields are better and the crops mature earlier. This lengthens the growing and harvesting period and makes it possible to raise two crops of some vegetable types in the same soil-bed during one growing season.

Learn More

- Home Seedling Production
  *See **Lesson 22: Seedling Production***
- Building an Inexpensive Seedling Greenhouse
  *See **Appendix D: Building a Seedhouse***
- Importance of the Greenhouse in Disease and Insect Control
  *See **Lesson 21: Common Plant Diseases***
  <u>*Food For Everyone*</u>
  (pp. 487-540)

In summary, plants transplanted in the garden from seedlings

- are stronger and more vigorous.
- mature earlier.
- produce more uniform and larger yields.
- cut costs on weed and insect control.

You can purchase seedling plants at nurseries or you can grow them yourself in your own inexpensive greenhouse.

Dr. Mittleider grows most crops first in the seed house and then transplants to the garden. However, he seeds certain crops directly into the soil. Most retail nursery stock is not fed and so is nutrient deprived when you buy it.

Refer to the *Transplanting/Planting Guide or Garden Planting* Details in Appendix C to learn which plants respond well to transplanting and which are best planted directly from seed.

Use the *Planting Guide* found in *Appendix B* to indicate which of your crops you will plant from seedlings and which you will plant from seed. Refer to the *Transplanting/Planting Guide and the Garden Planting Details in Appendix C,* as needed, to help you decide.

How should I space my plants?

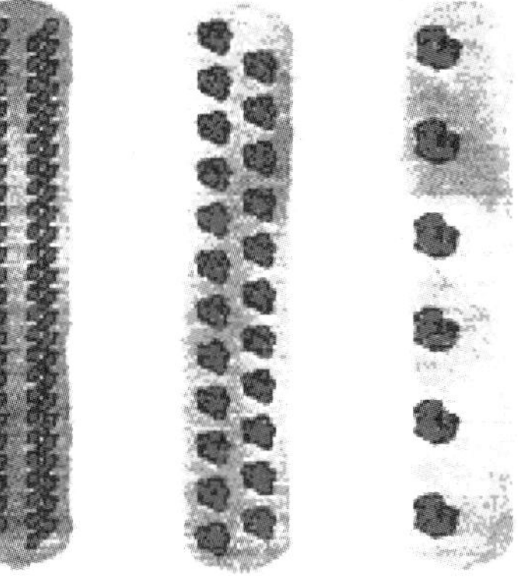

Spacing seedlings (or seeds) uniformly, tailored to their full-grown shape and size, will provide adequate space and light for them to mature. Remembering the first law of plant growth, at least 6-8 hours of sunlight is essential to produce high-yield crops.

Spacing between plants varies according to the type of plant. However, there are three basic patterns for arranging plants in 18-inch-wide grow-boxes.

- ***Double Rows*** are used for plants such as potatoes, corn, radishes, and leaf lettuce.
- ***Double-Alternating Rows*** are used for plants such as head lettuce, cabbage, broccoli and similar-size crops.
- ***Single Rows*** along one side of the soil-bed are used for tomatoes, melons and other large or vertically grown crops.

Refer to the *Transplanting/Planting Guide or Garden Planting* Details in Appendix C to learn about row arrangements and spacing requirements for many common crops.

Using a marker to mark your grow-boxes before you plant is the best way to ensure uniform spacing. You will learn about making a marker in the next section.

Go to the *Planting Guide* found in *Appendix B* and enter the spacing, row arrangements, and depth of planting seeds or seedlings for you crops. Refer to the *Transplanting/Planting Guide* and *Garden Planting Details in Appendix C* as needed.

Can I grow crops vertically?

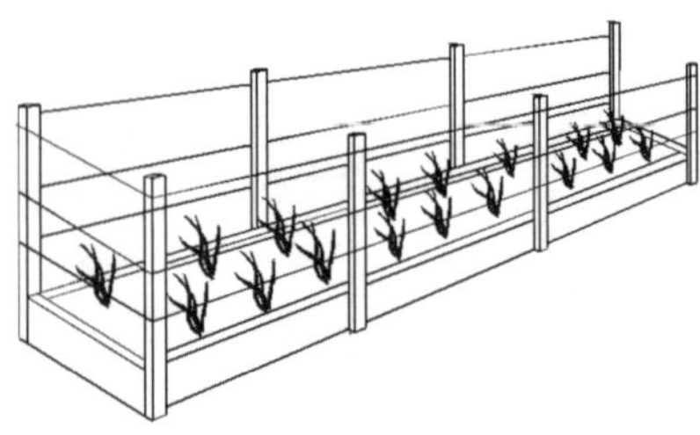

With Mittleider gardening, you can grow plants both horizontally and vertically. Some plants are normal climbers, for example: pole beans, pole peas, and certain squashes. Other crops can be made to grow vertically. These include tomatoes, cucumbers, and melons.

Growing crops vertically has these advantages:

- More plants can be grown in a small area.
- Better quality crops are produced because of the extra light each plant receives.
- Plants are easy to feed, water, prune, and harvest.
- The fruit does not sunburn and the vines and leaves are not damaged during harvesting.
- The fruit does not mildew, get eaten by bugs and animals, or get stepped on.

There are two ways of growing crops vertically. You can use stakes, or you can use T-frame structures (see Lesson 15).

Using Stakes

To grow crops vertically using stakes, you need 2" x 2" x 10' long stakes. These are driven 18 inches into the ground along both sides of the grow-box. Stakes should be 30 to 36 inches apart along each side of the box. Run string or wire between stakes to keep plants confined to the grow-box area.

> Tip Paint your stakes white before using to improve their appearance and durability.

After the growing season remove the stakes and store them for next year.

Learn More

- Using T-Frames
  See ***Lesson 15: Caring for Climbing Plants***
- Making Mini A-Frames
  Gardening by the Foot (pp. 120-123)
- Pruning
  See ***Lesson 15: Caring for Climbing Plants***
- Growing Tomatoes Vertically
  See ***Lesson 15: Caring for Climbing Plants***
  Let's Grow Tomatoes (pp. 64-69)
- Alternative Stake Method (Appendix F)

How do I make and use a marker?

Markers help you mark the soil to ensure uniform spacing between plants.

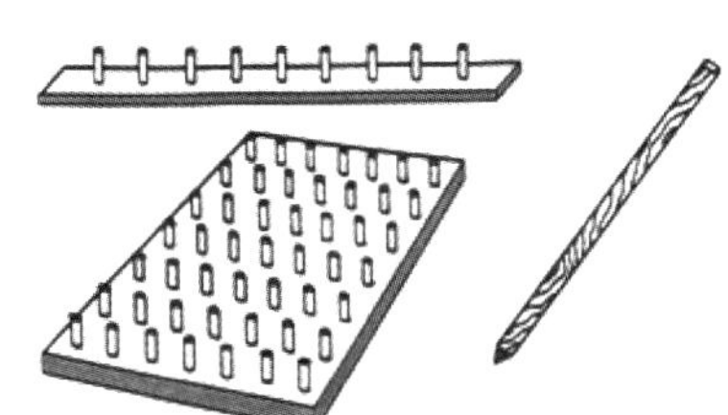

To make a marker for showing the placement of seedlings or seeds at 2-, 3-, 4-, 6-, 8-, 9-, 12-, 18-, 3½-, 7-, 14-, or 21 inch intervals, you will need the following materials and tools.

Materials

- several 4 ft. lengths of ½ in. wood doweling
- one 2"x 2"x 8' wood strip
- glue (preferably water-proof)

Tools

- a saw
- a drill and a ½ in. wood or steel drill bit
- a wood rasp or belt sander
- a tape measure

Procedure

1. Cut the doweling into 2 ½ in. pieces and sharpen one end of each with the wood rasp.
2. Drill ½ in. holes in the wood strip at 6 inch intervals on one side, and 7 inch intervals on the opposite side.
3. Glue the pieces of dowel in the holes (pointed ends out).

Using the Marker

- Transplanting in damp soil is preferred, but the same results can be achieved in dry soil if you water immediately after planting.

- With the marker, mark where the planting holes should be by dragging across the soil in the grow-box.
- Make the actual hole just before you set each plant.
- The holes should be large enough to accommodate the root ball without crowding.

Tip The 6 and 7-inch marker is the most useful as a universal marker. Use this marker to make reference points in your grow-boxes and then plant with other spacing increments (e.g., 2-, 3-, 3½ -, 4,- and 9- inches) by referring to the reference marks.

Garden Genius

Consider the spacing requirements for the crops you plan to plant. (Refer to your *Planting Guide*, if necessary.) Which markers do you plan to make?

- ***6-inch*** interval marker (for 2-,3-,4-,6-,9-,and 12-inch spacing)
- ***7-inch*** interval marker (for 3 1/2-,7-,14-, and 21-inch spacing)

Go to the *Tools and Materials List* in *Appendix B* and indicate which markers you plan to make.

How do I plant seeds in grow-boxes?

If you sow seeds directly into your grow-boxes, remember these points:

- Use certified seed, whenever possible. (Certified seed is produced under more rigid inspection.)

- Don't plant too early, while the soil is cold!

- Do not cover seeds deep. Use the following guidelines.

Covering Seeds

- Tiny seeds—cover only with sawdust, sand or peatmoss

- Medium seeds—cover ¼" to ½"

- Large seeds—cover ¾" to 1"

Tip Cover seeds 2½ times the thickness of the seed.

Planting Very Small Seeds

The following procedure permits you to plant small seeds evenly and quickly by hand so that thinning later is unnecessary.

Step 1: Mix Seed with Filler

Mix the desired amount of seed with sand. Mix 100 parts of sand with 1 part seed.

Step 2: Make Depressions

Using a piece of ¾" diameter plastic pipe, or something similar, make a depression in the soil along each length of the grow-boxes by pressing evenly on the pipe. The space between the depressions should be at least 10 inches and the depression ¼" to ¾" deep depending on the size seeds you are planting.

Step 3: Spread Seed

Take a small amount of the seed mixture in the hand. With a swinging motion of the hand and arm spread the seed in the furrows along the length of the beds.

> Tip Using a 16 ounce can may improve your accuracy in distributing seeds evenly throughout the length of the grow-box.

Step 4: Water Soil

Water the custom-soil gently after sowing the seeds.

Step 5: Cover Seeds

Cover the seed in the depression lightly with sand or grow-box soil mixture. Do not cover very deep. A good rule of thumb for seed planting depth is 2 ½ times the seed thickness.

Optional: Also cover the seeds with a layer of burlap or cheese cloth. This helps seeds stay moist and keeps them from moving.

Step 6: Keep Soil Wet

Keep the soil wet during germination. If the seeds are covered with burlap, gently water through the burlap covering until the seeds begin to sprout.

Step 7: Remove Burlap

Remove the burlap covering as soon as you see the first sprouts. Failure to do this will result in weak, thin seedlings. Seedlings require lots of light quickly.

How do I transplant seedlings?

After marking the grow-boxes, make holes at each mark. It's best if you make the holes right at the time of transplanting. The holes should be deep enough and large enough to accommodate the root-ball and plant stem without crowding.

> Tip Water the seedling plants heavily just prior to actual transplanting. Wet soil hydrates the plant and keeps the root-ball from falling apart when taken out of the pot.

Transplantin g/ Planting Guide

Refer to the *Transplanting/Planting Guide and Garden Planting* Details in Appendix C and for guidelines on how deep to transplant different crops.

To transplant:

Transplant seedlings as early in the day as possible to reduce transplant shock.

Step 1: Take Plant in Hand

Take a young plant in hand. Slip the plant stem between the index and middle fingers.

Step 2: Turn Pot

Keep the fingers in place and turn the pot upside down. Tap the bottom of the pot with the free hand. If the root ball is wet it slips easily from the pot.

Step 3: Make Hole

Hold the plant by a mark in the grow-box, and with your free hand make a hole large enough to accommodate the roots.

Step 4: Place Plant in Hole

Turn the plant right side up while lowering the roots into the hole.

Step 5: Position Plant

Set the plant deep, down to the crown (the top part of the plant), but do not plant the crown below the soil level in the grow-box frame. Dirt falling on the crown will kill the plant.

Step 6: Fill the Hole

After the plant is set properly in the hole, pull loose soil around the plant to fill the hole. Filling the hole with soil around the plant should take just one movement of the hand. Do not pack the soil around the plant.

Step 7: Repeat Procedure

Repeat the transplanting procedures and plant one plant at each mark.

Step 8: Apply Fertilizer

After a grow-box is planted, apply 8 ounces (1/4 oz/ft) nitrogen fertilizer in a narrow band between rows, avoiding plant stems.

Step 9: Water

Water promptly, thoroughly soaking the custom-soil to dissolve the granular fertilizer and keep the plants from wilting.

Step 10: Start Regular Fertilizing Schedule

Apply the regular application of Weekly-Feed Fertilizer 3 days after transplanting. You will learn how to do this in *Grow-Box Basics/Lesson 5: Fertilizing.*

Calculate how much nitrogen you will need when transplanting your plants. (Allow 8 ounces per 30-foot grow-box or 1/4 oz/ft).

Enter this information on your *~~Tools and Materials List~~* in *Appendix A*.

Lesson 11: Watering

In this lesson, you will learn how to answer these questions:

What should I know about plants and water?
How does this method conserve water?
How do I water my grow-boxes?

What should I know about plants and water?

- The 4th law of plant growth is water.
- Over 80% of a plant's weight is water. Tender, crisp, flavor-filled vegetables need water often, generally on a daily schedule.
- A continuous "pipe" runs from the tip of the deepest root to the end of the highest leaf in a plant.
- Every time a plant begins to wilt it has already stopped growing.
- In addition to keeping a plant from wilting, water is necessary to carry nutrients from the soil to the plant roots. Dry fertilizer can do nothing until it is dissolved.
- The larger the leaf area of a plant, the more water it requires for transpiration.
- Since soils are not dams for storing water, it is false economy to supply excess water during irrigation. Stop watering when you see water coming out from the bottom of the box.

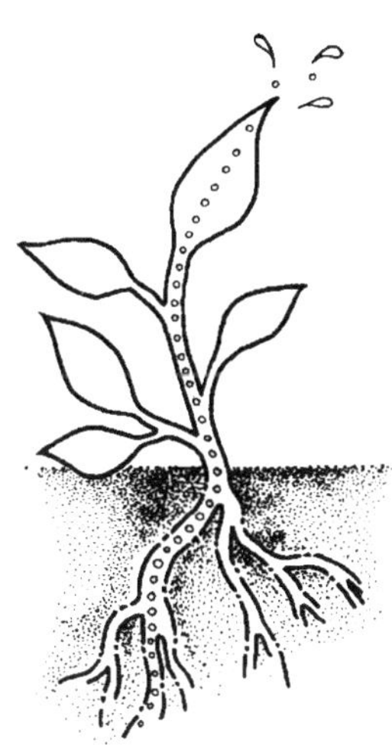

Learn More

Soil Water
*See **Lesson 19: Problem Soils***
Food For Everyone
(pp.106-116)

Is sprinkling a good way to water?

No. Water escapes through the leaves. The droplets you see on plant leaves in the early morning hours are water leaving the plant—this is called transpiration. (A wilting plant is somewhat helped by sprinkling, but usually not enough to support optimum growth.) Sprinkling wastes water and encourages weed growth in the aisles. Sprinkling also promotes fungus diseases such as mildew and mold growth on leaves.

How does this method conserve water?

The Mittleider grow-box method simplifies watering and conserves water. Grow-boxes

- are built above the soil surface, thus assuring excellent drainage all along the bottom edges of the frames. (This same feature makes it virtually impossible to over-water the crops.)
- keep the hard sub-soil damp and soft, allowing roots to penetrate and take advantage of sub-surface water.
- save water because water penetrates the soft custom-made soil uniformly, easily, and quickly.

How do I water my grow-boxes?

Here is the procedure for watering grow-boxes.

Step 1: Tie an 18" Towel to the Garden Hose

Wrap the towel **several times** around the hose, and extend the towel 12” past the end of the hose. This will modify the speed of the water coming out of the hose without affecting the water volume.

Step 2: Turn the Water on Full Volume

Every time you water, make sure to leave it on long enough—it’s the roots that need the water.

Step 3: Drag the Hose between the Rows of Plants

Slowly drag the hose between the two rows of plants to water. Leaving the end of the hose in one place will create a hole in the custom-made soil.

Step 4: Move the Hose to the Next Bed

Lift the hose and towel and move it to the next grow-box and repeat the watering procedure until done.

Step 5: Water Daily

Water the beds daily, except when it rains.

> Tip Less water is lost to evaporation if you water in the cool of the early morning. Water at any time of day if plants show a need for it. Don’t wait.

An alternative manual watering method. While soil is loose and before plants establish a root system, watering with a hose and wand may be the best option.

Learn More

- Automating Watering
See ***Lesson 16: Automated Watering***
- Effective Water Systems
Grow-Bed Gardening (pp. 103-108)

Lesson 12: Fertilizing

In this lesson, you will learn how to answer these questions:

Why do I need to fertilize?
What kind of fertilizers should I use?
How much fertilizer should I use?
How do I mix the Pre-Plant Fertilizer?
How do I mix the Weekly-Feed Fertilizer?
How often should I fertilize?

Why do I need to fertilize?

Plants are like people in that they require balanced nutrition. They get 3 essential nutrients - carbon, oxygen, and hydrogen -from the air, from which they produce carbohydrates. Hence the importance of air as the 3rd law of plant growth. Plants receive 13 more nutrients essential to healthy growth as water-soluble minerals through their roots, hence the importance of nutrition as the 5th law of plant growth.

The 13 essential natural mineral raw materials from which plants make food have come to be called fertilizers.

These natural mineral nutrients in soil can be compared with a checking account in a bank.

- Every crop reduces the amount of soil fertilizer just as writing checks reduces the amount in a checking account.

- If the amount of the check is more than the amount in the bank, the bank will not accept the check. Growing crops affect the soil in the same way. Planting a large crop when the supply of fertilizer is too low will result in crop failure.

- Applying fertilizer to growing crops is just like making a deposit to a bank account. Plants are just like people (and pets and animals)—they require balanced nutrition.

What nutrients do plants need?

There are 16 essential plant nutrients. They include:

- **Airborne Nutrients**

  Carbon (C)
  Oxygen (O)
  Hydrogen (H)

- **Primary or Macro-Nutrients**

  Nitrogen (N) A component of proteins & chlorophyll.
  Gives plants their green color, rapid growth, high protein, and yield.

  Phosphorus (P) Plays a vital role in plant reproduction.
  Affects early vigor, healthy roots, and quality.

  Potassium (K) Vital for plant growth. Produces healthy plants, high-quality seeds and fruit.

- **Secondary Nutrients**

  Calcium (Ca) An integral part of plant cell walls. Promotes early root growth, high vigor, and seed formation.

  Magnesium (Mg) Associated with chlorophyll formation, photosnthesis, and oil and fat formation.

  Sulfur (S) Component of proteins and vitamins.
  Aids root growth, green color, and seed production.

- **Trace Elements or Micro-Nutrients**

  Boron (B) Essential for seed and cell wall formation.

  Copper (Cu) Catalyzes several plant processes.

  Iron (Fe) Is associated with chlorophyll formation which gives plants their green color.

  Manganese (Mn) A part of certain enzyme systems.

  Zinc (Zn) Aids chlorophyll and carbohydrate formation.

Learn More

Hidden Hunger in Plants
*See **Lesson 17: Understanding Fertilizers***
Food For Everyone
(pp. 284-199)

Recognizing Plant Deficiencies
*See **Lesson 18: Nutritional Deficiencies***
The Garden Doctor
(Books 1-3)
Food for Everyone
(pp. 142-254)

Molybdenum (Mo) Plays a vital role in nitrogen fixation by microorganisms and nitrogen processes in plants.

Chlorine (Cl) Essential for plant growth.

What kind of fertilizers should I use?

No matter how the soil is fertilized, whether by compost, organic matter, or fertilizer from a bag, the elements used by plants are the same. On a molecular level, nitrogen is nitrogen, regardless of its source. What is important is that plants receive an accurate and proper balance of the required nutrients.

The elements used in Dr. Mittleider's fertilizers are obtained from commercial sources. Twelve of the thirteen nutrients plants get from the soil occur naturally in the soil and are mined and then packaged and sold commercially.

Dr. Mittleider recommends the following four-step strategy for applying fertilizers. You will learn how to mix Mittleider Magic Pre-Plant and Weekly-Feed fertilizers in Lesson 17.

Step 1: Pre-Plant Fertilizing

Before planting, start with an application of Pre-Plant Mix on the bottom of the grow-box. Then apply an application of the Pre-Plant Fertilizer and Weekly-Feed Fertilizer on top. These fertilizers are mixed thoroughly with the soil before planting.

Step 2: Transplant Fertilizing

After transplanting seedlings, apply 8 ounces (1/4 oz/lineal ft) of a nitrogen fertilizer in a narrow band between rows in each grow-box, avoiding plant stems. This will help jump-start the young seedlings.

Step 3: Weekly Fertilizing

After crops are in the soil, wait 3 days and then apply only the Weekly-Feed Fertilizer on a regular basis, every 7 days.

Step 4: Special-Need Fertilizing

Learn More

- Organic vs. Inorganic Gardening
  See ***Lesson 17: Understanding Fertilizers***
  6 Steps to Successful Gardening (pp.44-46)
  Food For Everyone (pp. 258-261)
- How Fertilizers Are Packaged and Sold
  See ***Lesson 17: Understanding Fertilizers***
- Recognizing Plant Deficiencies
  See ***Lesson 18: Nutritional Deficiencies***
  The Garden Doctor (Books 1-3)
  Food for Everyone (pp. 142-254)
- Corrective Treatments
  See ***Lesson 18: Nutritional Deficiencies***
  The Garden Doctor (Books 1-3)

If plants show symptoms of nutritional deficiencies (see Lesson 18), apply corrective fertilizing formulas in addition to the Weekly-Feed Fertilizer.

How much fertilizer should I use?

Pre-Plant Fertilizing

Before planting, evenly spread the following on each 30-foot soil-bed:

- **2 pounds** of the Pre-Plant Fertilizer (1 oz/linear ft)
- **1 pound** of the Weekly-Feed Fertilizer (1/2 oz/ linear ft)

Mix thoroughly with the soil.

Weekly-Feed Fertilizing

Apply **16 ounces (1 pound)** of the Weekly-Feed Fertilizer evenly down the center of each 30-foot grow-box.

Water after applying fertilizer to dissolve the granules.

Tip r

Weigh the amount of fertilizer needed; pour into can; mark a line on can; fill can to fill line for each feeding.

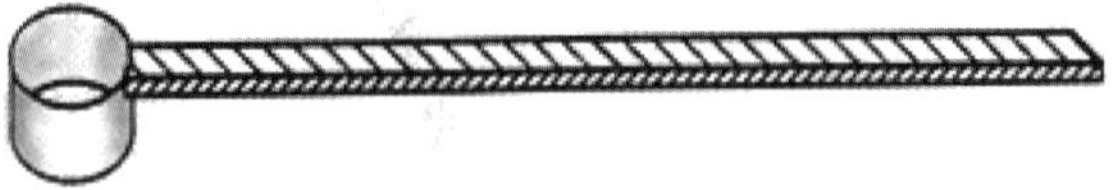

The can on your fertilizing tool holds enough fertilizer for a 18" x 30' grow-box. Hold the tool in your hands at an angle, start at one end, and gently shake the can to distribute the fertilizer. Walk along the grow-box distributing the fertilizer until you reach the other end. Refill the can with fertilizer and start on the next row.

Calculate how much of each fertilizer you will need for **one** application on all of the soil-beds in your garden.

- Pre-Plant Fertilizer

- Weekly-Feed Fertilizer

Enter these amounts on the *Fertilizing Schedule* found in Appendix B.

How do I mix the Pre-Plant Fertilizer?

Pre-Plant Fertilizer is of great importance to healthy plants. It helps seeds to germinate and gives seedlings a healthy start.

> Tip Be accurate in measuring and applying fertilizers to the soil. Overfed plants can produce poor yields just as underfed plants can.

To make ***Pre-Plant Fertilizer***, mix together the following:

- 5 pounds of lime or gypsum*
- 1 ounce boron (20 Mule Team Borax)
- 4 ounces magnesium sulfate (Epsom Salt)

It is easier to mix these ingredients evenly in these smaller amounts. (Doubling this mixture will sufficiently prepare five 30-foot grow-boxes.)

> Tip Remember, the most accurate feeding is done by weighing the needed amount and then marking the feeding container. Thereafter always feed that amount.

Should I use lime or gypsum?

Learn More

- What Are Commercial Fertilizers?
  See ***Lesson 17: Understanding Fertilizers***
  Food For Everyone
  (pp. 255-257)

- Calcium & Magnesium, Macronutrients
  See ***Lesson 18: Nutritional Deficiencies***
  Food For Everyone
  (pp. 192-200)

- Soil pH—Acidity and Alkalinity
  See ***Lesson 19: Problem Soils***
  Food For Everyone
  (pp. 132-136)

Lime supplies calcium to crops. Use different sources of calcium depending on whether you have acid or alkaline soils.

In areas where the annual rainfall is more than 20 inches, use agricultural or dolomite lime.

In areas where the annual rainfall is less than 18 inches, use gypsum (calcium sulfate).

Where do I get these ingredients?

Garden shops (nurseries), farm supply stores, and chemical shops usually carry packaged fertilizers, including gypsum and/or agricultural lime.

Boron and magnesium sulfate are frequently sold in supermarkets under the following names: *Twenty Mule Team Borax* (a detergent) and *Epsom Salt*—magnesium sulfate (a laxative).

Based on how much Pre-Plant Fertilizer you will need for your garden, calculate how much of each ingredient you will need.

- lime or gypsum
- boron (*Borax*)
- magnesium sulfate (*Epsom Salt*)

Enter these amounts on *Tools and Materials List* found in *Appendix B*.

How do I mix the Weekly-Feed Fertilizer?

Weekly-Feed Fertilizer provides for the on-going nutritional needs of growing plants.

To make 25 pounds of ***Weekly-Feed Fertilizer***, mix together the following:

Ammonium Nitrate *$AmNO_3$* (34-0-0)	10 pounds 8 ounces
Phosphorus *P* (0-45-0)	4 pounds 8 ounces
Potassium *K (0-0-60)*	6 pounds
Magnesium Sulfate *MgSO4 (Epsom Salt)*	3 pounds 12 ounces
Boron *B* (*Borax*)	3 ounces
Manganese *$MnSO_4$*	2 ounces
Zinc *$ZnSO_4$*	4 ounces
Iron(Fe) Chelate #330	½ ounce
Copper Sulfate *$CuSO_4$*	½ ounce
Molybdenum *Mo*	¼ ounce

Learn More

What Are Commercial Fertilizers?
*See **Lesson 17: Understanding Fertilizers***
Food For Everyone
(pp. 255-257)

What if I can't find these ingredients

You can order the Micro-Nutrients directly from us online at www.growfood.com/shop. Add 4# of Epsom Salt. And 25# of 16-16-16 will provide the Nitrogen Phosphorus, and Potassium needed.

For a short-term substitute to the Weekly-Feed Fertilizer, mix together

- 6 pounds fertilizer (16-16-16)
- 1 pound magnesium sulfate (*Epsom Salt*)
- 5 grams boron (*Borax*)

What do the numbers 16-16-16 mean?

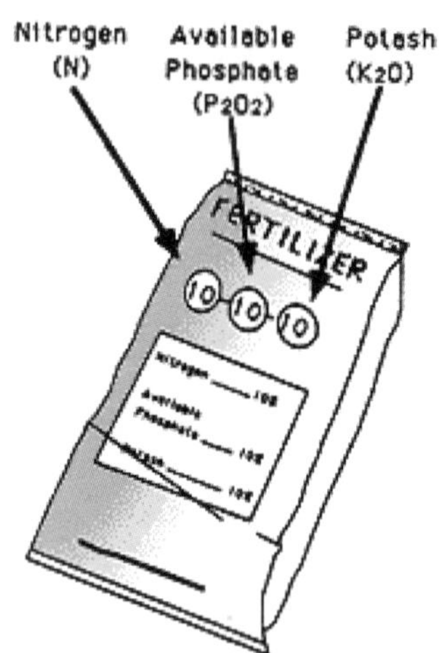

Throughout the world, fertilizer is sold using standard labels. The three numbers show the percent of nitrogen (N), phosphorus (P), and potassium (K) in the fertilizer. For instance, the fertilizer bag shown here contains 10% of each element.

What should I do if I can't find a 16-16-16 fertilizer?

Substitute one of the following mixtures, shown here in order of most acceptable substitute to least acceptable:

- 15-15-15 fertilizer
- 17-17-17 fertilizer
- 20-20-20 fertilizer

Garden Genius

Do you plan to use the standard Weekly-Feed formula listed above or to start by using the short-term-substitute formula?

Refer to the *Tools and Materials List* in *Appendix B* and check off the materials you need to get for the Weekly-Feed formula you have chosen to use.

How often should I fertilize?

Fertilize with the ***Weekly-Feed Fertilizer*** every 7 days, applying down the center of the bed and away from plant stems.

Learn More

- Recognizing Plant Deficiencies
  See ***Lesson 18: Nutritional Deficiencies***
  The Garden Doctor (Books 1-3)
  Food for Everyone (pp.142-254)

When to Begin

For transplanted plants, apply the first regular application of the Weekly-Feed Fertilizer 3 days after transplanting and on a weekly basis thereafter.

For crops planted from seed, do not fertilize until the seeds have sprouted.

How Many Applications

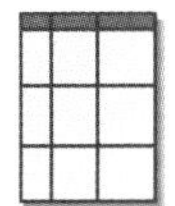

Suggested Fertilizer Applications

To see a table showing how many weekly applications are recommended for various crops, refer to *Suggested Fertilizer Applicationsand Garden Planting Details* in *Appendix C.*

These are only recommendations. Any time plants look like they are hungry, they should be fed. Judge by the visual appearance of the plants.

> Tip Fertilizing with Weekly Feed should continue until 3 weeks before harvest for single-crop varieties, and until 8 weeks before the first expected killing frost for ever-bearing plants. If not including lime in the Weekly Feed Mix ever-bearing crops should receive an additional Pre-Plant feeding after 8 weeks.

What are the signs of a hungry plant?

"Plant hunger" is shown by thin, weak looking plants, poor leaf color, blossoms not developing into fruit, and inferior quality of fruit.

Garden Genius

Go to the *Fertilizing Schedule* in *Appendix B* and enter the recommended number of Weekly-Feed Fertilizer applications for each of your crops. Use this schedule to record the dates you fertilize each crop.

Lesson 13: Weeding

In this lesson, you will learn how to answer these questions:

When do I start controlling weeds?
How can I prevent weeds?

When do I start controlling weeds?

The need to weed should be minimal when using custom-made soil in grow-boxes. Still, weeds can originate from under and around grow-boxes and can also be transferred to the grow-boxes through the air. These weeds can be easily eliminated by starting to control them before they control you.

Remember, there are two kinds of weeds—perennial and annual.

- ***Perennial*** weeds keep growing year after year from the same rhizomes (underground stems) and runners.

- ***Annual*** weeds start from new seeds every year.

There are two main times to control weeds.

Time One: When Preparing the Soil for Planting

This is the best time to attack perennial weeds. You should try at this time to remove the rhizomes and runners of all perennial plants. Some of the biggest weed nuisances spread through runners. Removing them will save a lot of unnecessary effort later.

Time Two: When the Weeds first Sprout

Usually about 5 to 8 days after planting your crop, annual weeds begin to sprout. This is the time to stop them.

How can I prevent weeds?

Using custom-made soil is one of the best ways to prevent weeds in the first place. Here are several additional ways to prevent weeds from coming up in your grow-boxes:

- Irrigate with well water.
- Use a domestic water supply (garden hose connected to water faucet).
- Do not walk in the grow-boxes. Shoes carry disease and weeds.
- Remove sprouting weeds from the aisles using the rake or scuffle hoe. Shallow tilling with a small garden tiller is also possible.

Lesson 14: Harvesting

In this lesson, you will learn how to answer these questions:

> How do I protect my harvest?
> When should I harvest my crops?

How do I protect my harvest?

You can protect and enhance a bountiful harvest by following a few simple rules:

- Consider growing crops vertically to protect fruit from pests and spoilage on the ground.
- When the days are hot, harvest vegetables in the cooler morning hours.
- Treat produce gently—avoid bruising.
- Keep freshly-picked produce out of the sunshine and wind. Cool it promptly to keep it from wilting.
- Keep produce clean—consider eye-appeal.
- For the ultimate in health, flavor and eating quality, allow crops to mature and ripen on the plants or vines.

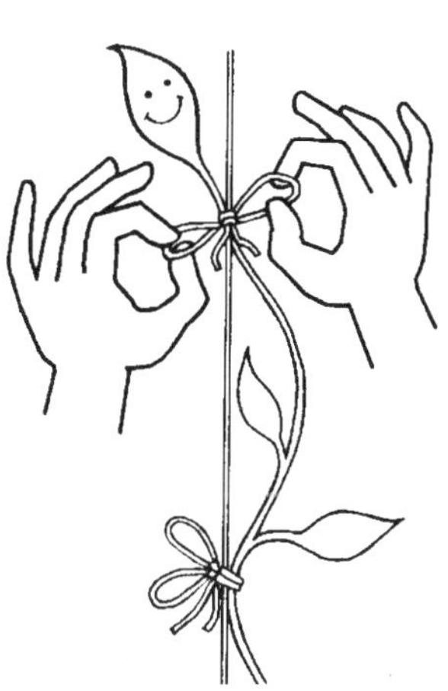

Learn More

- Pruning
  *See **Lesson 15: Caring for Climbing Plants***
- Growing Crops Vertically
  *See **Lesson 15: Caring for Climbing Plants***
  More Food From Your Garden (pp. 75-85)

> Tip Fruit picked too early will be lacking in vital nutrients, and if fruit is left on the vine past maturity the plant senses the completion of it life cycle and starts to die.
> Harvest at peak maturity to assure a long and delicious harvest of healthy fruit.

When should I harvest my crops?

To enjoy vegetables at their prime, you need to pick them at the right time.

Avoid harvesting in the middle of the day.

Do not leave crates of fresh produce in the sun or wind to wilt and heat up.

Harvest . . .

- ***peas*** when the pods are full - leaves at any time.
- ***broccoli*** and ***cauliflower*** just as the heads loosen and before flowers appear - leaves at any time.
- ***red beets at any size - leaves*** throughout the growing cycle.
- ***red and Swiss chard*** - Keep outer leaves picked all season.
- ***new potatoes*** while the skins slip easily. (Allow potatoes for winter use to remain until the vines dry out.)
- ***tomatoes*** best when red ripe - to individual taste.
- ***cucumbers*** before seeds develop.
- ***zucchini squash*** at any size, but before seeds develop.
- ***cabbage*** before the heads split - outer leaves all season.
- ***turnips*** while bulbs are solid and crisp - leaves any time.
- ***sweet corn*** when silk turns brown and kernals are plump.
- ***radishes*** before the bulbs are pithy—they are best in cool weather - leaves at any time.
- ***cantaloupes*** when the fruit separates easily from the stem.

Part IV: Mittleider Advanced Topics

Lesson 15: Caring for Climbing Plants

In this lesson, you will learn how to answer these questions:

When should I prune?
How do I make T-frames?
How do I train plants to grow vertically?
How do I prune cucumbers?
How do I prune melons?
How do I prune tomatoes?

Some crops such as pole beans and pole peas naturally grow very high. Other crops, such as tomatoes, must be trained to climb.

As you learned earlier (*see Lessons 3* and *10*), you can grow plants vertically by using either stakes or T-frames. You already learned about using stakes. In the following sections, you will learn more about making and using T-frames. Either method, stakes or T-frames, will increase your yields, enhance the quality of fruit, improve the appearance of your garden, and make harvesting easier.

When should I prune?

If you are using ***stakes*** to support tall-growing plants, less pruning is required. With plants farther apart 2 or 3 stems may be allowed to grow. Remove old leaves, leaves that touch the soil, and damaged leaves and vines growing outside the soil-bed or grow-box.

If you are using ***T-frames***, the purpose of pruning is to grow only one stem per plant and encourage it to set a maximum crop of fruit. To do this, remove all ***suckers*** from the main stem. Suckers are new shoots (buds) which grow out of the main stem just above the apex of each leaf (the place where the leaf is attached to the main stem).

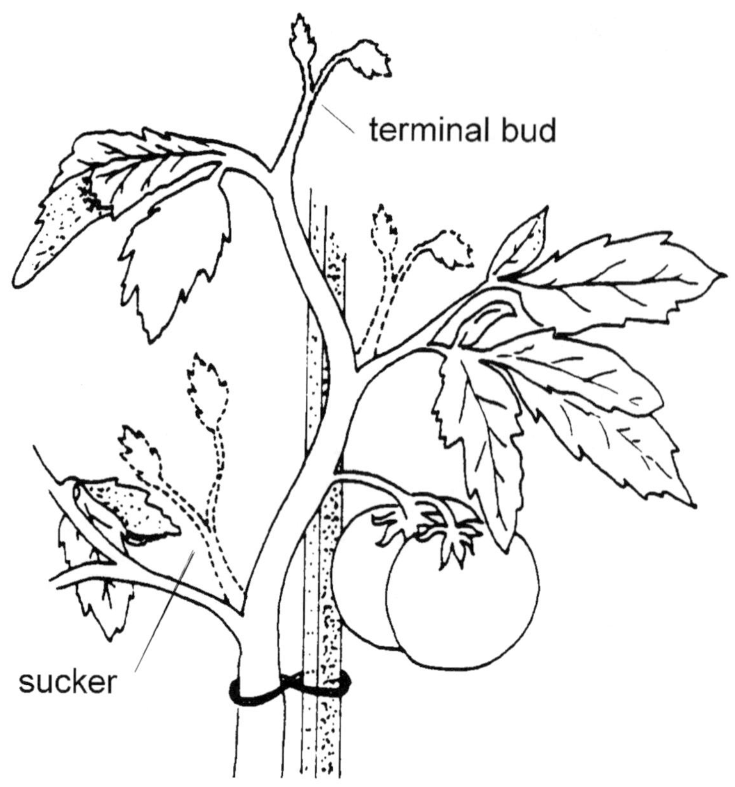

Remove suckers (dotted lines) from tomatoes plants. But leave the terminal bud, which is the growing-tip.

How do I make T-frames?

The main advantage of using T-frames is that once they are constructed they are trouble-free, fixed, and ready to use year after year. These structures are especially suitable for commercial tomato, cucumber, or melon production. Plants can be grown close together and yields are high.

Step 1: Construct T-frame Posts

To construct each T-frame for an 18" bed or box, start with an 8 foot tall 4" by 4" treated post and attach a 4 X 4 32" cross piece to the top supported by braces, as shown in the illustration.

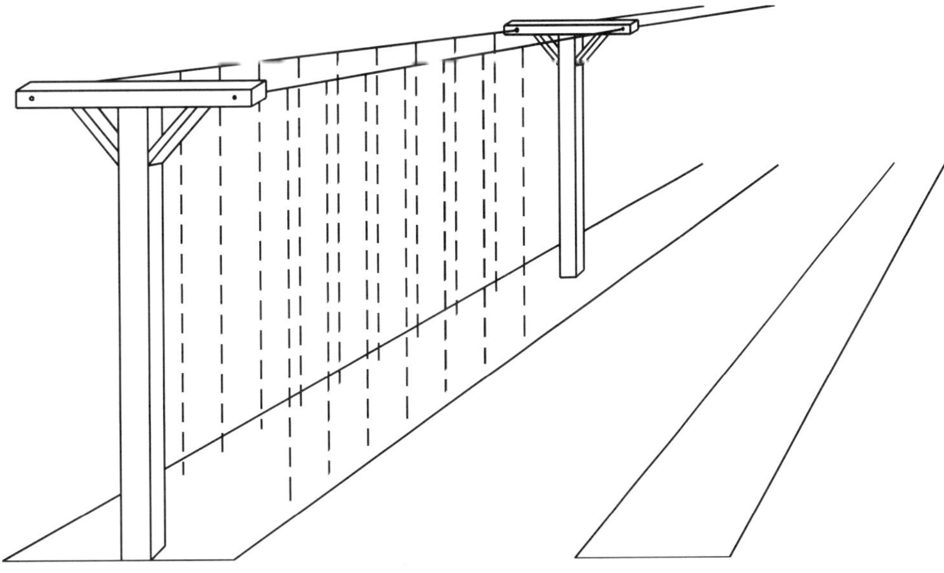

T-frames.

Step 2: Install T-Frames

To install, bury the posts with the outside edge of the post at the tip of the ridge farthest from the sun. Bury 15" deep, leaving the top of the T-Frame 7 feet above ground.

Step 3: Attach Overhead Wires

Attach overhead wires to the T-frames, one wire 1" in from each end of the cross piece. Use 8 or 9 gauge wire and tighten the wires with eye bolts. Braces will be needed on outside T's. Alternatively, ½" steel pipe or rebar can be used. If you are considering covering your T-frames for an in-the-garden greenhouse nail 2 x 4's vertically to the outside edges of the cross pieces. See illustrations in Appendix G.

Step 4: Attach Strings

Tie 10' pieces of 180# polypropylene (baling twine) strings to the overhead wires, pipe, or 2 x 4's, with a slip knot, one string for every plant in the row, but on alternating sides so that plants go to opposite sides of the T-Frame.

How do I train plants to grow vertically?

To train crops such as cucumbers, melons, and tomatoes to grow vertically using T-frames, use the following procedure. Guide the strings around your plant stems before they are tall enough to start falling over.

Step 1: Wrap String Around Stems

Very gently wrap a string around each stem two or three times.

Step 2: Tie to Wire at Base of Plant

Run a ground-level 16-18 gauge wire between nails attached to the inside face of the T-Frames and tie the strings to these wires with a simple slip knot.

Step 3: Guide Plants as Needed

Guide the string around your plants, as needed, carefully in a clockwise direction twice a week.

You do not need to train pole beans and pole peas to follow the strings. Just get them started and these plants will attach themselves to the strings and climb.

When plants reach the top wire help the stem turn back down, or loosen more string to let the plant sag in place.

Remove all growing tips 8 weeks before the first expected hard frost. Also stop fertilizing at this time.

How do I prune cucumbers?

When growing cucumbers vertically using T-frames, allow only one vine (stem) to climb the string. Do not prune the main stem.

Where leaves form along the stem, new vines develop. Allow these vines (also called runners) to grow to their first leaf. You will see a small cucumber (behind the female flower) and some male flowers developing. You will also see a bud (the growing tip of the runner).

Gently remove the growing tip but leave the new leaf, the developing cucumber and male flowers if they are present. After pruning, the new runner will have one leaf, a small cucumber with its flower and possibly some developing male flowers. The main stem will be carrying leaves, clusters of male flowers, and cucumbers along its entire length.

If you do not prune the new runners, they will grow like the main stem. They will produce more runners, and soon the entire vine becomes unmanageable. The mass of foliage will cut off light necessary to develop fruit, and the crop will fail. Pruning prevents this.

How do I prune melons?

When growing melons vertically using T-frames, prune them like cucumbers. As the vines grow, leave only two or three melons to grow and mature on each vine. Do this pruning while the melons are very small— the size of golf balls. In long growing seasons several melons can be produced on each vine.

Watermelons have no set pattern to set fruit. Therefore, allow each new sucker to grow six to ten inches long. If it sets fruit, cut the bud off and allow the melon to grow. If no fruit is set, remove the entire sucker. Varieties heavier than 6# are not recommended for growing vertically.

How do I prune tomatoes?

Here is the suggested procedure for pruning tomatoes when using T-frames (see illustration on page 120).

Step 1: Cut off Suckers

As the vine grows, gradually cut off all suckers and leaves that touch the ground. Be careful not to injure the main stem of the tomato plant.

Suckers grow above every leaf node (where the leaves join the main stem). All suckers should be removed from the stem, but save all the leaves on the main stem. Also, save the tomato flowers; these will bear fruit later.

> Tip If, by accident, the main stem is injured but still hanging to the plant, tie the broken end to the string to hold it securely in place. It will sometimes continue growing normally. Or hope a nearby sucker lives to take its place.

Step 2: Guide String around Vine

Gently guide the string around the tomato vine . Do not twist the vine. Guiding strings around the vines should be done as often as twice each week during the fast-growing period.

Step 3: Cut Growing Tip

When the vines reach the overhead wires (7 ½ feet high) unless you have more than 8 weeks in your growing season or plan to protect your crop with an in-the-garden greenhouse (Appendix G), cut off the growing tip of the vine. This stops the vine from growing longer. Feeding also stops 8 weeks before frost.

Lesson 16: Automated Watering

In this lesson, you will learn how to answer these questions:

Why use automated watering?
How do I install automated watering?

Why use automated watering?

Since more than 80% of a plant's weight is water, consistent and adequate watering is essential for healthy plants. If a plant begins to wilt, it has already stopped growing. That's why plants usually require water at least once a day during warm weather and sometimes more often in hot weather.

The aim in watering should be to provide a uniform amount of water at all times. This encourages uniform plant growth day after day. By installing an automated watering system, you can easily and consistently ensure that your plants are getting the water they need. You will also be able to distribute water evenly over the entire growing area so dry spots won't occur.

It's fairly easy and inexpensive to install an automated watering system in soil-beds and grow-boxes. After installing this system, fast-growing plants in soil-beds or grow-boxes can be watered in 30 to 60 seconds, even on low water volume and low pressure.

How do I automate watering?

Step 1: Purchase Pipe

Purchase ¾-inch (200 PSI) plastic pipe. Make up lengths 30 feet long (or the length to fit your soil-beds or grow-boxes).

Step 2: Make Three Rows of Holes in the Pipe

Make a simple jig to mark the pipe. Have a helper hold the pipe to keep it from turning. Slide the marking jig down the pipe to make a straight visible line down the full length of the pipe. Then turn the pipe 45° and make another line. Repeat a third time. Mark the pipe on 4-inch centers its full length across the lines.

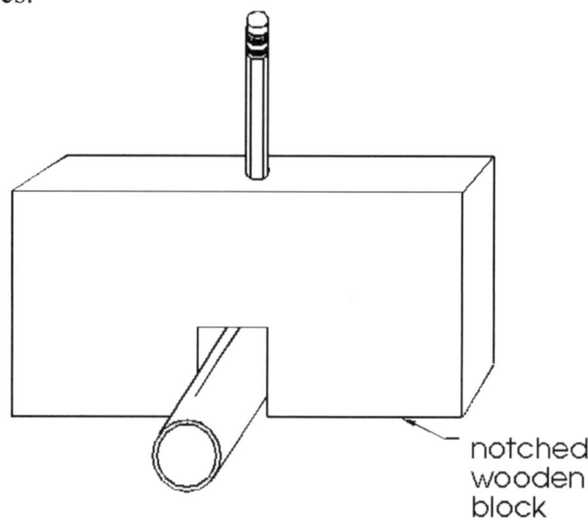

Marking plastic pipe using a simple jig.

Place a hand-held electric drill in a small drill press and make tiny holes in the plastic pipe. The proper drill size is smaller than $1/16^{th}$. It is sold as a no. 57. The holes should be on the pencil lines and the 4" marks.

If the soil-beds or grow-boxes are longer than the length of a pipe, glue the pipes together to make the right length before drilling holes in the pipe. Make certain the lines match. The holes in the pipe must be in straight rows or the system will not operate accurately. Glue a threaded (male) coupling on each end of the drilled pipe. Plug one end with a threaded female cap.

> Tip If your soil-beds or grow-boxes are longer than 30 feet, use the no. 57 drill for the first 30 feet and a 1/16th drill for the rest of the length.

Step 3: Plumb and Connect the Water

Plumb and connect the water to each soil-bed or grow-box. To do this, dig trenches in the soil and install ¾" threaded T-connections.

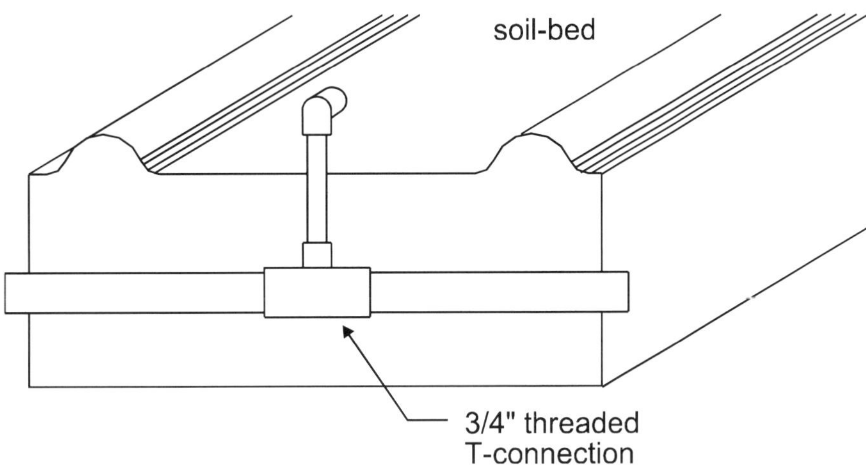

Installing threaded T-connections.

Step 4: Install Shut-Off Valve

Install a "quick shut-off" valve at the end of the soil-bed or grow-box by the water source. Using plastic pipe fittings, plumb the water source two inches above the end of the bed. Install a half-threaded plastic "L." The threaded portion should be female threads.

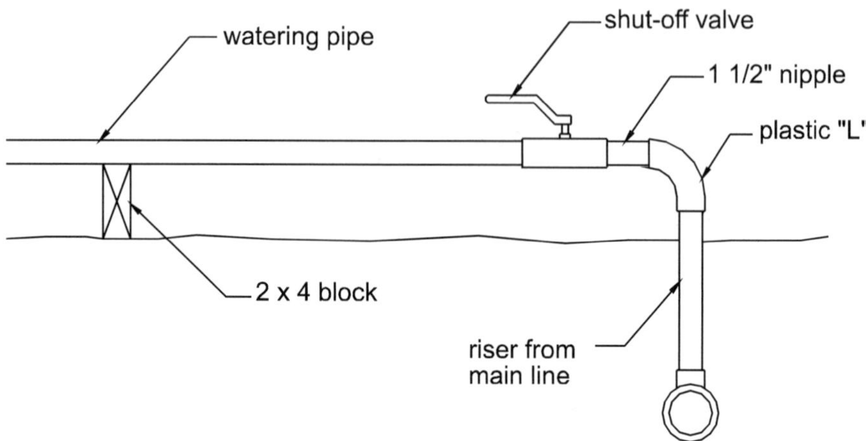

Shut-off valve assembly.

Step 5: Cover the Trenches

After the main line and risers are connected and glued in place, cover the trenches with soil.

Step 6: Connect Drilled Pipes

Mate the threaded couplings of the drilled pipe with the threaded "L."

Step 7: Prepare Blocks of Wood

From a 2" x 4" strip of lumber, cut off 6-inch blocks, 5 per 30-foot soil-bed or grow-box. Space them evenly down the center of the row. Lay the blocks across the beds, not length-wise.

Step 8: Attach Watering Pipes

Lay the pipe down the center of the beds on the 2" x 4" blocks and thread each into its water source. Turn the holes in the pipe so the center row faces straight downward.

> Tip To keep the pipe positioned on the blocks, drive two 1 ½" finish nails into the center of the block 1" apart.

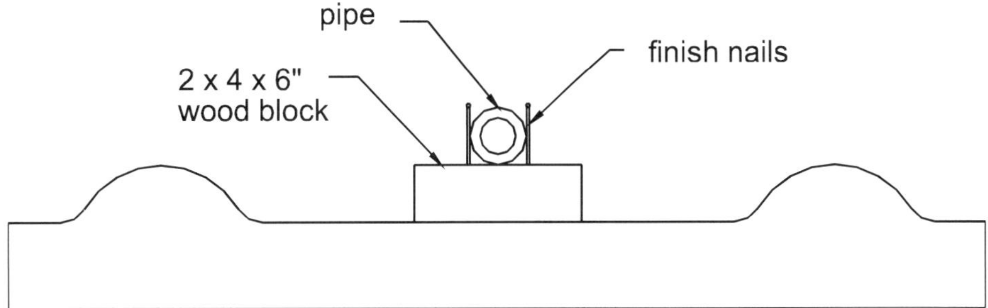

Drilled pipe should rest on 2 x 4 x 6" wooden blocks.

Refer to the scale drawing of your soil-beds or grow-boxes and calculate how much pipe and the number and kinds of fittings you will need to automate the watering in your garden.

Lesson 17: Understanding Fertilizers

In this lesson, you will learn how to answer these questions:

What are fertilizers?
Should I use organic or inorganic fertilizers?
How are fertilizers packaged and sold?
What are the benefits of fertilizing?
What can happen if I don't fertilize enough?
What can happen if I fertilize too much?

What are fertilizers?

There are 16 essential plant nutrients. In addition to the carbon, oxygen, and hydrogen found in the air, the essential plant nutrients include the following elements commonly found in the soil: nitrogen, phosphorus, potassium, calcium, sulfur, magnesium, zinc, boron, manganese, iron, copper, chlorine, and molybdenum.

None of the 16 essential nutrients which plants require can be used as single elements by the plants. They must be oxidized before plants can use them. For example:

- Pure nitrogen is an inert gas and cannot be used by plants.
- Pure phosphorus, when exposed to air, flashes into flame and cannot be used by plants.

- Pure metallic potassium must be kept under oil to prevent oxidation. Exposed to air, it oxidizes quickly and, combined with water, forms caustic potash, a highly toxic material.

Learn More

Plant Nutrients
Food for Everyone
(pp. 142-249)

Consequently, commercial natural mineral fertilizers are sold as water-soluble compounds. The most common fertilizer compounds are ones containing nitrogen, phosphorus, and potassium. Here is a list of commonly used fertilizer compounds for most of the essential plant nutrients. (The chemical symbol for each element is shown next to its name.)

Commonly Used Fertilizer Compounds

Nitrogen

Ammonium Nitrate	
Ammonium sulfate	(also contains sulfur)
Calcium nitrate	(also contains calcium)
Diammonium phosphate	(also contains phosphorus)
Urea	
Anhydrous ammonia	
Potassium nitrate	(also contains potassium)

Phosphorus

Mono-ammonium phosphate	(also contains nitrogen)
Diammonium phosphate	(also contains nitrogen)
Single superphosphate	
Triple superphosphate	
Phosphoric acid	

Potassium or potash

Muriate of potash or	
Potassium chloride	(also contains chloride)
Sulfate of potash	(also contains sulfur)
Potassium nitrate	(also contains nitrogen)

Calcium

Calcium sulfate (gypsum)	(also contains sulfur)
Dolomite lime	(also contains magnesium)
Calcium nitrate	(also contains nitrogen)
Calcium chloride	(also contains chloride)
Calcium carbonate	

Magnesium

Magnesium sulfate (Epsom Salt) (also contains sulfur)

Magnesium oxide
Dolomite lime (also contains calcium)

Sulfur

Single superphosphate	(also contains phosphorus)
Ammonium sulfate	(also contains nitrogen)
Sulfate of potash	(also contains potassium)
Magnesium sulfate	(also contains magnesium)
Ferrous sulfate	(also contains iron)
Gypsum	(also contains calcium)

Boron

Solubor
Boric acid
Borax

Iron

Ferrous sulfate (also contains sulfur)
Iron chelates

Manganese

Manganese sulfate (also contains sulfur)
Manganese oxide

Copper

Copper sulfate (also contains sulfur)

Zinc

Zinc sulfate (also contains sulfur)
Zinc oxide
Zinc chelates

Molybdenum

Sodium molybdate (also contains sodium)
Ammonium molybdate (also contains nitrogen)

Should I use organic or inorganic fertilizers?

Learn More

Organic vs. Inorganic Gardening
Food for Everyone
(pp. 258-261)

It makes no difference to plants whether you use commercial fertilizers or organic materials such as animal manure, compost, or crop residues. Regardless of the source, plants absorb nutrients as ***inorganic salt*** compounds, dissolved in water through their roots. What is important is that plants receive an accurate and proper balance of the required nutrients to sustain growth and yield.

To chemists, metals found in rocks or in rock fragments are ***chemicals*** or ***chemical compounds***. Others call these compounds ***minerals***. For the most part, chemical fertilizers are just minerals that are found, in varying concentrations, in soils and rocks throughout the world. They are minded from the earth, processed into individual components and conveniently bagged for farm or home garden use.

Of the 16 plant nutrients that plants require, 12 are mined from the rocks. These include: potash, phosphate, magnesium, sulfur, manganese, boron, calcium, zinc, copper, iron, molybdenum, and chlorine. Three nutrients come from the atmosphere: carbon, hydrogen, and oxygen. One nutrient, nitrogen, originally comes from the air and eventually returns to the air. Decaying and decayed organic materials in the soil are possible sources of nitrogen for plants. Presently, most commercial nitrogen fertilizer is captured from the atmosphere (like lightning does) or is a by-product from the refining of fossil fuels (God's compost piles).

Does Dr. Mittleider practice or believe in organic gardening?

Those who practice organic gardening generally adhere to the following tenets.

- Inorganic (chemical) fertilizers and pesticides are poisoning the soil and soil organisms.

  Crops grown with inorganic fertilizers and pesticides are harmful to humans and less beneficial than those grown with organic fertilizers.

Proponents of organic gardening usually claim extra and unusual virtues for natural organic sources of plant food and condemn most chemical sources. However J. I. Rodale, the publisher of Organic Gardening Magazine and Father of the organic gardening movement said "A plant cannot tell the difference between nitrogen from a leaf (compost/manure) and nitrogen from a fertilizer bag."

Dr. Mittleider believes:

- No matter how the soil is fertilized, whether by compost, organic matter, or fertilizer from a bag, the elements used by plants are the same.
- The elements used in Dr. Mittleider's fertilizers are *naturally occurring* elements—they are mined and then packaged and sold commercially.
- There is no evidence to support the notion that using commercial fertilizers is injurious to health. On the contrary, people live longer and enjoy higher levels of health where fertilizers are used.
- Dr. Mittleider doesn't usually teach practices such as composting because it is difficult to determine what amounts of specific nutrients are contained in these materials. All fertilizers must be used knowing exactly how much and what type of nutrient is being supplied, to assure that plants get the right balance of all 13 essential plant nutrients.
- Composting also often leads to other plant problems, such as disease, rot, bugs, and excessive weeds.
- Dr. Mittleider's gardening methods minimize the need for pesticides. However, situations arise where there is little alternative but to use pesticides in order to save a crop. In these cases, you should use pesticides carefully, following the suggested guidelines.

How are fertilizers packaged and sold?

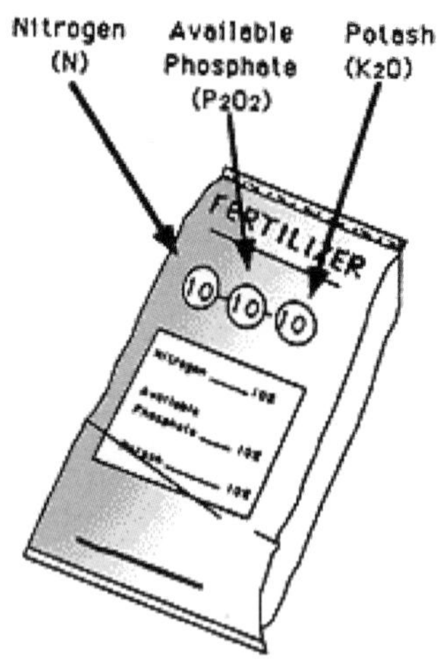

Throughout the world, fertilizer is sold using standard labels showing the percentage of nitrogen (N), phosphate (P), and potash (K) in the fertilizer mixture. The fertilizer formula 10-10-10 means 10 percent nitrogen, 10 percent phosphate, and 10 percent potash. This adds up to 30 percent plant food. Therefore, a 100-pound bag of 10-10-10 (N-P-K) fertilizer contains 10 pounds of nitrogen, 10 pounds of phosphate, and 10 pounds of potash nutrients, totaling 30 pounds out of the 100 pounds.

The other 70 percent of the fertilizer bag (70 pounds) is composed of the accompanying ions and inert materials that serve as carriers and spreaders. In potassium sulfate, for example, the weight of the sulfate ion would be part of the 70 percent in question. The actual amounts of the N-P-K nutrients are marked on the fertilizer bags.

Similarly, a bag of ammonium sulfate fertilizer will be marked 21 percent nitrogen, meaning 21 pounds in a 100-pound bag.

If you need to add 150 pounds of nitrogen to an acre of ground, remember that each 100-pound bag of ammonium sulfate fertilizer contains only 21 pounds of this element. To get 150 pounds of nitrogen when each 100 pound bag provides only 21 pounds, you must purchase seven 100 pound bags.

Urea fertilizer labeled 46 percent nitrogen contains 46 pounds of nitrogen in every 100 pound bag. If a soil-test calls for 150 pounds of nitrogen per acre, the farmer who uses urea needs to buy 150 divided by 46 or 3.3 bags per acre.

What are the benefits of fertilizing?

Each crop you raise and harvest on a plot of land removes many of the required nutrients from the soil. For example, one acre (150 bushels) of corn removes the following nutrients from the soil:

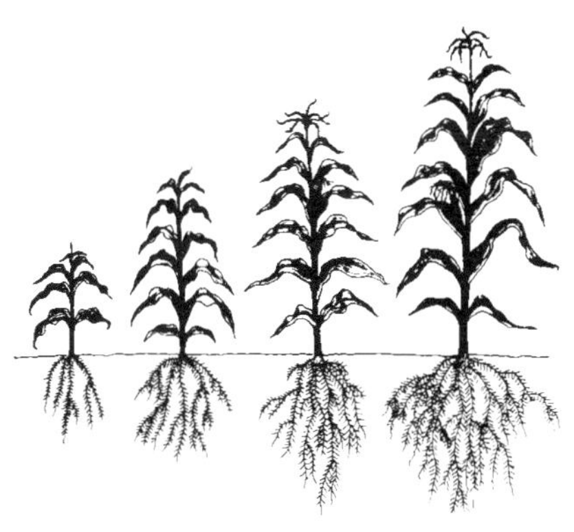

- 240 pounds nitrogen
- 90 pound phosphate
- 180 pounds potash
- 25 pounds sulfur
- 40 pounds magnesium
- 50 pounds calcium
- 2.5 pounds iron
- 2 pounds manganese
- 1 pound boron
- .5 pound zinc
- .1 pound copper

In addition, rain and erosion further deplete the soil.

Soils cannot always be rebuilt by simply adding organic matter. Although organic materials such as animal manure are very valuable, the fact remains that they do not always completely balance the soil. Since their exact nutritional content is unknown, you shouldn't rely on them to offset deficiencies in the soil.

Sometimes plants appear to be growing normally, without any noticeable deficiencies, but may not be growing or producing to their full potential. This often happens when essential nutrients are depleted in the soil and thus limit plant growth. This condition is known as ***hidden hunger***. For example, a field of corn may produce only between 75 and 125 bushels of corn, whereas well-fed plants in the same area could produce between 175 and 225 bushels of corn. Hidden hunger frequently reduces the quality and yield of plants without the gardener or farmer being aware of this lost potential.

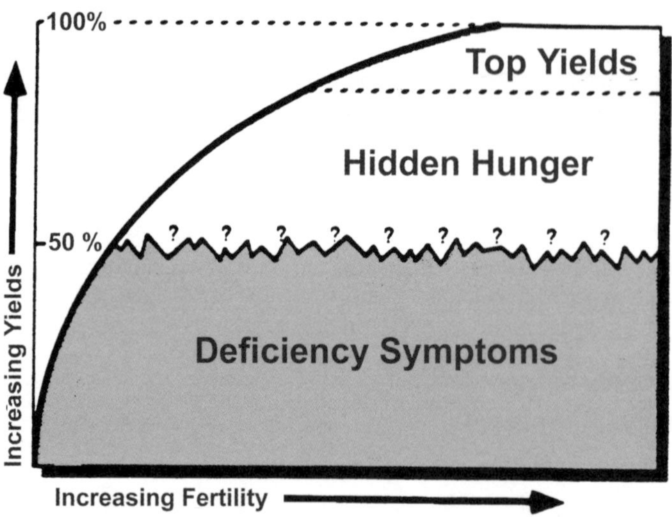

Hidden hunger in plants limits yields.

Based on years of research and experimentation, we now have a proven, accurate idea regarding nutrient requirements for different crops. Dr. Mittleider's fertilizing methods utilize this research to help you to avoid the obvious as well as not so obvious nutritional deficiencies in plants in order to maximize the potential of your garden.

What can happen if I don't fertilize enough?

The soil cannot produce beyond its most limiting factor, whether this is fertilizer, water, warmth, or sunlight. Yet plants will grow quite satisfactorily over a wide range of fertilizer deficiencies provided they are all uniformly low. The key is "the most limiting" factor.

For example, if one acre of land has no limiting (deficient) plant growth fertilizers, and has all the necessary factors for good crop yields, it will produce 40 tons of cabbages.

However, when one fertilizer (nutrient) amount is low enough to be a limiting factor, plant growth will be no greater than that allowed by this limiting factor.

In our example, suppose that our first limiting factor is phosphorous. The acre has only 1/8 of the required amount of phosphorus. This means that, when no fertilizers are used, crop yields on this acre of land will not exceed 5 tons (40 tons ÷ 8 = 5 tons).

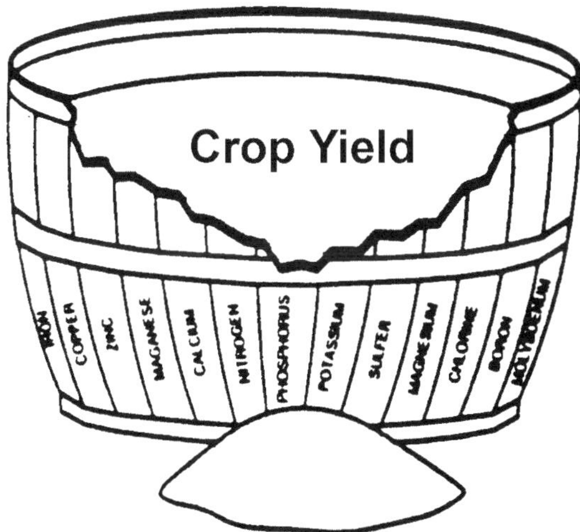

The most limiting factor is phosphorus.

To correct this problem and to make his farming more profitable, the farmer spreads 300 pounds of triple superphosphate on his land. By applying this phosphate, the farmer has corrected that deficiency, and it is now no longer a limiting factor. Production reaches 50 percent capacity, which is 20 tons. By applying the fertilizer, the farmer has increased his yield by 15 tons.

But 20 tons is a long way short of the 40-ton potential, and the farmer tries for higher yields. The next fertilizer he applies consists of 300 pounds of potassium chloride. By taking this step, the farmer finds that his yield increases to 30 tons. The increased yield made the purchase of potassium a wise investment.

Encouraged, the farmer tries for yet a higher yield.

The farmer purchases a 16-8-16 formula. This means it contains 16% nitrogen, 8% phosphorus, and 16% potassium. He adds an additional 400 pounds of this fertilizer to his acre of land.

Does the land require this type of fertilizer? Actually, the next most limiting factor may be calcium—not nitrogen, phosphorus, or potassium.

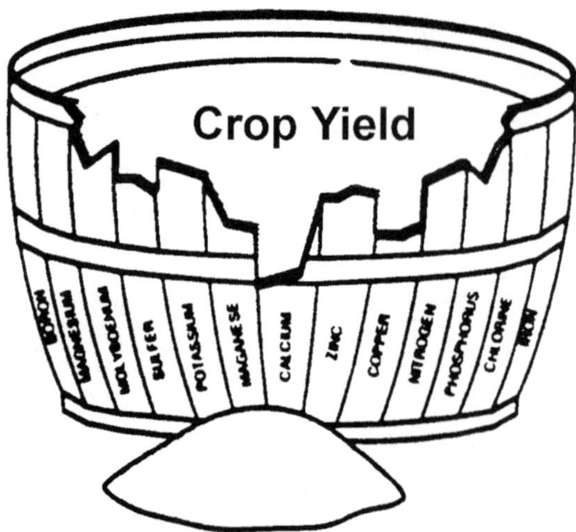

The most limiting factor is now calcium.

Since calcium is now the factor that limits production, the 16-8-16 formula is a mistake; this formula does not contain calcium and does not increase crop yield. In fact, the farmer runs the risk of reducing the yield of his crop. You will learn how this can happen in the next section.

So how can you avoid the problem of fertilizing too little? How do you know what the limiting factor may be in your garden? First of all, if you use the fertilizers and follow the fertilizing schedule recommended by Dr. Mittleider, you generally should be optimizing the productivity of your garden. However, there may be instances where your plants still are not getting adequate nutrients. Deficiency symptoms of each of the plant nutrients are well known. Plants always reveal nutrient deficiencies before serious damage is done to the crop. Healthy plants are known by their healthy appearance. You will learn how to recognize and treat the most common nutritional deficiencies in the Lesson 18: *Nutritional Deficiencies*.

Learn More

- Why Plants Starve *Food for Everyone* (pp. 81-97)
- Testing the Soil *Food for Everyone* (pp. 136-141)

> Tip Spend time getting acquainted with your plants. Learn the language of plants by studying and watching them closely day by day. If a nutrient deficiency develops, the plants will show it.

If you are gardening on a large scale, you may want to get a soil test to identify the limiting factors in your soil. Soil tests are conducted by experts and will describe the composition of your soil and make suggestions about fertilizing.

What can happen if I fertilize too much?

To understand what too much fertilizer can do to a crop, it is important to understand the principle of ***osmosis***. Osmosis is the process by which the cells in the roots of a plant absorb water and nutrients from the soil.

Here is how osmosis works. When two saline solutions are separated by a semi-permeable membrane (such as a cell wall), the heavier solution exerts a pull on the weaker solution and its volume increases as shown in the illustration below. Solution B is the lighter and solution A, the heavier. Because of the impermeable wall in beaker 1, the levels stay the same.

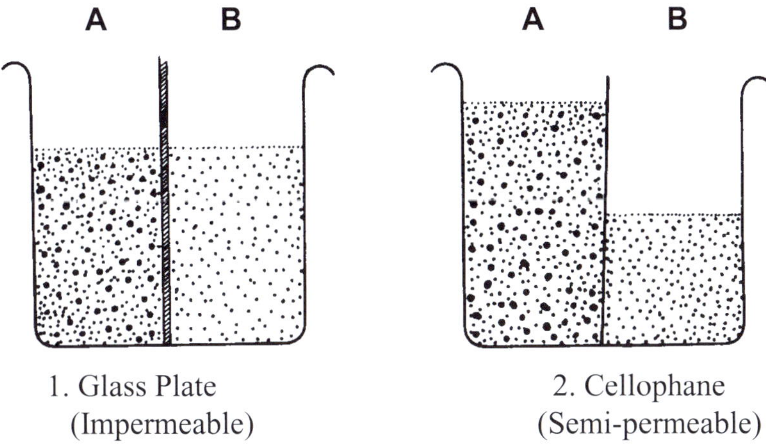

1. Glass Plate (Impermeable)

2. Cellophane (Semi-permeable)

The right beaker shows the result of osmosis.

Here is an everyday example of osmosis in action. Try this experiment. Peal an apple. Remove the core. Cut the apple into four or more pieces. Now sprinkle sugar (or salt—to chemists, these substances are both "salts") over the four pieces of peeled apple. Make sure all parts of the apple are coated with sugar or salt.

You will observe the following results to the apple experiment:

- After 5 minutes—the sugar on the peeled apple pieces will dissolve.
- After 10 minutes—drops of apple juice will fall from the pieces.
- After 4 hours—Almost all of the apple juice in the apple slices will be drawn out of the pieces and only pulp remains.

This is the effect of osmosis. The sugar, being more concentrated, pulls the juice out of the apple pieces.

Let's return to our fertilizing example from the last section where the farmer had applied 400 pounds of 16-8-16 fertilizer to his acre of land. This did not increase yields. Since all of the ingredients were salt, it means that 160 pounds of actual salt were spread on the acre of land (16 + 8 + 16 pounds of salt per bag = 40 pounds of salt per bag; then 40 pounds/bag x 4 bags = 160 pounds of salt). The plants did not need this salt (fertilizer), and the plants could not use it.

An extra 160 pounds of salt per acre will seldom have the effect of killing the crop outright, but it does have an adverse effect on crop yield. Rather than increasing yields, it reduces them.

Plant yields are reduced because plants take up nourishment and water through the soil solution by osmosis. To do this, of course, plant solution (juices) must be saltier than the soil solution. If the soil solution is equal in salt content to the plant solution, the plant stops absorbing water in the soil. If the soil solution is stronger in salt content than the plant juices, the soil solution will pull the plant liquids out of the plant. The plant wilts and, if not rescued, dies.

To illustrate an extreme case of over-fertilizing, suppose the farmer observes his plants doing poorly. He makes the very serious mistake of assuming that even more fertilizer is needed. He purchases urea and spreads an additional 184 pounds of salt on the already over-fertilized land. With the addition of 184 pounds to the existing 160 pounds of salt on the land, he now has a total of 344 pounds of excess salt. This is enough to not only reduce crop yield, but to dehydrate (pull moisture out of the plant), wilt, and maybe even kill the crop.

> Tip If you make a mistake and over-fertilize, apply enough water at a single watering to leach the fertilizers below the top 8 inches of the soil. Then replant if the first crop is extensively damaged or killed. Apply enough extra water for several subsequent waterings to keep the fertilizers at or below the 8-inch depth. Following this procedure will usually yield good results.

The example above clearly shows what can happen when fertilizers are used carelessly. Good intentions and good guesses are not a safe guide when using fertilizers. If fertilizers kill plants, it isn't because the materials are poisonous. They are simply raw materials from which plants make necessary plant foods. The fertilizer percentages printed on the bags tell that they are concentrated materials. When they are applied accurately, balanced correctly, and timed properly, the result will be high-quality, high-yield, and profitable crops. Guessing can be disappointing and even fatal to crops.

> Tip To avoid over-fertilizing, develop a procedure for accurately measuring and applying all fertilizers you use. Also, keep records of how much fertilizer you apply and when.

Use the *Fertilizing Schedule* provided in *Appendices A* and *B* for keeping track of how much and when you fertilize your garden.

Lesson 18: Nutritional Deficiencies

In this lesson, you will learn how to answer these questions:

What are nutritional deficiencies?
How do I recognize common deficiencies?
How do I correct nutritional deficiencies?

What are nutritional deficiencies?

Plants, like people, can get sick. Plant diseases, such as viruses, can attack and kill plants, but nutritional deficiencies are more common causes of plant "sickness." When properly using the Mittleider Magic™ Pre-Plant™ and Weekly-Feed™ Fertilizers as described in *Lesson 5*, you will rarely experience nutritional deficiencies. However, those around you may need your help, so be prepared.

Nutritional deficiencies result when plants fail to get the required nutrients (including nitrogen, phosphorus, potassium, calcium, magnesium, and sulfur) and trace elements (iron, boron, copper, zinc, molybdenum, manganese, chlorine). The soil cannot produce beyond its most limiting factor, regardless of the type of limitation.

No matter how many essential nutrients the soil may lack, you can correct all nutrient deficiencies without sustaining a loss of crop yield or quality. To successfully treat nutrient deficiencies, however, you must recognize them in the early stages of plant growth and promptly apply the proper corrective treatment. Obviously, this means accuracy in diagnosing and treating nutrient deficiencies is very important. Fortunately, nutritional deficiencies in plants are easy to correct once they are diagnosed.

If plants suffer from nutritional deficiencies, they indicate this very clearly with symptoms such as these:

- bright yellow color on the leaves
- hollow centers in the stems
- split heads or fruit

Even if plants have been started with good seed and planted in ideal soil, they can still develop nutritional deficiencies. Plants need a continuous supply of nutrients and water in order to develop and mature.

How do I recognize common deficiencies?

For the beginning gardener, recognizing nutritional deficiencies in plants is sometimes challenging. Making a diagnosis can be difficult if other types of problems exist. Before you try to make a nutritional diagnosis for problem crops, make sure that one or more of these factors isn't the reason for your problems:

- poor drainage
- too much shade
- excess fertilizer
- excess salinity in the soil
- sunburn
- damage from pesticides
- virus diseases
- fertilizer burn on leaves or fruit (caused by placing fertilizer too close to the plants)

Once you have eliminated or corrected these possible causes of your crop difficulties, you can more easily make a proper diagnosis for nutritional deficiencies should they arise.

Generally, plants are deficient in two or more essential nutrients at the same time. However, you can learn to diagnose specific individual symptoms accurately by visual inspection.

If you are a beginning gardener, play detective in your garden. Carefully observe the growth of your plants and note any day-by-day changes. Your observational abilities will increase and so will your ability to identify plant problems.

> Tip If you happen to have tomatoes in your garden along with several other crops, watch your tomatoes carefully. Tomatoes will tell you if your garden lacks particular nutrients. These clues from the tomato will help you treat your other crops as well.

How do I correct nutritional deficiencies?

When you spot a deficiency symptom, take corrective measures as soon as possible. After spotting the symptom, apply the corrective nutrient and water. Do ***not*** repeat the corrective application until several weeks have elapsed.

Be sure to correct deficiencies ***in addition to*** the regular feeding program, not along with it. Do not simply add the corrective nutrient to your regular feeding mixture. Instead, make a separate application (on a different day than your regular feeding application), followed by a separate watering.

> Tip Keep a written record of all your fertilizer applications, including the date of the application, the amount, and the kind applied.

A table of the symptoms and correctional treatments for thirteen of the nutrients needed by plants follows. If you wish to see color pictures illustrating the common symptoms of these nutritional deficiencies, refer to some of Dr. Mittleider's other reference sources.

Learn More

- Recognizing Plant Deficiencies *The Garden Doctor* (Books 1-3) *Food for Everyone* (pp. 142-254)
- Corrective Treatments *The Garden Doctor* (Books 1-3)

Common Nutritional Deficiencies and Treatments

Deficiency	Symptoms	Correction (per 30-foot bed)
Nitrogen **N**	General yellowing of the entire plant, including the leaf veins; weak, spindly plant stems and leaves; death of the older leaves; failure to fruit.	1 pound (1/2 oz/ft) nitrogen (34-0-0). (21-0-0). (46-0-0).
Phosphorus	Thin, weak, spindly	8 ounces (1/4 oz/ft

Deficiency	Symptoms	Correction (per 30-foot bed)
P	plants; red and purple colors on tops of leaves; purplish blotches on underside of tomato leaves between the leaf veins; poor fruit set and poor fruit quality.	8 ounces (1/4 oz/ft phosphate (0-45-0). (18-46-0). (11-53-0).
Potassium K	Firing (scorching) of the edges of the leaf or leaves; brown, dry blotches within the leaf and between the leaf veins; poor quality fruit set; poor root growth; grain stems weaken and filled heads bend downward and later fall to ground.	1 pound (1/2 oz/ft) potash (0-0-60). (0-0-50).
Calcium Ca	Death of terminal buds of the plants; quick and severe wilting, scorching, and death of large areas of a leaf or leaves; poor plant color and growth; enlarged leaves; poor flower set and poor fruit set.	1 pound (1/2 oz/ft) calcium (agricultural lime) (dolomite lime) (gypsum) (calcium nitrate)
Magnesium Mg	Interveinal yellow patches on maturing leaves; later these patches dry up; flower set turns yellow and drops off; fruits are poorly shaped and poorly developed; bright colors of reds, yellows, oranges, and purples appear on maturing leaves.	1 pound ((1/2 oz/ft) magnesium sulfate (Epsom salt—10% to 13%)
Boron	Death of the terminal	1 oz borax (1 gram/ft

Deficiency	Symptoms	Correction (per 30-foot bed)
B	bud; enlarged cotyledons (seed leaves) with leathery appearance and feel; rosette development about the terminal bud area; black hearts in tubers.	(sodium borate).
Iron Fe	Bleached yellow color between the veins of the young leaves; leaf veins remain dark green color; older leaves turn yellow, dry out, and fall off; stunted plant growth; leaves and flowers shed prematurely.	1 ounce (1 gram/ft) Sequestrene 330.
Molybdenum Mo	"Whiptail disease" (narrow long leaves with twisted patterns) in cabbage, broccoli, and cauliflower; cracked stem of celery; ruptured cells in leaves of affected plants; loss of living green color; flower drop, and poor fruit crop.	1 ounce (1 gram/ft) sodium molybdate.
Sulfur S	Creamy white to light yellow color of entire leaf or leaves of the terminal buds; creamy white color of older leaves; dying terminal buds; older leaves die and fall off the plant.	8 ounces (1/4 oz/ft) agricultural grade sulfur.
Manganese 	Predominant symptoms of manganese deficiency resemble those of iron	2 ounces (2 grams/') manganese sulfate.

Deficiency	Symptoms	Correction (per 30-foot bed)
	and sulfur. Usually, however, they are more clearly identified by their descriptive names, such as gray speck, white streak, dry spot, and yellow disease in spinach and beans.	
Copper **Cu**	Copper deficiency is rare. Copper deficiency has a characteristic pale yellow color or stripes, and curled leaves.	1 ounce (1 gram/ ft) copper sulfate.
Zinc **Zn**	Small terminal leaves referred to as "little leaf" in fruit trees; severely reduced fruit-bud formation; small, seedless pods in some vegetable crops; streaks of yellow and long bands of yellow in the leaves of some crops, red firing on orange-yellow leaves with green veins.	4 ounces (4 gm/ft) zinc sulfate.
Chlorine **Ch**	Unnatural wilting of the plants. Resembles the symptoms of excess nitrogen and excess salt.	Do not correct. When formulating the *Weekly-Feed Fertilizer*, use potassium chloride.

Lesson 19: Problem Soils

In this lesson, you will learn how to answer these questions:

What makes a good soil?
What are common soil problems?
How can I improve problem soils?

What makes a good soil?

We seldom experience ideal soil in actual growing, but most soils contain portions of the ideal and function surprisingly well in supporting plant growth. Nearly any kind of soil can be used to grow quality crops, if you know how to compensate for its shortcomings. Here are some characteristics of a good soil.

A good soil:

- is easy to manage;
- can be worked even when wet;
- does not harden, crust, or crack;
- warms up quickly in cool weather;
- has an insulating effect during hot weather;
- drains easily (retains soil air);
- takes water quickly and retains it;
- is low in soluble salts such as alkali;
- does not produce clods.

Because soils never wear out, high-yield crops can be grown on the same soil for generations by applying proper soil maintenance procedures.

What are common soil problems?

Here are some soil-related reasons crops can fail:

- Lack of adequate nutrients in the soil.
- Excess salts (chemicals) in the soil.
- Inadequate drainage.
- Unbalanced soil pH—too acidic or too alkaline.

Having too few nutrients in the soil or too many salts or chemicals in the soil are both problems most often related to fertilizing. In the first case, you may not be fertilizing enough, and, in the latter case, you may be fertilizing too much. We addressed both of these common soil problems in *Lesson 17: Understanding Fertilizers*. To address the problems of inadequate drainage and unbalanced soil pH, first you need to understand the concepts of soil structure and soil pH.

Soil Structure

The term ***soil structure*** refers to the arrangement of soil particles and the way in which the smaller particles are held together to form larger ones. Both soil fertility and moisture are affected by soil structure.

Soils hold moisture as a film of water surrounding each soil particle. When you water, this film thickens, and the volume of the soil expands. Then, as the moisture decreases, either from evaporation, plant use, or drainage, the film shrinks (gets thinner), and the soil volume contracts, often causing cracks to develop.

Humus is the fibrous residue left over from decomposed organic residue. Humus acts like a cushion to separate soil particles. Humus also acts like a sponge to absorb and hold soil moisture and mineral nutrients.

Almost all garden and field soils are depleted in humus content. If the land is deficient in humus, there is no cushioning effect and the ground sets hard. Wide cracks develop as it dries. Water penetration (percolation) is slow and restricted. The supply and quality of oxygen in the soil is also poor. Seeds planted in this type of soil develop roots slowly; seedling growth is poor; and when young plants are transplanted, considerable root damage results.

Garden soils vary widely in their soil structure—they come in many shades and compositions. ***Clay soils*** have the advantage of retaining moisture, but they are hard to till, and water penetration is slow. Also, the availability of plant food often is restricted in clay soils because their highly compacted nature limits the amount of oxygen in the soil. ***Sandy soils***, on the other hand, provide ample soil air, assuming the water table is low. The rapid movement of water through sandy soil, however, removes many needed nutrients.

An ideal soil structure avoids the extreme characteristics demonstrated by clay and sandy soils. ***Loam soils***, containing adequate amounts of humus (decomposed organic material), are closer to the ideal. They are easy to till; they absorb water readily; and evaporation losses are not excessive. In these soils, soil air moves easily in and out of the soil; root growth is not restricted; and loam soils do not shrink, crack, or set hard. Drainage is good.

Soil pH

The symbol ***pH*** is used to express a measure of the acidity or alkalinity of a soil. The measurement of a soil's pH is like a doctor's measurement of a patient's temperature—it is an indicator of the soil's chemical health. The pH scale goes from 0 to 14 and is a logarythmic scale, which means that a pH of 4 is 10 times more acidic than a pH of 5. On the pH scale, the strength (intensity) of acids is stated somewhat like the size or gauge of wire, in which the smaller the number in the scale the heavier the wire, as stated above. Thus, the smaller the pH value the more acidic the soil. For instance, a pH of 4.0 is about the extreme acidity for any soil. A pH of 7.0 is neutral, and above pH 7.0 a soil is alkaline and may contain free lime.

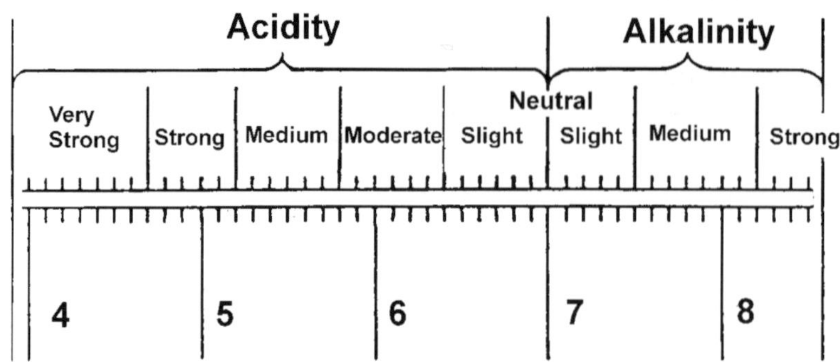

The pH scale showing ranges of acidity and alkalinity at which crops grow.

When plants fail to grow properly, one of the first questions you should ask is, "What is the pH of the soil?" The pH may indicate a serious chemical imbalance in the soil. Soils which are too acidic or too alkaline affect the availability of critical plant nutrients. It may be that what appears to be a serious nutrient deficiency is caused by the acidity or alkalinity of the soil—not by a deficiency of that nutrient in the soil. The diagram below shows how the availability of essential nutrients is affected by the soil pH.

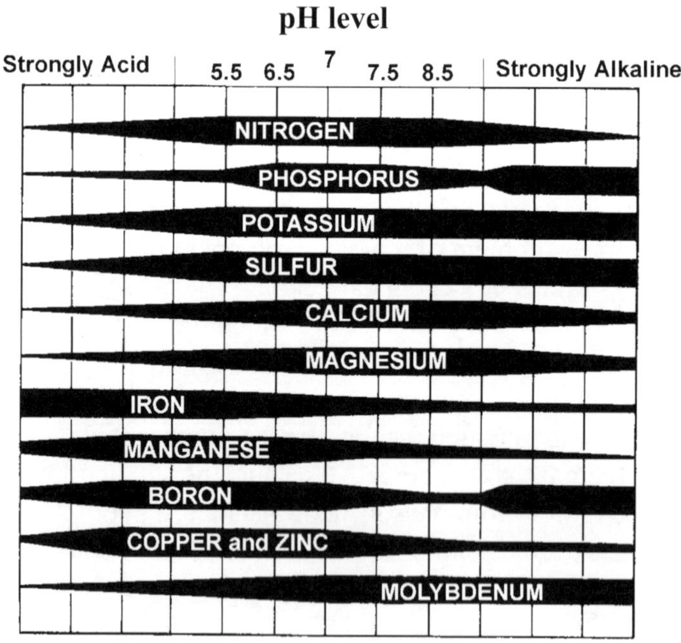

Soil pH affects availability of plant nutrients. The wider the bar, the greater the availability.

This diagram shows how most plant nutrients are optimally available when the pH is neutral or only slightly acidic.

How can I improve problem soils?

By properly using Mittleider Magic Pre-Plant and Weekly Feed Fertilizers as described in Lesson 5, you can grow excellent crops in almost any soil, even without amendments. However, amending some soils can make them easier to work with.

Amending the Soil

Both coarse, sandy soil and fine, clayey soil are poor. But they can be amended. Both can be reconstituted and improved by adding organic matter. Soil can also be amended by adding sand to clayey soil or clay to sandy soil.

Amend ***clay soils*** by spreading 25 percent sand over the surface and mixing it thoroughly with the clay. Another effective procedure is to mix 25 percent or more sawdust or peat moss with clay soil (see Appendix F).

Amend ***sandy soils*** by mixing 20 to 40 percent organic materials into the soil, such as peat moss, sawdust, or rice hulls.

> Tip One 30' long 18" wide bed 8" deep contains 3000+# or 1.1 cubic yards of soil by volume. Therefore, amending 10 clay beds will require 2.5 to 5 cubic yards of sand—with no sand going in the aisles.

If the water table is high and drainage is poor, try raising your garden bed 8 inches above the surrounding water level.

Sometimes gardeners try to retain soil moisture in their gardens by ***mulching***—spreading bark, grass, leaves, and other organic material on top of their soil. Dr. Mittleider generally doesn't recommend this practice, however. Mulching and covering the soil area between the plants with sheets of black plastic helps reduce moisture losses from evaporation. But placing lawn clippings, peanut shells, leaves, manure, and other organic materials on top of the soil has esthetic disadvantages, plus there's the labor cost. Moreover, mulching is a potential haven for insects to live and to multiply. A weed-free and clean garden is good insurance against plant disease epidemics and insect buildup.

Correcting Soil pH

The pH value of a soil indicates the intensity or strength of an acid but tells nothing about the amount or quantity that may be present. For example, vinegar, a weak acid, has a pH of about 2.0 whether you have a quart or a gallon. But it will take 4 times as much limestone to neutralize a gallon as it will take to neutralize a quart.

In a similar way, soils may have the same pH value and still differ greatly in lime requirements. A sandy loam with a clay content of 12 percent would not require much lime to change its acidity from pH 5.0 to 6.5, but a clay loam with a clay content of 24 percent would require about twice as much lime to produce the same change in pH.

As a rule of thumb, plants perform best when the soil pH-level is between 6.5 and 7.0. If the pH is 6.5 or less, broadcast lime on the land to raise the pH to the desired level. On sandy soils, use between 800 and 1000 pounds of lime to raise one acre from a pH of 5.5 to 6.5. On clay soils, use between 1200 and 1800 pounds to achieve the same results.

Alkaline soils are usually encountered in semi-arid regions where the annual rainfall is less than 18 inches. You can lower the pH of alkaline soil by adding 200 to 300 pounds of sulfur per acre. This will usually lower the pH by one point.

Garden Genius

Evaluate the structure of the soil in your garden. Would you characterize it as clayey, sandy, or loamy? Do you need to amend it in any way? If so, decide how you plan to amend it and how much material you will need for amending it.

Try to find out the pH of your garden soil. Does it tend to be acidic or alkaline? (Remember, areas where annual rainfall is less than 18 inches tend to have alkaline soils, and areas with more than 18 inches per year tend to have acidic soils.) Refer to the diagram showing how pH affects nutrient availability. Given the pH tendency of your soil, which nutrient deficiencies are most likely to show up in your plants? Refer to *Lesson 18:*

Nutritional Deficiencies and review which symptoms you may want to be especially careful to watch for as your crops mature.

Soil testing is not needed in a Mittleider garden because it receives regular small balanced applications of all 13 essential plant nutrients, and the soil pH stays in the ideal range for optimum plant growth.

Lesson 20: Destructive Insects

In this lesson, you will learn how to answer these questions:

How do I prevent insect damage?
How do I recognize destructive insects?
How do I control destructive insects?

How do I prevent insect damage?

Insect control is as necessary to gardening success as planting seeds and performing other essential gardening tasks. You should become acquainted with the common insects which invade the garden and frequently leave it looking like a disorganized battlefield.

The surest way to minimize insects all through the growing season is to keep a weed-free garden, and prune and remove old and dying leaves. This keeps the insect population at a minimum because it leaves them no place to feed and multiply.

Not all insects are bad, though. You should try to protect beneficial insects, such as the mantid (praying mantis), lady bug, and others which prey on insects destructive to food crops —these insects are your friends.

If you do notice destructive insects implement control measures at once—at the first signs of insect activity.

Next in importance in preventing insect damage is feeding your plants the balanced Mittleider fertilizer on a weekly basis. Healthy plants naturally resist pests and diseases.

How do I recognize destructive insects?

There are many types of destructive insects. For control purposes, common garden insects (and other small pests) fit neatly into four groups: chewing insects, sucking insects, soil maggots, and bait eaters. These four groups are described below.

Chewing Insects

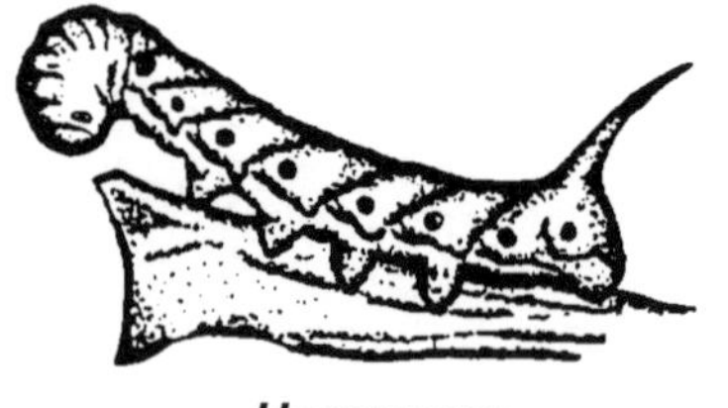
Hornworm

Description	*Plant Symptoms*
Hornworms. Hornworms are brown or green in color. Brown hornworms are called *tobacco hornworms*, and the green-colored hornworms are known as *tomato hornworms*. Hornworms have a notable horn on their backs. They have a ferocious appetite and grow very fast. The adults are brown, heavy-bodied butterflies. The females lay clusters of eggs on plant leaves such as potatoes and tomatoes.	Chewed or ragged-looking leaves or stems without leaves.
Cabbage and tomato fruit worm. The common imported cabbage worm is about one inch long. These worms are generally green in color. The adults are white butterflies. They lay eggs on the underside of leaves.	Cabbage worms eat holes in the leaves of vegetable crops. They also eat holes in cabbage heads—spoiling them for marketing. The tomato fruit worm specializes in eating holes in the tomato fruit.

Description

Plant Symptoms

Leaf miners. There are many species of leaf miners. As their name suggests, they mine their way between the upper and lower skins of leaves. Leaf miners are very common and several generations occur in one season.

Trails between the upper and lower skin of the leaf.

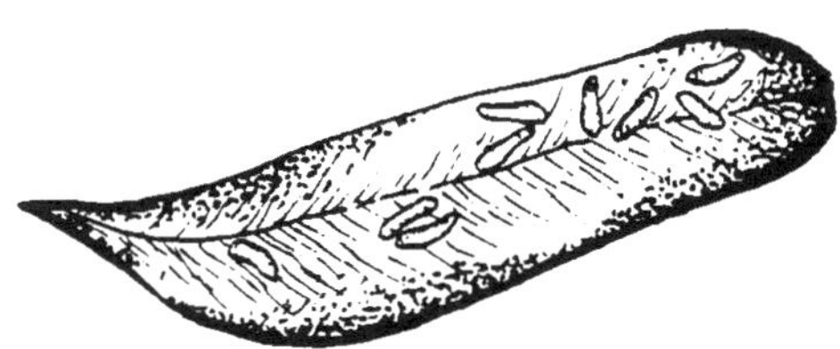

Leaf miner larvae are very tiny, white or yellow maggots. The adults are flies of varying colors. The females lay clusters of eggs on the under surface of the leaves or inject the eggs under the skin of the leaf.

Cutworms and armyworms. Cutworms are about 1 inch long. They are brown, gray, or black in color. Mature cutworms are somber-colored moths. Moths are night-flying butterflies. They lay their eggs during the night.

Cutworms and armyworms are active throughout the year, but in arid regions, they are more active in the early spring season.

Cutworms feed at night. During the daytime, they hide just under the soil surface, about ¾ inch deep.

The common cornborer is also a type of cutworm. It enters the corn ear by eating through the newly emerged silk.

During night hours, cutworms feed on tender parts of plants. They are particularly destructive of young seedlings by cutting them off about 2 inches above the soil surface.

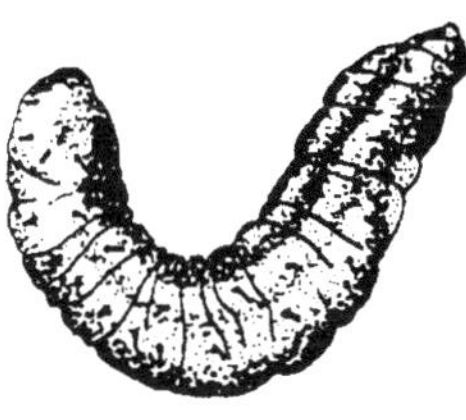

Cutworm

Sucking Insects

Examples of sucking insects include spider mites, thrip, earwigs, aphids, and leaf hoppers.

Spider mite

Description	*Plant Symptoms*
Spider mites. Spider mites are not spiders. They are not even related, but they are a serious pest and very destructive. Spider mites are very tiny and prefer the underside of the leaves. They probably got their name from the fact that they spin a weblike substance under the leaves. To the untrained eye, spider mites appear as mere dots on the leaves. The adult mites are either a rusty-red color or gray with two black dots (these are called two-spotted mites). The two-spotted mite is the most destructive. Young females are a bright red color.	Leaves infested with spider mites are sickly and pale in color. Mites affect both the size and quality of crops.
Thrip. Thrip are juice suckers and carriers of disease. They are slender, very tiny, and often light-greenish in color. There are many species of thrip. They are of primary concern in greenhouse crops.	Thrip damage both vegetable and ornamental crops, primarily by the diseases they introduce.
Earwigs. Earwigs are easy to identify by a pair of prominent forceps at the rear of the body. Earwigs breed in the soil and multiply rapidly. They can ruin the market value of a celery crop anytime—even just before harvesting.	Tender parts of plants are eaten.
Aphids. Aphids are tiny, soft-bodied, somewhat rounded insects. There are many kinds and colors. Aphids multiply so rapidly they completely cover the parts of the infested plant. They live by sucking the sap from	Disfigured flowers and curling leaves. Can destroy an entire crop.

Earwig

plants.

Leaf hoppers. There are many species of leaf hoppers. They are very small, slender, and green, yellow, or brown in color. They are primarily of concern in greenhouse crops.

Leaf hoppers suck the sap from plants.

Leaf hoppers attack all kinds of plants, but their worst threat to the grower is in the diseases they spread.

Deformed flower buds.

Leaf hopper

Soil Maggots and Grubs

For control purposes, maggots and grubs can be grouped together.

Description

Soil maggots. While in the larvae stage, soil maggots are tiny white worms. They are very destructive to many crops, especially during cold weather in early spring.

Cabbage maggots have black needle-pointed heads. They attack cauliflower, early onions, early peas, turnips, radishes, and other crops.

Soil maggots can destroy crops anytime through their growing cycle, but are more severe in the early stage. Soil maggots attack plant stems either at the soil surface or just under the surface. They eat the cambium layers, bark, and tender white roots, and burrow into plant stems both above and below the soil surface.

When maggots mature, the adults

Plant Symptoms

On vegetable crops during the early spring season, watch for plants that develop a dull-gray-green color, wilt easily, and fail to respond to fertilizer and water. Possibly maggots have moved in and are destroying the bark on the underground stems and small roots. Be your own detective and inspect a plant by taking away the soil around the stem to a depth of 1½ to 2 inches deep. If maggots are active, they are easy to

Description	*Plant Symptoms*
become small flies. The females lay eggs in the soil near the stems of plants. The eggs hatch in 5 to 7 days. Several generations can occur in one season simultaneously. There are many different kinds of maggots. Different varieties attack different plants or different parts of plants: • The European corn-borer attacks both corn ears and stock • The apple fruit maggot bores holes in apples • The seed-corn maggot attacks newly planted corn seed, beans, squash, melons, and others Some maggots are active throughout the year, even when fruit trees are dormant.	detect.
White grubs. White grubs are beetle larvae. Their size corresponds to the size of the adult beetles. For example, large grubs will emerge as large beetles. Grubs feed on decomposing vegetation and tender white roots.	Plant dying; roots are eaten off.

White Grub

Bait Eaters

For control purposes, sowbugs, beetles, ants, slugs, and snails can be grouped together. Although, slugs and snails are not insects (they're mollusks), they are included here because they are common garden pests, and they can often be controlled along with the other bait eaters.

Description	*Plant Symptoms*
Sowbugs or pillbugs. Sowbugs are small gray, brown or black in color. They are wingless insects with a flattened body, capable of rolling into a round ball shape. They feed on roots and on the tender parts of crops.	Leaves are eaten off.
Beetles. There are many kinds of beetles: • Banded cucumber beetle • Striped cucumber beetle • Mexican bean beetle • Colorado potato beetle • Squash beetle The bean beetle has 16 black spots on its back. The squash beetle is very destructive to vining crops. They have an obnoxious odor when crushed.	Leaves are eaten off.
Ants. Ants are a nuisance in the house, garden, and field. They carry aphids and deposit them on tender plants such as roses and peppers, sucking the juices.	Plant dies—dries up.
Slugs and snails. Slugs are soft, slimy creatures. They are brown, black, gray, or spotted. They feed on plant leaves. Snails leave a glistening, shiny trail behind them. They also feed on plant leaves.	Corn silk eaten off; new leaves eaten off.

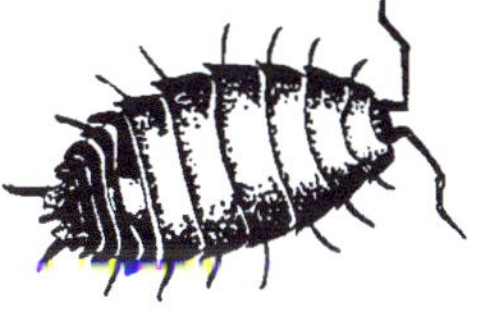

Sow Bug

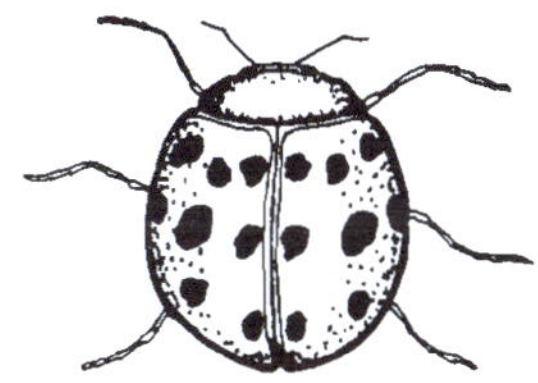

Mexican Bean Beetle

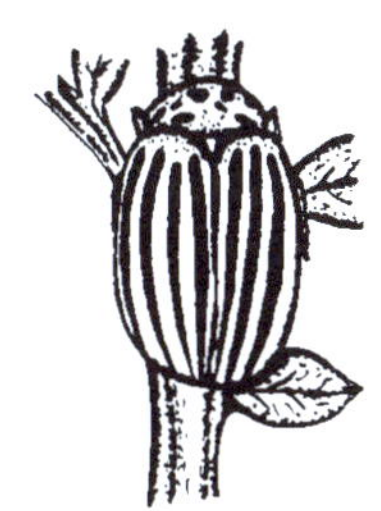

Colorado Potato Beetle

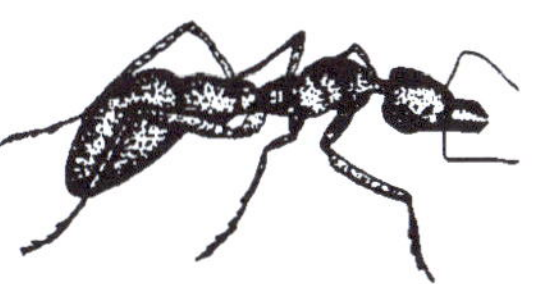

Ant

Slug

Snail

How do I control destructive insects?

The best control is prevention, and the Mittleider garden employs several cultural practices that help, such as bare, dry aisles and perimeter, keeping plant leaves off the ground, transplanting healthy seedlings into the garden, growing plants healthy and fast, and harvesting at peak maturity.

Daily inspection of your plants lets you discover insects as soon as they appear. Physically remove them at every stage of development, including rubbing egg clusters from the under-side of leaves.

Use pesticides only when the foregoing measures fail to solve the problem

> Tip To find the most effective types of insecticides to use where you live, call your county agricultural agent. Insecticides and laws change often. Find out the most recent recommendations and application instructions for your area.

Purchase a reliable insecticide. Use the insecticide purchased to kill one insect to kill other destructive insects that belong to that same group. For example, an insecticide that kills cabbage worms will also kill nearly all other worms, such as hornworms, cornborers, measuring worms, or army worms. Likewise, an insecticide which kills spider mites will also kill white fly and all other sucking insects. You can destroy chewing insects by poisoning the leaves, stems, and fruit which they eat. A soil drench will kill soil maggots and also lawn moth, wireworms, griubs, and other similar insects. Use a poisoned bait to kill slugs, snails, and sowbugs.

In many situations, a regular spray program is essential in order to harvest a crop. Under these conditions, use the proper material to keep insects under control. Keep in mind that insecticides are poisons and should be stored in a safe area away from children and extremes of heat and cold. Read and follow the instructions on the labels carefully.

Lesson 21: Common Plant Diseases

In this lesson, you will learn how to answer these questions:

What kinds of diseases can plants get?
How do I identify common plant diseases?
How are plant diseases spread?
How can I prevent plant diseases?

What kinds of diseases can plants get?

Plant diseases are a common concern of gardeners. There are three main types of diseases that can attack plants:

- A ***virus disease*** enters the plant's blood stream (the plant sap). Once it is in the blood stream, it is next to impossible to eradicate.
- A ***bacterial disease*** enters a plant from outside through an injury such as a scratch or bruise. The infection is usually localized in the early stages, but can kill the plant.
- A ***fungus*** is a parasite. A fungus such as *Rhizoctonia* is relatively unspecialized, which gives it the ability to attack many kinds of plants.

Plant diseases are spread like diseases that affect humans—through contact and contamination. When a virus or parasite comes into physical contact with a healthy plant, the disease spreads to the healthy plant.

There are several ways of protecting your crop from plant diseases. One method is to grow special disease-resistant plant varieties, specifically bred by scientists for that purpose. Another method is to grow your own healthy plants in a seedhouse, because healthy plants naturally resist infection from disease. The seedhouse has often played a significant role in preventing diseases from developing in the garden.

How do I identify common plant diseases?

Symptoms of disease are very different than symptoms of nutrient deficiency. Learn to recognize the difference.

Knowing the names and symptoms of common plant diseases may help you diagnose what happens with your crop. Here are some brief descriptions of a few of the more common plant diseases.

Curly-Top Disease (on tomatoes)

The first symptoms of this disease appear on the growing tip. The living-green color of healthy plants changes to yellowish-green. The growing tip curls and the youngest leaves are deformed. The leaves just below the growing tip tend to curl. Older leaves develop yellow and brown areas. The plant deteriorates and dies.

Curley-Top disease is spread from one plant to another by insects such as thrips.

There is no satisfactory treatment for *Curely-Top* disease. Destroy any infected plants and spray to control the insects.

Early and Late Blight Disease

These are infectious fungus diseases which can invade a growing tomato crop at any time, but infection usually occurs after the plants are carrying fruit. Blights also attack peppers, eggplant, squash, and beans.

Early Blight attacks the leaves but not the fruit. It affects both old and young leaves. Symptoms are brown-to-black spots on the leaves with thin, gray whiskers around the perimeters (the gray whiskers are the spores by which the disease spreads). Sunken spots on leaves vary in size from mere dots to one-half inch or larger.

Late Blight disease looks like *Early Blight* in the early stages of infection. As the infection progresses, black lesions develop along the midribs of the leaves and along the stems. Dark brown-to-black spots develop on all parts of the plant, including the fruit. The spots on the tomatoes become watery, and the tomatoes rot and fall off. The black lesions on the stems and midribs of the leaves increase in size and penetrate the healthy tissues. Later the stem becomes watery, decays, and the plant dies.

Fungicides can be used to control this disease, but results of treatment can be disappointing.

Yellows Virus and Tobacco-Mosaic Virus Disease

These viruses attack many varieties of vegetables. Plants infected with *Yellows Virus* are stunted and have an even, yellow discoloration. Plants infected with the *Tobacco-Mosaic Virus* lose the dark-green color of healthy plants and practically stop growing. Terminal bud cells and leaflets are deformed, fruit has brown streaks, sunken areas, and ridges and grooves. The surface of the stem end of tomatoes is rough.

All infected plants should be destroyed promptly, preferably by burning.

Anthracnose

Anthracnose is a fungus disease that frequently occurs in wet weather. Anthracnose attacks beans, tomatoes, cucumbers, melons, peppers, potatoes, pumpkins, squash, and watermelons. It is especially serious on beans. Symptoms resemble those of *Early Blight Disease*: depressed dead areas on the leaves and fruit with a slightly raised edge.

This disease can be controlled with fungicides and losses need not be severe. The best means of control is prevention. If you have suspect bean seed, you can immerse the seed in hot water at 130 degrees Fahrenheit for 30 minutes.

Damping-off Disease

"Damping-off" refers to the sudden wilting and death of seedling plants. In the seedhouse, seed decays before it germinates, or seedling plants may rot before they emerge from the soil. Damping-off diseases also affect older, more mature plants. Cuttings may rot from the cut end.

Rhizoctonia is a damping-off disease which destroys the cambium layer (on the surface of the stem) of plants. The decay originates near the soil surface, rather than at the plant's root tip. With the aid of a hand lens, you can observe coarse brown fungus mycelium on the decayed parts. ***Mycelium*** are a mass of interwoven thread-like structures forming the vegetative portion of the fungus body.

Soil and planting equipment infested with Rhizoctonia remain infected for months even though they are stored in dry conditions.

Water Molds

Water molds are also a fungi. The mycelium on the roots is fine, colorless, and difficult to see with a hand lens. It is so delicate that it does not hold to soil particles, as does Rhizoctonia. The mycelium grows between soil particles and in organic matter in the soil. Therefore, it is in an ideal position to invade the root tips. This disease is generally damaging to plants only when the soil is wet, hence the name "water molds."

If plants are grown under relatively dry conditions, losses from these fungi may be delayed and the death of plants will occur several years after the plant has been planted in the home garden. Since the soil becomes infested from such plants, healthy stock planted in the same soil also becomes diseased and dies.

How are plant diseases spread?

As explained before, most plant diseases are spread through physical contact. Here are the most common ways plant diseases are spread.

- **Rain or watering.** Rain, overhead irrigation, or watering of flats can spatter bits of soil containing fungus strands to nearby uninfested plantings.

- **Dipping plant cuttings in water.** Diseases spread from dipping cuttings in water. Water is an efficient carrier of many kinds of pathogens.

- **Soil in watering hose.** The soil under benches in greenhouses is often infested. When a hose is dropped on the ground after use, bits of infested soil get into the open end and get washed into a clean planting when the hose is next used.

- **Infested containers.** Rhizoctonia and other fungi commonly live over between crops in bits of soil, on wood, and in corner joints of flats. When treated soil is placed in such flats and watered after planting, the fungi resume growth and cause damping-off in the corners or along the sides of the flat.

- **Infested tools and equipment.** Exposed surfaces and cracks in equipment such as shovels, trowels, dibbles, replanting tools and wheelbarrows also afford a place for the survival and spread of disease.

- **The gardener's hands and feet.** The fingers of the gardener may carry bits of soil and the fungus from flat to flat while testing for moisture or knocking plants out of pots for root examination. A green thumb may actually be the black hand for seedlings!

  Equally dangerous is walking on the edge of flats in ground beds while watering. Infested soil particles often drop from shoes into clean flats.

- **Placing containers on the ground.** It is poor practice to place clean flats on the ground. Infested soil may be kicked or splashed into flats, or the roots grow through the bottom and become infected. The fungus then spreads to the plant above.

- **Unsterilized covers.** Placing old, unsterilized canvas or sacking over seed flats may cause infestation of clean soil. Unsterilized lath frames placed over flats can also be dangerous.

- **Infected plants or seed.** Disease may also be carried to clean soil by infected (but healthy appearing) plants or seed.

How can I prevent plant diseases?

Once diseases spread, they are difficult to control. For this reason, you must prevent diseases rather than fight diseases. Plan your prevention methods well in advance. Don't wait until trouble comes.

If you encounter diseases in your garden, it is usually best to eliminate disease by destroying the plants.

To prevent diseases in your garden, apply the following measures:

- Treat soils. Sterilize all soil mixes and propagating media used in the seedhouse to destroy microorganisms and weed seeds.

- Use healthy seed and planting stock. There is no point in planting infected stock in treated soil.

- Follow a sound sanitation program.

Follow the same type of sanitation practices in the garden or in the seedhouse as in your home. For example, we wash our food and our dishes; we don't eat food dropped on the ground; we do not sneeze or cough in the open; we use our own toothbrushes and towels; and we do not visit friends who have an infectious disease. By the same token, follow these "Do's and Don'ts" in gardening:

Do

- Segregate the clean treated pots and flats from untreated ones.
- Place clean planting material on treated surfaces of benches, flats, or baskets.
- Discard seed flats with any diseased seedlings.
- Segregate areas of plant propagation from areas of crop production.
- Treat tools with disinfectants.
- Use clean cloths or papers to cover seed flats.
- Place flats above the ground on treated timbers.
- Hang the hose nozzle on a hook on the side of the bench when not in use.
- Place plants of uncertain health in an isolation ward until you know they are healthy.
- Wash your hands after working with any soil or planting stock not known to be clean, before handling clean materials.

Don't

- Place an untreated pot or flat among clean containers.
- Store clean pots on the ground.
- Place treated soil in untreated containers.
- Transplant infested seedlings into treated soil.
- Use cuttings taken from plants at or near soil level unless you are sure they are free of disease.
- Dip clean planting material in water unless absolutely necessary.
- Use overhead sprinkling or watering.
- Handle treated soil unnecessarily.
- Handle your plants unless your hands are clean.
- Walk over treated flats of soil, expose treated soil to blowing dust, or kick dust into treated soil.
- Place flats of plants directly on the ground. (Never!)

Obtaining Clean Stock

You can obtain clean stock:

- From a source you trust.
- From plants known to be healthy.
- By using tip cuttings produced 12 or more inches above the soil.
- By growing plants from seed.

Treating Seed

Many kinds of seeds carry disease, even common vegetable seeds. The best protection is to treat seeds using a protective fungicidal coating or by using a hot-water treatment. Both methods are described below.

Method 1: Protective fungicidal coating. To 1,000 seeds (almost any kind in the smaller seed groups) add 1 pinch of copper oxichloride and 1 pinch of *Zineb-65* or *Captam* (but not both), and just enough water (usually just a few drops) to make a paste. Roll the seeds in the paste to coat them thoroughly. Then add sufficient lime to absorb the excess moisture in the paste on the seed; roll the seeds gently to thicken the fungicidal coat, and plant in the usual way.

Method 2: Hot-water treatment. Plunge the seeds into 125 to 130 degree Fahrenheit water for 25 to 30 minutes, depending on the variety of plants, the size of the seed, and the thickness of the seed coat. For some specific seeds and plants, the required temperatures and length of treatment have been worked out (see your agricultural agent).

Sterilizing Soil

Proper sterilization frees the soil of fungi, bacteria, nematodes, as well as weed seeds and insects.

Use an oven to sterilize small portions of gardening soil. See Lesson 22: Seedling Production.

For large-scale operations, use methyl bromide gas. Fill the flats with soil, then stack them along with pots, cans, and tools. Cover the stack with a tight plastic tarpaulin and release the gas from pressurized cylinders at the rate of one to two pounds per 100 cubic feet. Preferably, the temperature should be 80 to 100 degrees, but any temperature over 50 degrees Fahrenheit will work. Leave the stack covered for 24 to 48 hours. Remove the tarpaulin and the flats can once again be used in the seedhouse.

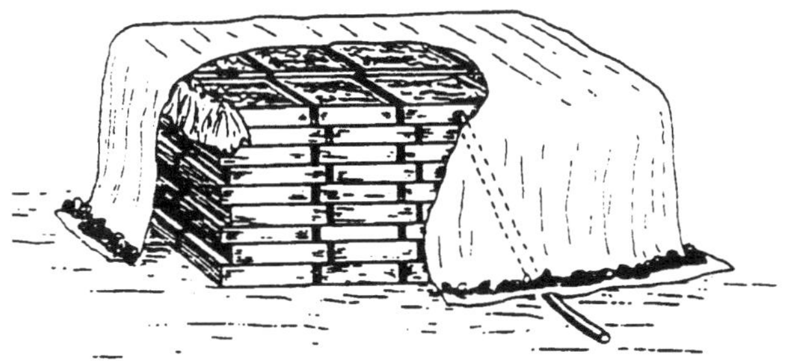

Lesson 22: Seedling Production

In this lesson, you will learn how to answer these questions:

Why build a seedhouse?
How do I plan and operate a seedhouse?
What should I use for a growing medium?
How do I produce seedlings?
How do I transplant seedlings into pots?
How do I transplant seedlings into flats?
How do I care for transplanted seedlings?
How do I care for large-container plants?

Why build a seedhouse?

A ***seedhouse*** is a structure for germinating seed and growing seedling plants. But, why would you want to build your own seedhouse?

Building a seedhouse will allow you to:

- Save on the cost of buying from a nursery.
- Obtain better quality plants for transplanting.
- Lengthen the growing season.

In this lesson, you will learn how to use a seedhouse to help you produce mature seedling plants with strong root systems, stocky stems, and flowers ready to pollinate. This will give you a very substantial head start in harvesting vine-ripe fruit.

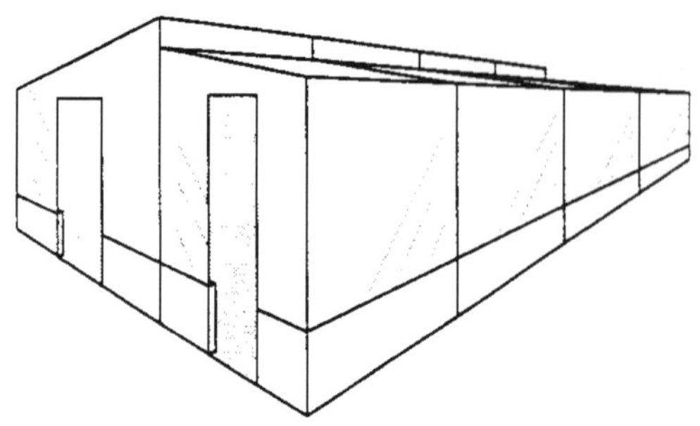

A Mittleider seedhouse

How do I build and operate a seedhouse?

Seedhouse construction is both simple and economical. There are many sizes, styles, and shapes of seedhouses.

To decide what size and style of seedhouse you should build, evaluate the size of your garden and your ongoing need for seedlings. Experience is a good teacher. Time will indicate what kind of seedhouse is best for your operation. Instructions for constructing a good 20' x 40' x 8.5' seedhouse are found in *Appendix D: Building a Seedhouse (***scale to your own needs***)*.

You can also build mini A-frames over soil-beds and grow-boxes to lengthen the growing season and to protect crops during cold temperatures. See *Lesson 23: Cold-Weather Gardening* for more information.

Location

Seedhouses should be located in a flat area where there is room for expansion. They should be built in a location with full sunlight, avoiding shadows. Facing your greenhouse length-wise north and south assures direct sunlight on both sides - one side gets morning sun and the other sides gets afternoon sun.

Layout

In planning a seedhouse, make sure propagating facilities are adequate so seedlings have plenty of light, oxygen, moisture, essential nutrients, and warmth. An effective seedhouse provides uniform light and ventilation.

A seedling greenhouse should be equipped with a peaked roof (top) to allow fast drainage from rain and snow and level tables 30 inches high. Tables are necessary to hold flats of seedlings off the ground and provide a good growing environment for both the plants and the grower. Provide similar tables outside the seedhouse to ***harden-off*** the seedlings (to allow seedling to become used to the sun and outside temperature changes) before transplanting to the field.

Temperature and Ventilation

A seedhouse should have sufficient heat to keep plants from freezing. The seedhouse should also be equipped with ventilators, since plants require fresh air.

Maintain the temperature inside a seedhouse above 32 degrees Fahrenheit, since plants die when they freeze. For all practical purposes, plants stop growing at 50 degrees Fahrenheit. Ideally, temperatures in the seedhouse should be between 70 and 90 degrees.

When temperatures inside the greenhouse reach above 100 degrees, you can pull shade cloth over the seedhouse to lower the temperature.

Expelling stale air with fresh air is important to the health of the plants. Close the ventilators in the greenhouse during freezing weather both day and night. But during the daytime, when the outside temperature is above 32 degrees, some ventilation should occur, even if this is only for a short period of time.

What should I use for a growing medium?

Seeds perform best in a light, soft, and granular soil medium. You can use sterilized garden soil as a growing medium, but only as a second choice (see below to learn how to sterilize garden soil). Artificial soil is actually better, since it comes very close to meeting the characteristics of ideal soil.

To make artificial soil, you can mix together two or more of the following types of organic materials:

- Sawdust—any kind, fresh or aged, except walnut

- Sand—washed concrete sand is best (do not use sand containing traces of clay)
- Perlite—also known as rock wool (available from nursery suppliers)
- Bark—finely ground from Douglas Fir and other pine trees
- Styrofoam—small pellet size
- Peat moss—also called sphagnum moss

Here are some suggested artificial soil combinations:

- 25% Sand with 75% Peat moss
- 75% Sawdust with 25% Sand
- 15% Perlite with 50% Peat moss or Sawdust and 35% Sand
- 50% Sawdust with 25% Styrofoam Pellets and 25% Sand

> Tip When you combine materials to make artificial soil, measure the materials by volume, not by weight.

You can use common garden soil as a growing medium for seeds, but only after the soil has been sterilized.

To sterilize garden soil:

Step 1: Spread Soil on Cookie Sheet

Spread the soil evenly ½ to 1" deep on a metal cookie sheet.

Step 2: Place Soil in Oven

Place the soil in the oven for 45 minutes at 250 degrees.

Step 3: Remove and Mix

Take the soil from the oven and promptly mix it thoroughly.

Step 4: Put in Oven Again

Spread the soil evenly on the cookie sheet again and put it back in the oven for another 45 minutes at 250 degrees.

Step 5: Remove from Oven

Take the soil from the oven and use when cool, or store it in a clean container for use later.

How do I produce seedlings?

Step 1: Fill Flats with Soil

Fill plastic or wooden flats with a good soil medium such as described on the previous page.

The size of the flats and their shape can vary, but a common size of wooden flats is 18” x 18” x 2 ¾” (these are outside dimensions). The two sides and the bottom are made of ¼” x 2 ¾” boards called shook. The ends are 1/2" X 2 3/4" X 17 1/2". The shook for the bottom is separated (spread apart) 1/8 inch for drainage and free air movement.

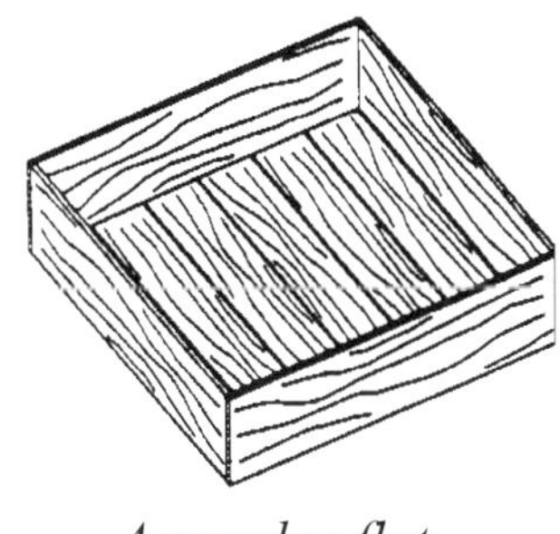

A wooden flat.

Fill flats level-full with the soil mix. Set them side by side on tables in the seedhouse.

Step 2: Spread Fertilizer

Spread 1 1/2 ounces of the Pre-Plant Fertilizer formula over the surface of each flat.

Step 3: Mix Soil and Level

Mix the soil and fertilizers together by hand. After mixing, spread the soil evenly over the flat.

Step 4: Water the Soil

Gently and moderately water the soil in the flats.

Step 5: Scatter the Seed in Rows

To make rows in the soil mixture, take a piece of ¾-inch plastic pipe 17 inches long or a ¾-inch thick board 17 inches long. Lay the pipe in the flat or lay the board on edge in the flat. Use a slight rocking motion to make uniform depressions in the flat. Make depressions 2 inches apart.

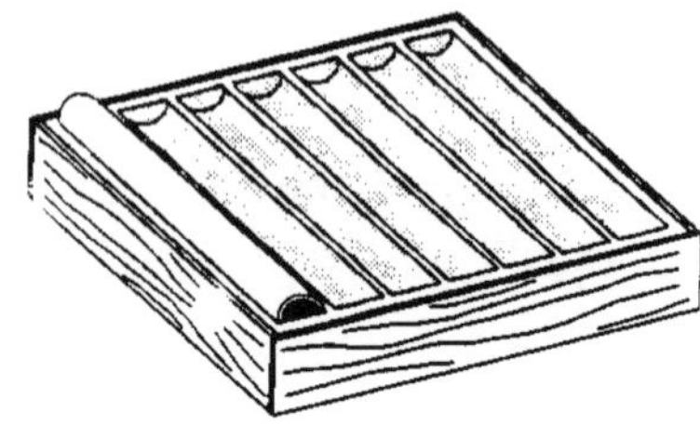

Using ¾ -inch pipe, make uniform depressions in the flat.

Scatter the seed evenly in a wide band along the bottom of the depressions. Limit the number of seeds to 600 or 800 per flat.

The size of the seed determines the depth of planting. Plant seeds 2 ½ times their thickness (not their length).

Step 6: Cover Seeds

Cover the seed in the depressions with coarse sand, or use the soil mixture.

Step 7: Cover Flats

Cover the planted seed flats with burlap or cheesecloth. Keep the seed flats moist at all times. Whenever you water the flats, apply the water through the burlap cover.

Some seeds germinate within 12 hours of planting. Others sprout in 3 to 7 days. And some take 2 weeks or longer. Much depends on the variety of seed planted and the temperature.

Step 8: Water Flats

Gently water the flats sufficiently to settle the loose soil, but do not float the seed to the surface.

Use only water on unsprouted seed. Do not use any kind of fertilizer solution to water unsprouted seeds. All fertilizer solutions are saline (salty) and, as such, retard and delay germination.

Step 9: Remove Burlap after Sprouts Appear

While seeds are sprouting, they do not require light. However, be alert. Know when the seeds have sprouted and remove the burlap immediately after sprouts appear. Just before taking off the burlap, water the flats with a dilute fertilizer solution (described below) through the burlap.

Step 10: Set Flats in Full Light, then Water

Set the flats in full light before the new plants break through the soil completely. As long as seedlings remain in the seedhouse or on the hardening-off tables outside, they should be watered with the dilute fertilizer solution every time they are watered.

> Tip To produce short, strong seedlings, it is important to provide maximum light and to water regularly with a dilute fertilizer solution.

To feed growing seedlings, use the *Weekly-Feed Fertilizer*. To make a dilute fertilizer solution called the "constant feed" solution, dissolve 1 ounce (30 grams) of Weekly-Feed Fertilizer mixture in 3 gallons of water. Apply the solution using a sprinkler can.

When a sprinkler can is not available, you can make an effective sprinkler using a 16-ounce tin can as follows:

1. Cut out one end of a 16-ounce can.

2. Using a hammer and a small-size nail, make holes in the closed end of the can. Make about 125 small holes.

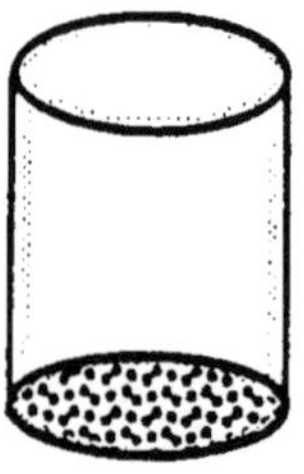

An effective, home-made sprinkler

To water, dip the dilute fertilizer solution out of the drum with a 2-gallon pail. Hold the pail with one hand the same height as the seed flats on the table. Hold the can in the other hand. Dip it in the solution and spread the fertilizer solution over the seedlings. Fill the can with solution before each pass over the flats. Water adequately, but do not move or roll the sprouting seeds. After watering, give the seed flats full light.

How do I transplant seedlings into pots?

After seedlings germinate in flats, they must be transplanted into individual pots to grow and mature. Pot-grown plants are stronger, and thus they grow faster and mature earlier. This lengthens the fruiting season for some crops. When potted plants are transplanted in the garden or field, there is virtually no shock to the plant.

Seedlings can be grown in flats as well as pots. Wooden, 18-inch flats are usually used when thousands of seedlings are needed. Transplanting procedures are the same whether you transplant seedlings in pots or flats. We will first explain how to transplant seedlings into pots.

Pots come in various sizes and shapes. They are made of different materials such as clay, peat moss, styrofoam, plastic, or pressed pulp. Plastic pots are recommended. Use the two-inch square plastic pots for early plants when seedhouse space is scarce.

Here is how to transplant into pots:

Step 1: Place Pots in Flats

Set 2-inch square pots side-by-side in empty wooden flats. Each 18" square flat holds 72 pots.

Step 2: Mix Soil and Fertilizer

Mix the soil and the fertilizer together using 1 1/2 oz Pre-Plant and 3/4 oz Weekly Feed per ½ cubic foot of soil (1 18" flat). Use the same soil mixture as before when you were filling the wooden flats. Fill all the pots in a flat in one operation. Dump two shovels of the soil on the pots.

Step 3: Fill the Corner Pots by Hand

Fill the corner pots by hand, pulling soil from the center.

Step 4: Remove Excess Soil

Take a 1 x 3 x 20-inch board and pull it over the filled pots to remove the excess soil.

Step 5: Water the Pots

Water the filled pots gently and lightly. If possible, water the pots one day <u>before</u> transplanting.

Step 6: Make a Dibble

Make a dibble (see illustration). From a ½-inch doweling rod cut off a 6-inch long piece. Point the end of the dibble.

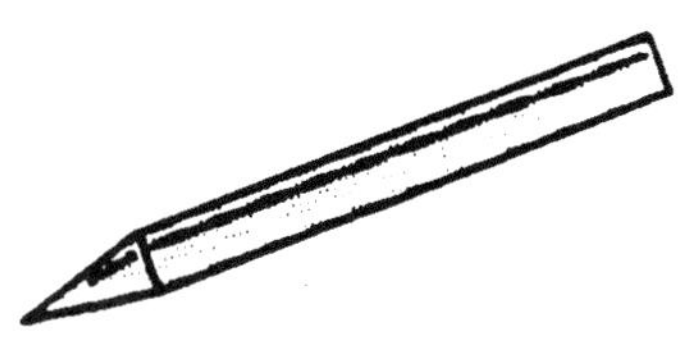

A dibble

Step 7: Check the Soil Moisture

Before transplanting, check the soil moisture by pushing the dibble deep in a few pots. If the holes do not cave in, the moisture is adequate.

Do **not** transplant seedlings in ill-prepared, half wet soil.

Step 8: Loosen Soil in Seed Flat

Use the dibble to loosen the soil around the root areas of the seed flat.

Step 9: Remove One Seedling at a Time

Gently lift up one seedling at a time. Always lift seedlings from the seed flat by their seed leaves (cotyledons). If you handle seedlings by their stems to take them from the seed flat, their stems can easily bruise and the plant may die. However, if a leaf tears during transplanting, the plat recovers quickly by making new leaves.

Step 10: Make a Hole in the Pot

Make a hole in the pot using a dibble. The hole should be large enough and deep enough to accommodate the stem and roots comfortably.

Step 11: Set the Seedling in the Hole

Set the plants deep in the hole—down to the crown. Do not allow the soil to cover the crown. Soil on the crown will kill the plant.

In transplanting, also avoid turning the roots upward on the plant stem as it is lowered in the hole.

Step 12: Anchor the Seedling

Anchor the seedling around the root area by pushing the dibble on an angle beside the plant stem. Soil pressure against the roots encourages faster moisture uptake by the plant. Check this point by gently pulling on the leaf of the seedling. It should be firmly anchored.

Step 13: Place Plants in Light and Water

Each pot usually contains one plant. Place the pots on tables in plenty of light. Water promptly before plants wilt. Use the dilute fertilizer solution recommended above.

The first watering during transplanting should be heavy but gentle. This watering should settle the soil around the plants in the pots.

How do I transplant seedlings into flats?

If you are producing large quantities of seedlings, you may wish to transplant seedlings into flats instead of using individual pots for each seedling.

Here is how to transplant seedlings into flats:

Step 1: Fill Flats with Soil

Fill 18" square flats level full with soil mix. Set the flats on level tables in the seedhouse.

Step 2: Fertilize Soil in Flats

Broadcast 1 1/2 ounces of Pre-Plant Mix and 3/4 ounce of Weekly Feed Mix over the flats:

Note that details for mixing the Pre-Plant and Weekly Feed Mixes were given in lessons 5 and 12.

Use agriculture or dolomite lime in areas getting more than 20 inches of rain annually. Use gypsum (calcium sulfate) in areas getting less than 20 inches rain annually.

Step 3: Mix Soil and Fertilizer

After spreading the fertilizer, mix the soil and fertilizer together adequately.

Step 4: Level the Soil and then Water

Level the soil in the flats and water lightly. The soil should be quite damp.

Step 5: Use a Marker to Mark Each Flat

Use a suitable seedling marker to mark each flat. Seedling markers are easy and fast to make, and marking gives each plant equal space to develop.

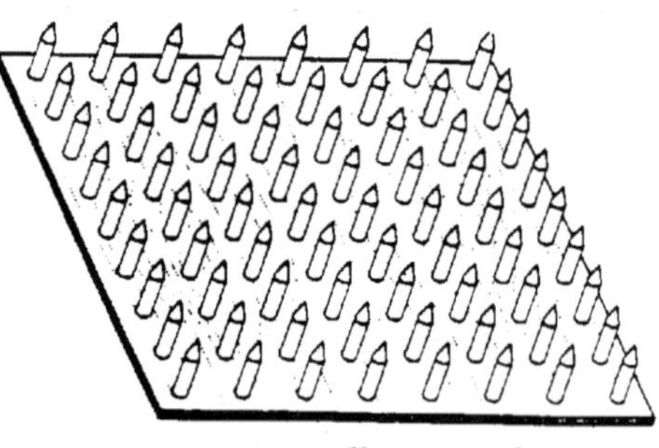

A seedling marker.

To make seedling markers:

1. Take a sheet of plywood 18” x 18” x ¾”.
2. Drill 72 equally-spaced ½” holes 8 rows x 9 holes.
3. From ½-inch doweling rods, cut off pieces 2 ½ inches long. Point one end of each piece.
4. Glue the pieces in the holes on the plywood sheet.
5. When gluing, insert the pieces so the flat end is flush with the plywood.

Set the marker over the filled flat and press down on the marker. Lift the marker and the flat is marked uniformly—giving each plant an equal amount of space. Notice that if the soil in the flats is sufficiently wet, the holes keep their shape. The soil does not cave in.

Step 6: Transplant Seedlings One at a Time

Take the seedling plants from the seed flat, one plant at a time. Plant at once—one plant in each hole. A recommended number of seedlings for a flat is 72. Be sure to lift plants by their leaves, not their stems. Also, do not turn the plant roots upward when you transplant.

How do I care for transplanted seedlings?

Under normal conditions, transplanted seedlings in the seedhouse overcome transplanting shock in two or three days, and start growing fast in seven to ten days.

Quality is largely determined by the care given seedlings during the first two or three weeks after transplanting. Robust, healthy seedlings are **produced**; they do not come by accident.

All plants in the seedhouse should be watered with the dilute liquid "constant feed" solution every time they are watered.

Provide sufficient heat to keep the temperature in the seedhouse above 32 degrees Fahrenheit. When the outside temperature is above 50 degrees, open the ventilators to supply fresh air. Fresh air is essential to healthy plants.

When temperatures permit, move seedling plants from the seedhouse to the tables in full sun.

Tomatoes are one of the most popular crops that can be started from seed and transplanted in pots or seedling flats. We will use tomatoes to illustrate proper cultural practices to develop sturdy seedhouse plants.

Two or three weeks after growing in two-inch pots or seedling flats, the leaves begin touching the leaves of the other plants. When this occurs, each plant begins vying for light and starts stretching. If the plants are allowed to stretch, they very quickly get tall and spindly with weak stems. To prevent this from happening, you have two choices:

1. If you have space, you can move the plants into a colder area and expose them to cold, fresh air. The colder temperature retards growth. Or,

2. You can pinch off the first set (the lower) of true leaves. Do not pinch off the growing tip (called the terminal bud).

Pinching off the leaves is a shock to the plant, and it stops growing for up to 7 to 10 days. But, during this stopped period the stems thicken and this is desirable.

If neither option is satisfactory, you can shift the plants from 2-inch pots to 4- or 6-inch pots, or move half to another flat.

Hardy plants, such as cabbage, celery, broccoli, cauliflower, lettuce, red beets, and spinach can tolerate some frosty weather and can be moved out of the seedhouse onto hardening-off tables where they will develop slowly into sturdy plants. They can remain in the seedling flats or small pots for 2 to 3 weeks without stunting their growth and affecting their harvest.

If you choose the second option, pinching off plant leaves, you will notice that after about two weeks new leaves are once again touching other leaves. This time, the lowest leaves are again pinched as before, and any other overlapping leaves should be pinched back.

Tomato plants in seedling flats or 2-inch pots can be pinched two times before they must be shifted into larger-size pots, or else they must be moved to cool growing temperatures. Be sure not to pinch off the leaves more than two times while the tomatoes are in 72-count seedling flats or 2" pots.

Be very gentle with the plants when you transplant them into larger pots.

By the time plants are 6 to 8 weeks old they are ready for a third pinching and need shifting to large pots.

Here is how to transplant into larger pots (6-inch, gallon-size pots):

Step 1: Prepare Soil

Prepare the soil as describe previously.

Step 2: Water the Soil

Add enough water to the soil so it holds its shape.

Step 3: Water Plants before Transplanting

Water the plants in the small pots quite heavily regardless of the variety planted.

Step 4: Transplant Plants in Larger Pots

Shift the plants to larger pots. Be careful not to damage the root ball on the plants.

Take a plant in the 2-inch pot in the left hand and slide the stem of the plant between the index and middle fingers. While keeping the fingers in place, turn the plant upside down and tap the edge of the pot slightly against the edge of a table, or just give it a sharp rap. If the soil is properly wet, the root ball slips easily from the pot.

Turn the plant right-side up and lower it in the 6-inch (gallon-size) pot. The crown (the top of the plant) should be set even with the rim of the large pot. If necessary, put some soil in the pot to raise the crown to the proper height.

Step 5: Fill Pot with Soil

Fill the pot with soil and press it firmly around the root ball.

Step 6: Water the Plants

Water the planted large pots promptly using the liquid fertilizer "constant feed" solution to settle the soil around the plant.

In areas where the growing season is short, shifting plants to large-size pots can produce plants eight to twelve weeks old by the time weather conditions permit planting in the garden or field.

How do I care for large-container plants?

Under normal conditions, two weeks after shifting plants into gallon-size containers the leaves of the plant begin crowding the leaves of other plants. This time do not cut off the leaves. Instead, start spacing the containers.

The first spacing between gallon-sized pots should be about 2 inches. It is important to provide ample light between the plants. Light is essential to producing short, sturdy plants.

Every week thereafter, spread the containers farther and farther apart, as long as plants are in the seedhouse.

When the plants are 12 to 14 inches tall, stake and tie them to keep from falling over. Use stakes 24 inches long.

Along with staking, remove all suckers as soon as they appear. Cut the suckers off close to the stem. They will not grow again.

As the plant gets more leaves and then height, cut off the lowest leaves which touch the ground. Save all flowers—no flowers, no fruit!

Proper spacing of the pots and prompt removal of all suckers will result in strong, healthy plants.

Timing Your Harvest

It takes approximately eight weeks from the time tomato flowers are pollinated until the fruit is red-ripe.

Greenhouse space is usually limited and the number of early gallon-size plants you can have is also limited. If you need many plants, plant seed so as to produce 4- to 6-week-old seedlings (up to 8 weeks for tomatoes, eggplant, & peppers), by the time it is safe to move the plants outside. Timing to accomplish this is very important. If seedlings are properly grown, they will be short and strong when moved outside. The plants will be excellent for transplanting to the garden.

Garden Genius

Refer to your *Planting Plan* and *Planting Guide* from Appendices A or B. And the *Garden Planting Details* in Appendix C is especially helpful. Calculate how many seedlings you will need for your garden and how much it would cost to purchase these seedlings from a commercial nursery. How much could you save each year by producing your own seedlings?

Lesson 23: Cold-Weather Gardening

In this lesson, you will learn how to answer these questions:

What is cold-weather gardening?
How can I cover soil-beds?
How can I cover grow-boxes?
How do I care for plants in cold weather?
Should I use a seedhouse to grow crops?

What is cold-weather gardening?

In cold-weather areas, you can grow frost-tolerant plants under plastic in order to protect the plants from cold winds, snow, and freezing weather. You can plant broccoli, cabbage, chard, lettuce, onions, radishes, peas, carrots, and other hardy plants several weeks earlier than usual, extending the length of the growing season and the yield from your garden.

The Mittleider Method is very versatile. You can choose from several cold-weather options, depending on whether you use soil-beds or grow-boxes, or whether or not you have a greenhouse.

You can:

- Shelter your soil-beds or mini grow-boxes with A-frames.
- Shelter larger-size grow-boxes with plastic frames.
- Build a seedhouse to raise seedling plants or to raise crops to maturity.

How can I cover soil-beds?

Here is how to create plastic frames for soil-beds:

Step 1: Prepare Wire

Using non-rusting 8 gauge wire, cut the wire into five-foot sections. These will become the frames for the soil-beds.

Step 2: Build Soil-Beds and Plant Seedlings

Build your soil-beds and plant seedlings from the seedhouse or sow seed.

Step 3: Shape Wire

Taking the five-foot sections of wire, shape the wire to construct frames over the soil-beds.

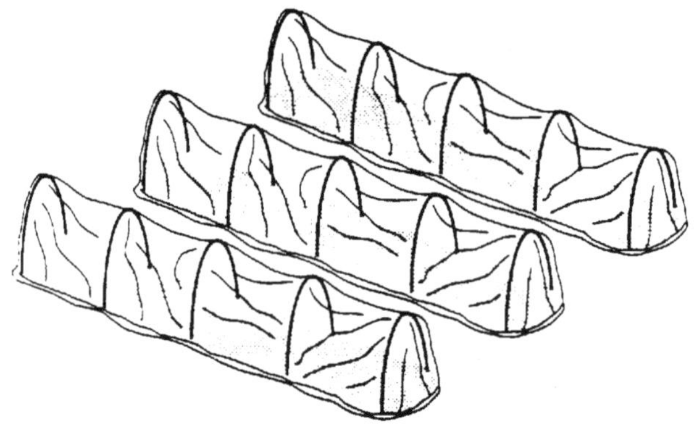

Plastic frames for soil-beds

Step 4: Cover Frames with Plastic

Cover the frames with clear sheets of 6 mil greenhouse (NOT construction) plastic, 4 feet wide.

Step 5: Secure Plastic Covers

Secure the plastic over the soil-beds with a 2" to 3" layer of soil along the edges. This film of soil spread along both sides and the ends will hold the plastic in place.

How can I cover grow-boxes?

If you have grow-boxes, you can construct a plastic frame fitting over the grow-box for cold-weather gardening. The grow-box itself serves as a base for the plastic frame. Use plastic PVC pipe to construct the structure's frame. PVC is lightweight, strong, and easy to use (works for soil-beds also).

Step-by-step instructions for building these plastic frames are found below. Our example is a U-shaped, mini A-frame for grow-boxes 18 inches wide. This is the best type of plastic frame for grow-boxes.

Once your A-frame structure is in place, cover it with 6 mil greenhouse plastic.

On mini A-frames, there is no need to attach the plastic to the frame—just leave it loose and secure the plastic with soil along the sides like the frames used with soil beds. Alternatively, you can sandwich the plastic between 1" X 2" boards, and hold those next to the box with stakes.

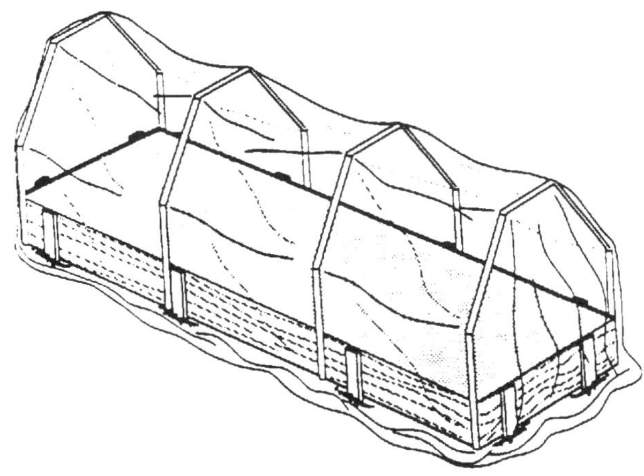

Plastic frames for grow-boxes

Here is how to make mini A-frames:

Step 1: Cut Plastic Pipe for Anchor Supports

Cut ¾-inch 200 psi plastic pipe into 15-inch lengths. These pipes will be driven into the ground, down beside the grow-box, to be anchor supports for holding the A-frames in place.

Step 2: Mark Grow-boxes

Starting at the corners, mark the grow-boxes every 24-30 inches.

Step 3: Drive in Anchor Pipes

Drive pipes at every mark. The top of the pipes and the top of the grow-box frames should be even across the top. Use a 2 x 4 block of wood on top of the pipe when pounding it to protect it from the hammer.

Step 4: Drill Holes in Grow-box

Drill a 1/16th hole into the grow-box on each side of the pipe, two inches down from the top of the grow-box.

Step 5: Wire Anchor Pipes to Grow-box

Take short pieces of No. 14 wire and wire the pipes to the grow-box frames. If you prefer, you can use metal u-clamps instead of wire.

Step 6: Drill Holes in Anchor Pipe

Make marks 6 inches below the top of the pipe and drill a 1/8th hole through both sides of the pipe. Insert a 2-inch nail through the hole. Be sure the nail sticks through the pipe. This nail controls the depth of the legs of the A-frame when it is installed.

Step 7: Cut Pipe for Top-Piece

Cut lengths of ½-inch pipe 60 inches long. Mark each pipe 14 inches up from each end. Make another mark 12 inches after the first mark on each end, leaving 8 inches in the center.

Step 8: Bend Pipe to Form "U"

Press the marks against a sharp corner, or make a nailed pattern on plywood, and bend the pipe, using a heat gun to soften the pipe.

Step 9: Slip U-shaped Pipe into Anchor Pipe

Slip the legs of the "U" into the ¾" pipes so the top-piece straddles the grow-box.

Step 10: Cover Frame with Plastic

From a roll of greenhouse plastic 6 feet wide, cut a piece 4 feet longer than one grow-box. Pull the plastic over the A-frames, pulling the plastic out evenly all along the sides of the grow-box.

Step 11: Secure the Plastic Cover

Cover the plastic edges with garden soil to secure the cover in place, or sandwich between 2 strips of 1" X 2" wood..

How do I care for plants in cold-weather?

The sun will warm up the soil quickly through the plastic, stimulating plant growth. When outside temperature is above 50 degrees open the ends of the plastic. On warm days above 70 degrees, lift the plastic from one side and fold it back, uncovering the plants so they can benefit from the full sunlight. Later, if the weather changes abruptly, recover the frames with plastic to protect the plants.

During cold-weather periods, don't water your plants daily. When the weather is cold, there's not much plant transpiration. Watering twice, or even once a week may be sufficient, but check soil moisture daily.

Also, don't apply as much fertilizer. One application of Weekly-Feed Fertilizer every 14 days is enough.

Should I use a seedhouse to grow plants?

A seedhouse (greenhouse) plays a crucial role in the development of strong, healthy seedlings in time for spring planting. A seedhouse also helps control pests and diseases, improve the nutritional quality of your crop, and allows you to produce more food in a smaller space.

In the winter, if your area has daytime temperatures between 45 and 75 degrees Fahrenheit, and night time temperatures no lower than 27 degrees Fahrenheit, plants can grow steadily in a seedhouse without artificial heat of any kind.

If you have a 12-week cold season with daytime temperatures between 40 and 60 degrees Fahrenheit and night temperatures no lower than 13 degrees Fahrenheit, you can grow hardy plants in the seedhouse all winter long, but the costs of heating during the coldest weeks may make your project economically unsound.

Serious about growing year-round? Consider a geo-thermal greenhouse using air circulated through pipes 4'-6' underground (learn more at www.growfood.com).

With careful planning, you can have two out-of-season crops with a minimum amount of expense. First, grow an early spring crop and harvest in time to plant again for summer. Then, start your fall crop so plants reach maximum fruit set and vegetative growth by the end of autumn. During the cold months of December and January, supply only enough artificial heat to keep the plants from freezing (above 32 degrees Fahrenheit). Plants will grow at a reduced rate during these cold months, but they will gradually mature.

Growing Plants to Maturity in a Seedhouse

Producing seedlings using a seedhouse was discussed in *Lesson 22: Seedling Production*. If you're interested in growing plants to maturity in the seedhouse (for example, tomatoes or cucumbers) build the seedhouse and follow these steps.

1. Construct grow-boxes, leaving 4 foot aisles for adequate light to plants. (See *Part III: Grow-Box Basics starting on page 63.*

2. Prepare grow-boxes for planting by fertilizing, filling the box with custom-made soil, mixing the soil, and watering.

3. Sow seeds or transplant seedling plants into the grow-boxes.

4. Care for plants, train them to grow vertically, and prune. (***1/2" plumbing pipe attached to ceiling replaces T-frames***)

5. Heat the seedhouse with a supplemental heat source to prevent plants from freezing, or use a geo-thermal system.

6. Ventilate when daytime temperatures are above freezing. When temperatures inside the seedhouse exceed 100 degrees Fahrenheit, use shade cloths to cool the seedhouse.

7. Water when needed.

If you are using the seedhouse to grow plants to maturity, hand-pollination may be required for some crops.

Learn More

Hand Pollination
More Food From Your Garden

Garden Genius

If you are planning on using cold-weather gardening by covering soil-beds or grow-boxes, determine which materials you will need and how much you will need of each item.

If you are planning on using a seedhouse, consider the cost of supplying artificial heat to the seedhouse versus the benefits of an earlier and continuous harvest.

Appendix A:

Soil-Bed Garden Genius Planning Forms

- Garden Plot Plan
- Planting Plan
- Tools and Materials List
- Gardening Cycle Calendar
- Planting Guide
- Fertilizing Schedule

Garden Plot Plan

Location:

Approximate dimensions: feet by feet

Scale: Each = feet

Instructions:

1. Describe your site, list its dimensions, and figure a scale for your grid.
2. Draw the outline of your garden (with a pencil).
3. Show the layout of your soil-beds. Remember:
   - Make soil-beds 18" wide x 30' long (or varying length)
   - Allow 3 ½ feet for aisles
   - Allow 5 feet at the ends of soil-beds
4. Label your soil-beds (1, 2, 3...).

Planting Plan

Average Day of Last Frost: ☐ ☐

Month *Day*

Soil-Bed	Portion of Bed	Type of Plant	How Many? *(# of plants)*	When to Plant

Instructions:

1. Enter the average day of last frost for your area.
2. List the soil-bed (1, 2, 3…) where each crop will be planted.
3. Designate what portion (full, ¾, 2/3, ½, 1/3, ¼) of each bed will be planted in a crop.
4. List the type of plant, how many plants you will need, and when to plant each crop. (Refer to *Appendix C: Yields for Common Garden Crops & Garden Planting Details* to complete your plan.)

Tools and Materials List

Things I Need to Get	Amount
For Gardening	
Round-headed shovel	
12" or 14" garden rake	
Straight-edged hoe (2-way hoe)	
Two five-gallon buckets	
Garden hose	
18" towel for end of hose	
Home-made fertilizing tool	
For Making Soil-Beds	
1"x 2" stakes (wooden or metal) 18 inches long, with one end pointed (4 stakes per soil-bed)	
Nylon string or mason line	
One 2-pound hammer	
Pick-ax for hard soil	
For Planting and Transplanting	
6-inch interval marker (for 2-, 3-, 4-, 6-, 8-, 9-, and 12-inch spacing)	
7-inch interval marker (for 3½-, 7-, 14-, and 21 inch spacing)	
Nitrogen (for transplanting)	
For Pre-Plant Fertilizer	
Lime or Gypsum	
Boron (Borax)	
Magnesium Sulfate (Epsom Salt)	
For Weekly-Feed Fertilizer (25 pounds)	
Nitrogen (34-0-0), (46-0-0), or (21-0-0)	10 pounds 8 ounces
Phosphorus—*P* (0-45-0), (18-46-0), or (11-53-0)	4 pounds 8 ounces
Potassium—K (0-0-60), (0-0-50)	6 pounds
Magnesium Sulfate—$MgSO_4$ (*Epsom Salt*)	3 pounds 12 ounces
Boron—B (*Borax*)	3 ounces
Manganese—$MnSO_4$	2 ounces
Zinc—$ZnSO_4$	4 ounces
Iron (Fe) Chelate #330	½ ounce
Copper Sulfate—$CuSO_4$	½ ounce
Molybdenum—Mo	¼ ounce

Things I Need to Get	Amount

For Short-Term-Substitute Weekly-Feed Fertilizer (7+ pounds)

Fertilizer (16-16-16)	6 pounds
Magnesium Sulfate (*Epsom Salt*)	1 pound
Boron (*Borax*)	1 teaspoon

Gardening Cycle Calendar

Month	To Do

Instructions:

List the gardening tasks you plan to complete each month. To see an example, refer to *Soil-Bed Basics/Lesson1: Planning/How much time will it take?.*

Planting Guide

Soil-Bed	Portion of Bed	Type of Plant	Seedling or Seed?	Spacing in Row	Rows per Soil-Bed	Depth of Seed/ Seedling *(inches)*

Instructions:

1. List the soil-bed (1, 2, 3…) where each crop will be planted.

2. Designate what portion (full, ¾, 2/3, ½, 1/3, ¼, or number of feet) of each bed will be planted in a crop.

3. List the type of plant, whether you will plant it as a seedling or seed, the row spacing, how many rows per bed, and the depth to plant the seed or seedling. (Refer to the *Transplanting/Planting Guide and Garden Planting Details* in *Appendix C*, as needed.)

Fertilizing Schedule

One Application:

Pre-Plant Fertilizer		pounds
Weekly-Feed Fertilizer		pounds

			Application Dates						
Soil-Bed	**Type of Plant**	**Suggested # of Applications**	**1**	**2**	**3**	**4**	**5**	**6**	**7**

Instructions:

1. Enter the amounts needed for one application of Pre-Plant and Weekly-Feed Fertilizers.

2. List the soil-bed (1, 2, 3…) where each crop will be planted.

3. List the type of plant and the suggested number of fertilizer applications for each type of plant. (Refer to *Suggested Fertilizer Applications & Garden Planting Details* in *Appendix C*, as needed, to complete your plan.)

4. Use this form to keep a record of your fertilizer applications by recording the date of each feeding in the designated column.

Appendix B:

Grow-Box Garden Genius Planning Forms

- Garden Plot Plan
- Planting Plan
- Tools and Materials List
- Gardening Cycle Calendar
- Planting Guide
- Fertilizing Schedule

Garden Plot Plan

Location:

Approximate dimensions: feet by feet

Scale: Each ⬚ = feet

Instructions:

1. Describe your site, list its dimensions, and figure a scale for your grid.
2. Draw the outline of your garden (with a pencil).
3. Show the layout of your grow-boxes.
   - You can make grow-boxes any length (Standard size: 18" x 30')
   - Allow 3 ½ feet for aisles and 5 feet at the ends
4. Label your grow-boxes (1, 2, 3…).

Planting Plan

Average Day of Last Frost: ______ ______

Month *Day*

Grow-Box	Portion of Bed	Type of Plant	How Many? *(# of plants)*	When to Plant

Instructions:

1. Enter the average day of last frost for your area.
2. List the grow-box (1, 2, 3…) where each crop will be planted.
3. Designate what portion (full, ¾, 2/3, ½, 1/3, ¼, or number of feet) of each box will be planted in a crop.
4. List the type of plant, how many plants you will need, and when to plant each crop. (Refer to *Appendix C: Yields for Common Garden Crops & Garden Planting Details* to complete your plan.)

Tools and Materials List

Things I Need to Get	**Amount**
For Gardening	
Round-headed shovel	
12" or 14" garden rake	
Straight-edged hoe (2-way hoe)	
Two five-gallon buckets	
Garden hose	
18" towel for end of hose	
Home-made fertilizing tool	
For Making Grow-Boxes	
Regular claw hammer	
Three-pound hammer or mall	
A level at least two feet long	
100 feet of strong cord	
2" x 8" treated lumber	
1"x 2"x 18" pointed stakes	
For Making Custom-Made Soil	
50% Concrete sand with 50% Peat Moss	
75% Sawdust with 25% Sand (clean)	
15% Perlite with 50% Peat Moss or Sawdust and 35% Sand (clean)	
50% Sawdust with 25% Pine Needles and 25% Sand (clean)	
Other	
For Preparing Grow-Boxes	
Gypsum or Lime	
For Planting and Transplanting	
6-inch interval marker (for 2-, 3-, 4-, 6-, 8-, 9-, & 12-" spacing)	
7-inch interval marker (for 3 1/2-, 7-, 14-, & 21-" spacing)	
Nitrogen (for transplanting)	

Things I Need to Get	Amount
For Pre-Plant Fertilizer	
☐ Lime or Gypsum	
☐ Boron (Borax)	
☐ Magnesium Sulfate (Epsom Salt)	
For Weekly-Feed Fertilizer (25 pounds)	
☐ Nitrogen (34-0-0), (46-0-0), or (21-0-0)	10 pounds 8 ounces
☐ Phosphorus—*P* (0-45-0), (18-46-0), or (11-53-0)	4 pounds 8 ounces
☐ Magnesium Sulfate—$MgSO_4$ (*Epsom Salt*)	3 pounds 12 ounces
☐ Potassium—K (0-0-60), (0-0-50)	6 pounds
☐ Boron—B (*Borax*)	3 ounces
☐ Manganese—$MnSO_4$	2 ounces
☐ Zinc—$ZnSO_4$	4 ounces
☐ Iron (Fe) Chelate #330	½ ounce
☐ Copper Sulfate—$CuSO_4$	½ ounce
☐ Molybdenum—Mo	¼ ounce
For Short-Term-Substitute Weekly-Feed Fertilizer (7+ pounds)	
☐ Fertilizer (16-16-16)	6 pounds
☐ Magnesium Sulfate (*Epsom Salt*)	1 pound
☐ Boron (*Borax*)	1 teaspoon

Gardening Cycle Calendar

Month	To Do

Instructions:

List the gardening tasks you plan to complete each month. To see an example, refer to *Grow-Box Basics/Lesson 8: Planning/How much time will it take?*.

Planning Guide

Grow-Box	Portion of Bed	Type of Plant	Seedling or Seed?	Spacing in Row	Rows per Grow-Box	Depth of Seed/ Seedling *(inches)*

Instructions:

1. List the grow-box (1, 2, 3…) where each crop will be planted.

2. Designate what portion (full, ¾, 2/3, ½, 1/3, ¼, or number of feet) of each bed will be planted in a crop.

3. List the type of plant, whether you will plant it as a seedling or seed, the row spacing, how many rows per bed, and the depth to plant the seed or seedling. (Refer to the *Transplanting/Planting Guide & Garden Planting Details* in *Appendix C*, as needed.)

Fertilizing Schedule

One Application:

Pre-Plant Fertilizer		pounds
Weekly-Feed Fertilizer		pounds

.

Grow-Box	Type of Plant	Suggested # of Applications	Application Dates 1	2	3	4	5	6	7

Instructions:

1. Enter the amounts needed for one application of Pre-Plant and Weekly-Feed Fertilizers.

2. List the grow-box (1, 2, 3…) where each crop will be planted.

3. List the type of plant and the suggested number of fertilizer applications for each type of plant. (Refer to *Suggested Fertilizer Applications & Garden Planting Details* in *Appendix C*, as needed.)

4. Use this form to keep a record of your fertilizer applications by recording the date of each feeding in the designated column.

Appendix C:

Reference Tables for Planning Your Garden

- Yields for Common Garden Crops
- Plant Hardiness and Planting Times
- Transplanting/Planting Guide
- Suggested Fertilizer Applications
- Garden Planting Details

Yields for Common Garden Crops

(Based on 18" by 30' beds)

Plant Type	# Plants *(full bed)*	Expected Yield *(full bed)*
beans, bush	240	68 lbs.
beans, pole	180	180 lbs
beets, red + leaves	360	120 lbs.
berries, black & rasp.	27	2.5 gal.
broccoli + leaves	52	80 lbs.
cabbage + leaves	60	150 lbs.
carrots	720	190lbs
cauliflower + leaves	52	160 lbs.
celery	62	120 lbs.
chard	124	250 lbs.
corn	92	115 ears
cucumbers	26	410 lbs.
cucumbers - bush	62	248 lbs.
eggplant	41	400 lbs.
kohlrabi	240	120 lbs.
lettuce, head	62	112 lbs.
lettuce, leaf	122	45 lbs.
melons, cantaloupe	41	245 lbs.
melons, honeydew	41	245 lbs.
melons, watermelons	16	320 lbs.
onions, green tops	1440	144 bunches
onions, large bulb	360	135 lbs.
parsley	120	23 lbs.
parsnips	240	175 lbs.
peas, bush + leaves	362	90 lbs.
peppers, all types	62	320 peppers
potatoes	92	145 lbs.
potatoes - sweet	60	300 lbs.
radishes + leaves	722	90 bunches
spinach	122	46 lbs.
squash, crooked-neck	18	135 lbs.
squash, vertical	41	154 lbs.
squash, yellow	18	135 lbs.
squash, zucchini	18	150 lbs.
tomatoes - bush	52	208 lbs.
tomatoes indeterminate	26	615 lbs.
turnips + leaves	240	120 lbs.

Plant Hardiness and Planting Times

Plant Type	Hardiness	When to Plant *relative to average day of last frost (ADLF)*
beans, bush	frost-sensitive	On ADLF
beans, pole	frost-sensitive	On ADLF
beets, red	moderately-hardy	2-3 weeks before
berries, black & rasp.	moderately-hardy	2-3 weeks before
broccoli	hardy	4 weeks before
cabbage	hardy	4 weeks before
carrots	moderately-hardy	2-3 weeks before
cauliflower	hardy	4 weeks before
celery	moderately-hardy	2-3 weeks before
chard	moderately-hardy	2-3 weeks before
corn	frost-sensitive	On ADLF
cucumbers	frost-intolerant	2-3 weeks after
cucumbers - bush	frost-intolerant	2-3 weeks after
eggplant	frost-sensitive	On ADLF
kohlrabi	hardy	4 weeks before
lettuce, head	hardy	4 weeks before
lettuce, leaf	hardy	4 weeks before
melons, cantaloupe	frost-intolerant	2-3 weeks after
melons, honeydew	frost-intolerant	2-3 weeks after
melons, watermelons	frost-intolerant	2-3 weeks after
onions, green tops	hardy	4 weeks before
onions, large bulb	hardy	4 weeks before
parsley	moderately-hardy	2-3 weeks before
parsnips	moderately-hardy	2-3 weeks before
peas, bush	hardy	4 weeks before
peppers, all types	frost-intolerant	2-3 weeks after
potatoes	moderately-hardy	2-3 weeks before
potatoes - sweet	frost-intolerant	2-3 weeks after
radishes	hardy	4 weeks before
spinach	hardy	4 weeks before
squash, crooked-neck	frost-intolerant	2-3 weeks after
squash - vertical	frost-intolerant	2-3 weeks after
squash, yellow	frost-intolerant	2-3 weeks after
squash, zucchini	frost-intolerant	2-3 weeks after
tomatoes, bush	frost-sensitive	On ADLF
turnips	moderately-hardy	2-3 weeks before

Transplanting/Planting Guide

(Based on a 18" by 30' bed)

Plant Type	Seedling or Seed *(most effective)*	Spacing in Row *(inches)*	Rows per Bed *(full bed)*	Depth of Seed/Seedling *(inches)*
beans, bush	either	3	2	0.5
beans, pole	either	2	1	0.5
beets, red	either	2	2	0.25
berries, black & rasp.	seedling	14	1	6
broccoli	seedling	14	2 alt.*	deep
cabbage	seedling	12	2 alt.	deep
carrots	seed	1	2	0.125
cauliflower	seedling	14	2 alt.	deep
celery	seedling	12	2 alt.	deep
chard	either	6	2	0.25
corn	seed	8	2	0.5
cucumbers - bush	seedling	12	2	deep
cucumbers - pole	seedling	9	1	deep
eggplant	seedling	14	2	deep
kohlrabi	either	3	2	0.25
lettuce, head	either	12	2 alt.	0.125
lettuce, leaf	either	6	2	0.125
melons, cantaloupe	either	9	1	0 5
melons, honeydew	either	9	1	0.5
melons, watermelons	either	9	1	0.5
onions, green tops	either	1	4	0.125
onions, large bulb	either	4	4	1.0
parsley	either	6	2	0.125
parsnips	seed	3	2	0.125
peas, bush	either	2	2	0.5
peppers, all types	seedling	12	2 alt.	deep
potatoes - Irish	seed	8	2	1.5
potatoes - sweet	slip	12	2	3.0
radishes	seed	1	2	0.125
spinach	either	6	2	0.25
squash, crooked-neck	either	21	1	0.5
squash - vertical	either	9	1	0.5
squash, yellow	either	21	1	0.5
squash, zucchini	either	21	1	0.5
tomatoes	seedling	9	1	deep
tomatoes - bush	seedling	14	2	deep
turnips	either	2	2	0.125

* alternating rows

Suggested Fertilizer Applications

Plant Type	Suggested # of weekly applications
beans, bush	5-6
beans, pole	10-12
beets, red	8
berries, black & rasp.	6
broccoli	6-8
cabbage	5-6
carrots	6
cauliflower	6-8
celery	5-6
chard	7-8
corn	6
cucumbers - bush	6-8
cucumbers - vertical	8-12
eggplant	10-12
kohlrabi	5
lettuce, head	5
lettuce, leaf	3-4
melons, cantaloupe	8-10
melons, honeydew	8-10
melons, watermelons	8-10
onions, green tops	3
onions, large bulb	7
parsley	5-7
parsnips	7
peas, bush	4-5
peppers, all types	8-12
potatoes	6-7
potatoes - sweet	16
radishes	2
spinach	4
squash, crooked-neck	8-12
squash - vertical	8-12
squash, yellow	8-12
squash, zucchini	8-12
tomatoes - bush	6-8
tomatoes - indeterminate	10-12
turnips	5

Garden Planting Details

Garden Planting Details for Mittleider Garden (www.growfood.com)

Plant Type (Not all vegetables are listed. Plant non-listed vegetables at the same time as listed vegetables in the same family.)	**Seedling or Seed** (most effective)	**Hardiness:** (Hardy: frost tolerant); (Moderately: handle a little frost); (Sensitive: protect from frost); (Intolerant: will not survive frost)	**When to Plant Outdoors** (ADLF=Average Day of Last Frost)	**Spacing** (inches)	**Rows per Bed** (18 "x 30' bed or box) (* = alternate rows)	**Planting Depth** (inches) (deep = Remove all but top 2-3 sets of leaves. Plant to depth of leaves)	**Expected Yield** (18" x 30' bed or box)	**# Plants** (full box/bed) (18" x 30' bed or box)	**Fertilizer Application** (Mittleider weekly feed)	**Plant Height** (inches)	**Plant Indoors** (weeks +/- ADLF)	**Plant in Garden** (weeks +/- ADLF)	**Days to maturity**	**Harvest Length** (weeks)
Beans, bush	either	frost-sensitive	On ADLF	3	2	0.500	68 lbs.	240	5-6	20	-2	+0	65	3
Beans, pole (vertical)	either	frost-sensitive	On ADLF	2	1	0.500	180 lbs.	180	10-12	84	-2	+0	75	16
Beets, red - + leaves	seed	moderately-hardy	2-3 weeks before	2	2	0.250	120 lbs.	362	6-8	12		-2	55	20
Broccoli - + leaves	seedling	hardy	4 weeks before	14	2 alt.*	deep	80 lbs.	52	6-8	20	-8	-4	60	4
Cabbage - + leaves	seedling	hardy	4 weeks before	12	2 alt.	deep	150 lbs.	60	5-6	15	-8	-4	60	2
Carrots	seed	moderately-hardy	2-3 weeks before	1	2	0.125	90 lbs	720	6	12		-2	75	16
Cauliflower - + leaves	seedling	hardy	4 weeks before	14	2 alt.	deep	100 lbs.	52	5-6	20	-8	-4	65	4
Celery	seedling	moderately-hardy	2-3 weeks before	12	2 alt.	deep	120 lbs.	62	5-6	18	-6	-2	80	2
Chard	either	moderately-hardy	2-3 weeks before	6	2	0.250	150 lbs.	124	7-8	12	-6	-2	50	20
Corn	seed	frost-sensitive	On ADLF	8	2 alt.	0.500	115 ears	92	6	72		+0	65	2
Cucumbers (bush)	seedling	frost-intolerant	2-3 weeks after	12	2	deep	248 lbs.	62	6-8	18	-1	+2	55	16
Cucumbers (vertical)	seedling	frost-intolerant	2-3 weeks after	9	1	deep	410 lbs.	41	8-12	84	-1	+2	60	4
Eggplant (vertical)	seedling	frost-sensitive	On ADLF	14	2	deep	400 lbs.	41	10-12	72	-8	+0	90	16
Kale	either	moderately-hardy	2-3 weeks before	3	2	0.125	50 lbs.	122	6-8	12	-7	-2	40	12
Kohlrabi - + leaves	either	hardy	4 weeks before	2	2	0.250	120 lbs.	360	5	12		-4	65	4
Lettuce, head	either	hardy	4 weeks before	12	2 alt.	0.125	112 lbs.	62	5	12	-7	-4	55	2
Lettuce, leaf	either	hardy	4 weeks before	6	2	0.125	45 lbs.	122	3-4	12	-7	-4	45	6
Melons, cantaloupe (vert.)	either	frost-intolerant	2-3 weeks after	9	1	0.250	246 lbs.	41	8-10	84	-1	+2	85	10
Melons, honeydew (vert.)	either	frost-intolerant	2-3 weeks after	9	1	0.250	246 lbs.	41	8-10	84	-1	+2	85	8
Okra	either	frost-intolerant	4 weeks after	12	1	0.500	100 lbs.	31	10-12	84	-4	+4	65	12
Onions, green tops	either	hardy	4 weeks before	1	4	0.125	144 bunches	1440	3	12	-7	-4	65	2
Onions, large bulb	either	hardy	4 weeks before	4	4	1.000	135 lbs.	360	7	15	-7	-4	85	4
Parsley	either	moderately-hardy	2-3 weeks before	6	2	0.125	23 lbs.	120	5-6	12	-6	-2	60	24
Parsnips	seed	moderately-hardy	2-3 weeks before	3	2	0.125	160 lbs.	175	7	12		-2	65	12
Peas, bush - + leaves	either	hardy	4 weeks before	2	2	0.500	90 lbs.	362	4-5	18	-7	-4	60	3
Peppers, all types	seedling	frost-intolerant	2-3 weeks after	12	2 alt.	deep	320 peppers	62	6-8	16	-7	+2	85	12
Potato, Irish, red	seed	moderately-hardy	2-3 weeks before	8	2 alt.	1.500	145 lbs.	92	4-5	16		-2	65	8
Potato, sweet	slip	frost-intolerant	6 weeks after	12	2	3.000	300 lbs.	60	16	12	-2	+6	120	1
Radishes - + leaves	seed	hardy	4 weeks before	1	2	0.125	60 bunches	722	2	8		-4	25	3
Spinach	either	hardy	4 weeks before	6	2	0.250	46 lbs.	122	4	8	-7	-4	45	4
Squash (vertical)	either	frost-intolerant	2-3 weeks after	9	1	0.500	154 lbs.	41	8-12	84	-1	+2	90	14
Squash, crooked-neck	either	frost-intolerant	2-3 weeks after	21	1	0.500	135 lbs.	18	8-12	24	-1	+2	50	14
Squash, yellow	either	frost-intolerant	2-3 weeks after	21	1	0.500	135 lbs.	18	8-12	24	-1	+2	50	14
Squash, zucchini	either	frost-intolerant	2-3 weeks after	21	1	0.500	150 lbs.	18	8-12	24	-1	+2	50	14
Tomatoes (indeterminate)	seedling	frost-sensitive	On ADLF	9	1	deep	615 lbs.	41	10-12	84	-8	+0	90	16
Tomatoes, bush	seedling	frost-sensitive	On ADLF	14	2	deep	208 lbs.	52	6-8	24	-8	+0	80	6
Turnips - + leaves	seed	moderately-hardy	2-3 weeks before	2	2	0.125	120 lbs.	240	5-6	12		-2	45	4
Watermelons	either	frost-intolerant	2-3 weeks after	21	1	0.250	320 lbs.	16	6-8	16	-2	+2	90	3

To learn more about the Mittleider gardening method go to www.growfood.com

Updated: 11/25/2014

Appendix D:

Constructing a Seedhouse

- Seedhouse Features
- Building the Seedhouse Frame
- Seedhouse Tables
- Seedhouse Ventilators
- Covering the Frame
- Finishing the Seedhouse

Seedhouse Features

Growing plants from seed ahead of the normal planting season has a number of advantages, including stronger and more vigorous plants, earlier maturation, larger yields, and reduced costs on weed and insect control.

There are many types, sizes, and shapes of greenhouses, but not every design or shape or structure is best suited to grow quality seedlings.

This appendix provides instructions for constructing a seedhouse which is simple in design, easy and quick to construct, inexpensive, and highly functional. This seedhouse design simplifies growing procedures, produces strong, healthy seedlings, and minimizes effort and care.

Features of this seedhouse include:

- A seedhouse frame made with 4 x 4 posts and 4 x 4 stringers.
- Plastic covering.
- Three rows of tables inside the greenhouse for growing seedlings.
- The same types of tables outside the seedhouse for hardening plants off before transplanting.
- Ventilators along the length and south side of the seedhouse for adequate circulation.

Building the Seedhouse Frame

Step 1: Select a Building Site

Select a level area large enough to accommodate the seedhouse with additional space for expansion, should the need arise.

Avoid shadows from trees and buildings. Full sunlight is essential to produce healthy plants.

Facing the length of the structure east and west gives the broadside a southern exposure and captivates more of the sun's heat during the winter season. Facing the length north and south equalizes sun exposure on both sides, with begtter light on the east side in the morning and better light on the west side in the afternoon.

Step 2: Purchase Materials

Purchase your materials. The size of the seedhouse can be scaled to fit your needs. We will illustrate with a seedhouse 20' wide, 40' long, and 8 ½ feet high at the peak.

> Tip If you plan to paint your seedhouse, it will be easier, faster, and you won't get paint on the clear plastic cover if you paint it now!

The table on the following page shows the materials you will need to build either a 20'x 40' or 15' x 30' seedhouse.

Seedhouse Materials List

Material Description	Seedhouse Size 20' x 40'	15' x 30'
4" x 4" - 8' Side Posts (all treated)	20	8
4" x 4" - 10' Center Posts "	5	4
4" x 4" - 20' Stringer "	8	6
2" X 12" - 20' Base Boards "	6	5
2" x 3" - 10' Rafters & End Studs	60	46-8', 4-10'
2" x 3" - 6' Wall Studs & Doors	40	30
2" x 3" - 3' Table Legs (in & out)	200	180
2" x 4" -16' Table Base	25	20
1" x 8" -10' Skirting	12	9
1" x 4" - 10' So. Side Vent. Base	4	3
1" X 4" - 8' Doors	4	4
1" x 4" - 6' Table Tops	320	300
1" x 4" - 4' Cross Braces	17	12
1" x 2" - 10' Ventilators	16	12
4" D Hinges	4	4
20' x 42' Plastic Side Covering (6 mil or better)	2	2(15' x 32')
20' x 42' Plastic End Covering	1	2 (15' x 32')
3" Box Nails or exterior screws	15#	12#
5" Box Nails or exterior screws	15#	12#
1 ¼ " Lathe Nails or ext screws	10#	8#
6" Spikes or lag screws	15	12
Black Roofing Paper (3')	120'	90'
1 ¾" x 48" Lathe	325	200
White Exterior Paint	3 gallons	2 ½ gallons

Step 3: Measure and Stake the Structure

After clearing and leveling the site, measure and stake the size of the structure.

Step 4: Mark Spots for Posts

Mark the spots for the 4 x 4 posts used to frame the building. The space between the posts is 10' each way.

Step 5: Dig Post Holes and Install Posts

Dig the holes and install the 4 x 4 side posts along the sides of the seedhouse. Set the 8' long posts in the holes 18" below the level of the floor (soil) surface. The top of the posts on the sides of the structure are 6 ½ feet above the floor level.

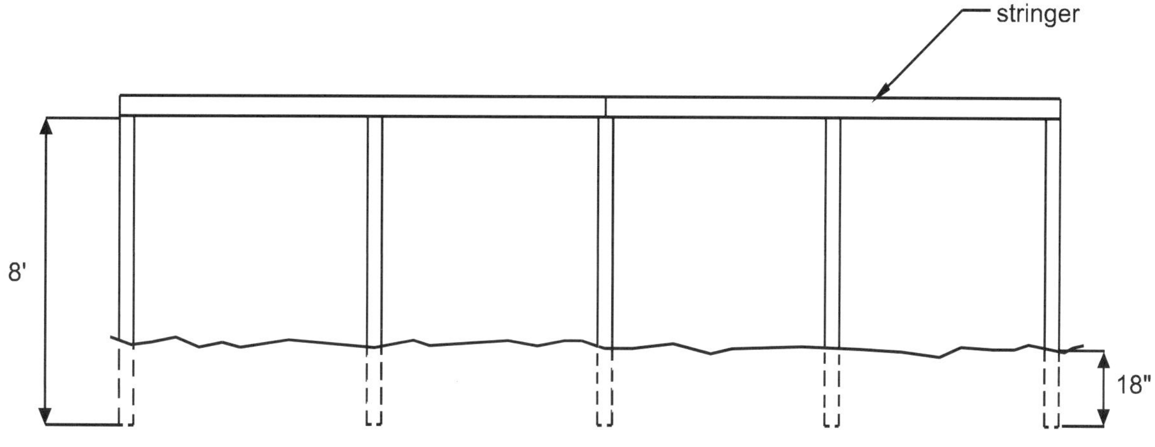

Side Posts

Step 6: Nail or Screw Stringers on Top of Posts

After the side-posts are secure, nail or screw 4 x 4 stringers 20 feet long on top of the posts.

Step 7: Prepare Center Posts

Prepare the center posts. Before the center posts are lowered into the holes, they need to be notched. Measure 21.5" from one end of the posts on one side of the 4 x 4's and cut a notch 1 ¾ inch deep x 3 ¾ inches wide above the 21.5" mark. Do this on one side only of all center 4 x 4 posts.

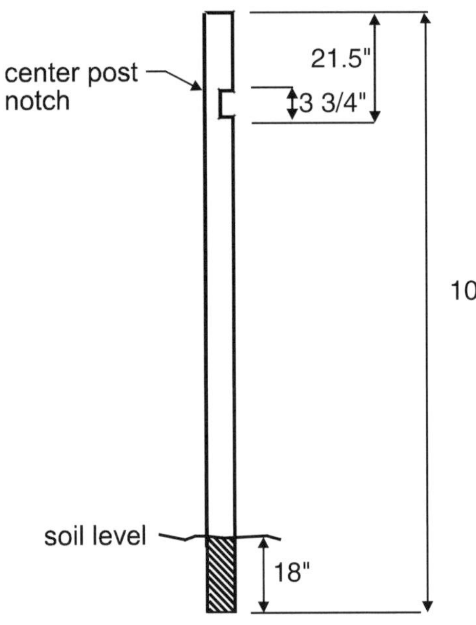

Center post with notch

Step 8: Place Center Row of Posts

Place the row of posts in the center of the structure. When the posts are set in place, the notches should face south, (or east if building north-south). The posts are 10' long set 18" deep in the ground. They are 8 ½ feet high above the floor level.

Step 9: Nail or Screw Stringers to Tops of Center Posts

After the posts are secure, nail or screw one row of 4 x 4 stringers 20' long on top of the posts.

Step 10: Nail or Screw Second Row of Stringers

Nail or screw a second row of stringers 18 inches below the first row of stringers. Before nailing or screwing the second row of stringers to the posts, notch one side of the stringers to match the notches made on the posts. Match the notches to fit into each other and nail or screw securely.

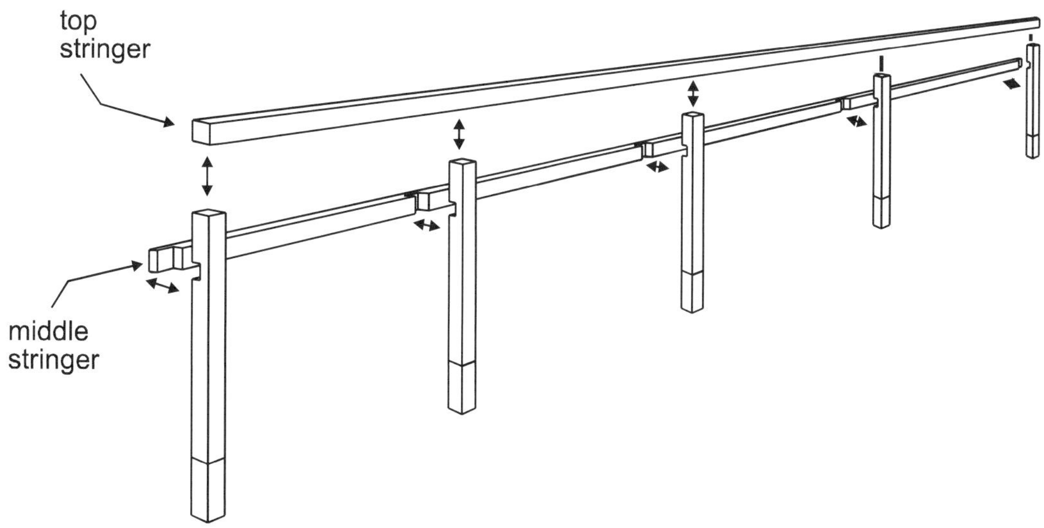

Center posts and stringer assembly.

Step 11: Make the Roof

Make the roof of the building of 2 x 3 wood rafters 10' long. The space between the rafters is 24".

Make the roof support for the north slope. Cut the rafters for the north slope to fit and toe-nail one end into the 4 x 4 stringer at the peak, flush with the top edge. Nail or screw the lower end on top of the 4 x 4 stringer flush with the outside edge.

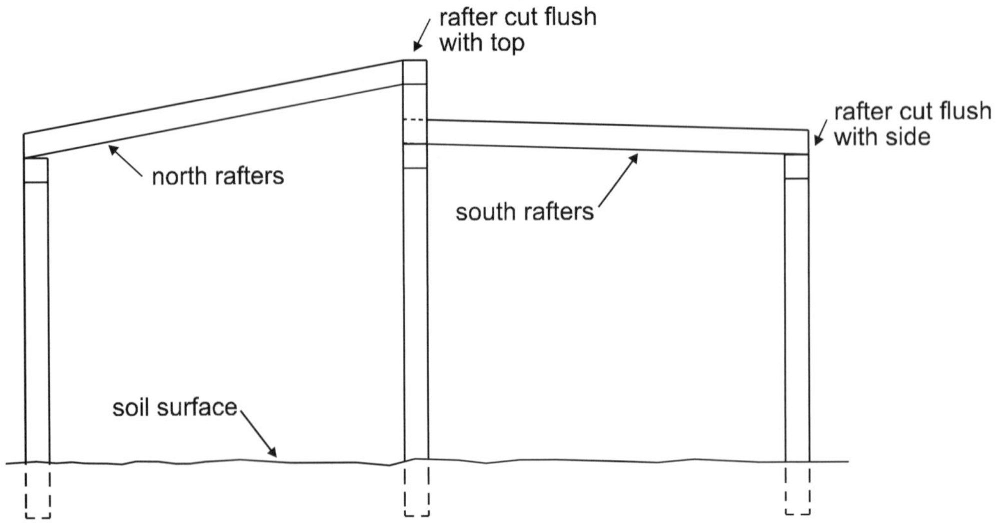

Roof assemby.

Step 12: Nail or Screw Side Studs to Frame

The studs along the sides of the frame are 2 x 3's that are 6' long. Space them 24" apart to match the roof rafters.

Nail or screw the top end of the stud to the underside of the 4 x 4 stringer and flush with the outside edge. Nail or screw the lower end of the studs to a 1 x 12 board 20' long attached near the floor level to the 4 x 4 posts on the outside of the frame.

Step 13: Make Roof Support for South Slope

Make the roof support for the south slope by nailing or screwing both ends of the 2 x 3 rafters on top of the 4 x 4 stringers. Nail or screw the rafters for the south-sloped roof to the second (lower) row of 4 x 4 stringers. Nail or screw the ends flush with the outside edges of both stringers.

Step 14: Frame the Ends of the Building

Frame the ends of the building with 2 x 3 studs. Cut to fit and nail or screw the studs in place. The space between the studs is 24 inches, except for the doors.

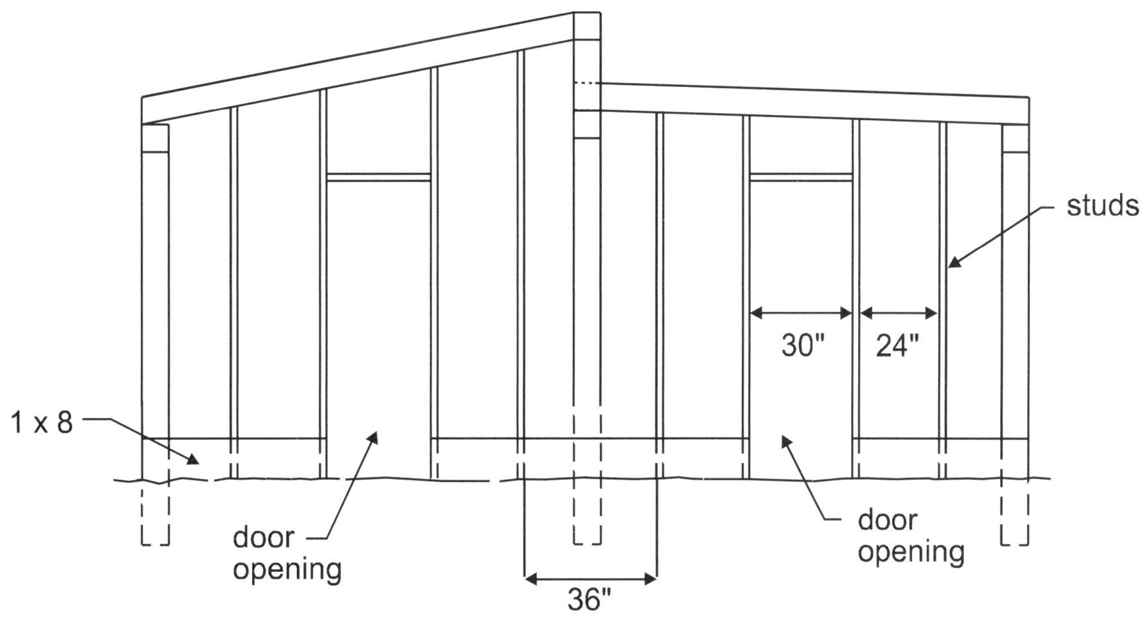

Studs are 24 inches apart on center.

Step 15: Install Doors

Doors should be at least 30" wide x 6' high. Construct the outer frame from 2 x 4's. Then notch 1 x 4 diagonal braces into the back of the door.

Cold winds blow from the northwest or north. Therefore, the door hinges should be installed on the north side of the door frame. When the doors are opened, they will tend to block the wind from blowing on the plants in the greenhouse.

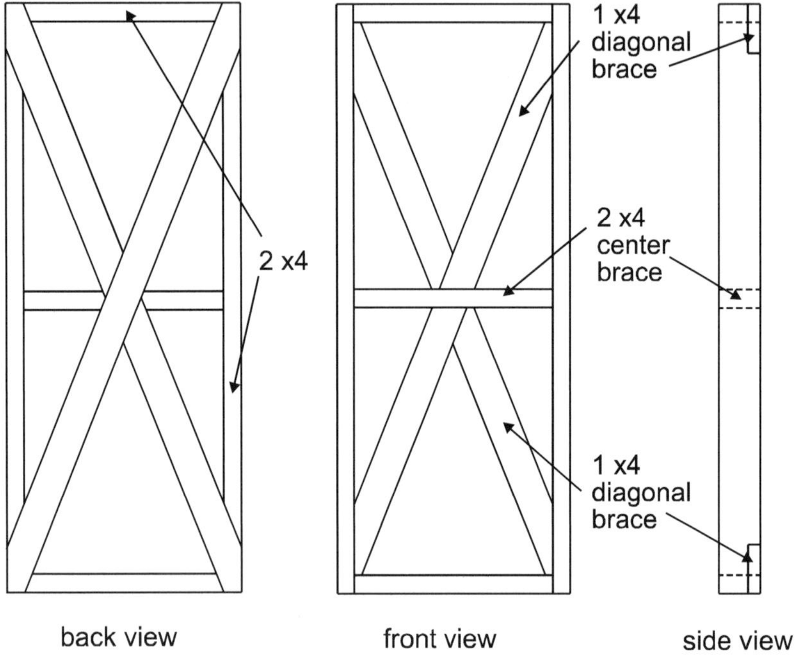

Door assembly.

You have now completed the frame of the seedhouse.

Seedhouse Tables

Constructing a seedhouse without tables would be a mistake. Seedlings should never be placed on the ground, even when growing in full sun.

Here is how the tables should be configured when completed:

- The tables are 30" high
- There are two side tables 36" wide
- There is one center table 72" wide
- The aisles between tables are 44" wide

Follow these steps to construct the tables:

Step 1: Stretch a Chalk Line for Tables

Measure 30" from the inside edge of the 4 x 4 side posts. Stretch a chalk line tight the length of the seedhouse.

Step 2: Drive Studs into Ground for Table Legs

Point one end of the 2 x 3 studs which are 36" long. Drive the studs 10" into the ground in line with the chalk line. Drive a stake every 28 inches.

Step 3: Level the Table Leg Studs

Check the top of the table legs. They must be level. Each table along the sides of the seedhouse has two rows of table legs. The center table has three rows of table legs.

Step 4: Nail or Screw 2 x 4's to Table Legs

With the table legs in place and level, nail or screw 2 x 4's standing on edge to the top of the table legs.

Step 5: Nail or Screw Top Boards on Side Tables

Nail or screw 1 x 4's that are 36" long across the two rows of 2 x 4's. Put a space of 1" between the 1 x 4 boards.

Step 6: Construct Center Table Legs

Construct the center table the same way, except use only one row of table legs along the center row of 4 x 4 posts.

Step 7: Nail or Screw on Center Table Tops

Nail or screw 1 x 4 boards 72" long across the three rows of table legs. Put a space of 1" between the boards. There will be a 6" overhang along each side of the table.

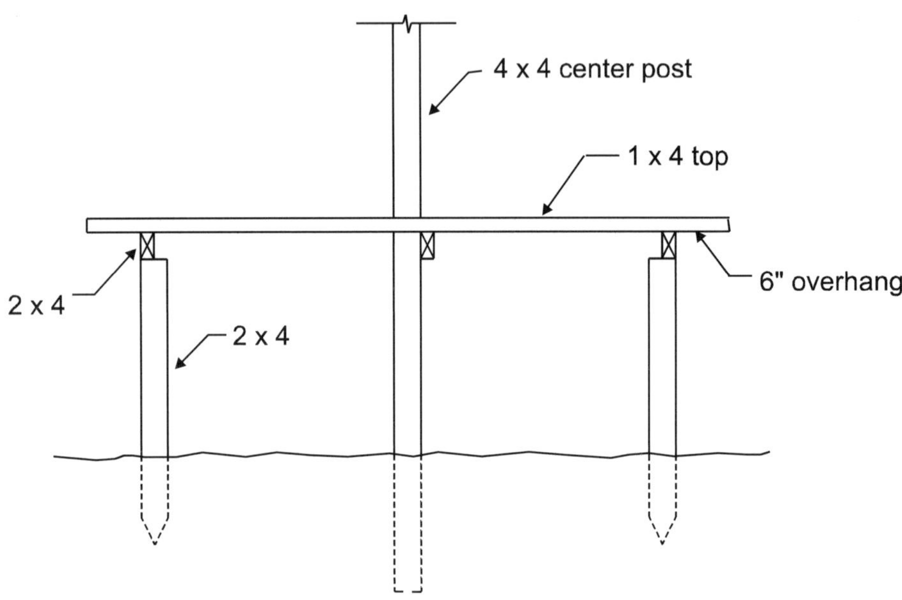

Center table assembly.

You have now completed building seedhouse tables.

If you intend to grow crops to maturity in your greenhouse the tables need to be removable. Consider hinges for attaching to walls, and folding legs.

Seedhouse Ventilators

Uniform, adequate, and even ventilation throughout the seedhouse is essential to uniform growth of plants.

The ventilators are located at two openings along the full length of the seedhouse: one just below the peak and another along the south side of the seedhouse.

The 18" opening along the length and ridge of the building, just above the south-slope roof is a continuous ventilator. This simple ventilator eliminates fans and cooling pads, yet effectively controls the temperature throughout the seedhouse.

To Make the Ventilator at the Peak

Step 1: Get Sheet of Plastic

Take a sheet of clear 6 mil plastic 24" wide x 40' long.

Step 2: Nail or Screw 1 x 2's to Plastic

Lay 1 x 2's of random length in a straight line on and along the length of the center table. Place one edge of the plastic sheet on the 1 x 2's. Place another row of 1 x 2's on top of the plastic and on top of the first row of 1 x 2's. Nail or screw the two 1 x 2's together securely with the plastic between.

Step 3: Attach Other Edge of Plastic to Stringers

Take the other edge of the plastic and, using lath, nail or screw the plastic to the 4 x 4 stringers at the peak. The ventilator is in place.

To Open and Close the Ventilator

Step 1: Fasten Metal Pulleys on North-Slope Rafters

Fasten a metal pulley on each north-slope rafter in line with each center 4 x 4 post. Fasten the pulley 24" down from the peak.

Step 2: Fasten Hooks on Center Posts

Approximately 14" above the table top fasten a hook or nail on each center 4 x 4 post.

Step 3: Attach Clothesline Rope

Take a length of clothesline rope and fasten one end securely to the 1 x 2 strip holding the plastic sheet (ventilator). Thread the rope through the pulley on the rafter and bring the end down to the hook on the post. Give the rope 18" extra length and cut it off.

Step 4: Tie Loops in Rope

Tie three loops on the rope; one on the end and the other two 12" apart from the end.

Use the ropes to regulate the amount of ventilation desired in the seedhouse.

To provide full ventilation, pull the ventilator to the full opening and anchor the ropes to the hooks on the posts.

To close the ventilator, simply unhook the ropes. The ventilator closes automatically. Because it is on the inside of the seedhouse, it is not affected by the wind.

To Make the Side Ventilator

Follow these steps to build the 18” ventilator along the south side of the seedhouse.

Step 1: Attach 1 x 8 Boards

Before you pull the cover over the seedhouse frame, nail 1 x 8 boards 20’ long in a straight line 18” below the top of the studs.

Step 2: Tack 1 x 2 Boards in Place

On the top edge of the 1 x 8’s place 1 x 2’s running the full length. Tack the 1 x 2’s only enough to stay in place.

This ventilator is not yet completed until after the seedhouse cover is installed.

Covering the Frame

Only two operations remain to complete the seedhouse. You will need cross bracing to strengthen the frame structure, and you will need to cover the frames with clear plastic film.

For added strength and stability, use 1 x 4's that are 48" to 60" long for cross-bracing in the building. Nail or screw these to the posts, rafters, and stringers.

Special formulated transparent plastic at least 6 mil thickness is sold in rolls of varying widths and lengths. The best materials have a life span of 6 to 9 years. To cover the sides and roof of a 20' x 40' seedhouse will require two sheets 18' wide x 40' long. To cover the ends of the seedhouse will take two sheets 9' wide and 20' long.

Covering a structure with plastic film is fast and easy—providing some precautions are used.

> **IMPORTANT:**
> Cover the north side and north roof with one sheet first. Attempt this only during the part of the day when the air is very still.

Step 1: Pull the Plastic Sheet over the Frame

Pull the sheet over the frame. Have the lath ready and very quickly lath the plastic to the rafters.

Step 2: Nail Plastic Sheet in Place

Use 1 ¼" lath nails or screws and nail or screw a lath to every 3rd or 4th rafter and upright stud as quickly as possible. This is a precautionary measure to hold the plastic in place in case of wind.

Step 3: Secure Plastic on Every Rafter

Nail or screw lath on every rafter and stud. The plastic must be secured with lath on every rafter and stud.

Nails or screws on the lath should be 8 to 12 inches apart. When nailed or screwed to the rafters, the lath should be tight to hold the plastic secure against flexing between the lath and the rafter or stud. When lathed to the rafters and studs as recommended, the plastic will not flex or tear and will weather strong winds for many years.

Step 4: Secure Plastic to South Side

After securing the plastic on the north side, pull a sheet of plastic over the south roof and side.

Follow the same procedure in fastening it securely as outlined for the north side.

Step 5: Secure Plastic to Ends of Structure

After completing the south side, take a sheet of plastic 9' wide x 20' long and cover each end of the building. Nail or screw lath to every upright stud. Before covering the end, hang the doors in place. The plastic covers the end including the doors.

Use lath to secure the plastic to the doors. After lathing the end and doors, cut the plastic along the door frames. The doors are free to move open and shut on their hinges.

Inspect to be sure the plastic is securely lathed to every rafter and stud.

You have now completed the seedhouse frame with plastic.

To Complete the South-Side Ventilator

Step 1: Nail or screw 1 x 2 Strip and Cut Plastic

Previously, you placed a 1 x 2 strip of lumber on the top edge of the 1 x 8 board along the south side of the structure. The plastic covers the 1 x 8 board and the 1 x 2 strip.

Take 1 x 2's and nail or screw a strip over the 1 x 2 strip under the plastic. Nail or screw the 1 x 2's securely together. Next, cut the plastic along the line separating the 1 x 2 from the 1 x 8 board. This separates the plastic and frees the 1 x 2.

Step 2: Roll Up Plastic to Open Ventilator

To open the ventilator, turn the 1 x 2 strip and roll the plastic up. When rolled up, you can hold the ventilator open using short lengths of clothesline rope attached to the rafters and hooked.

Step 3: Unhook Ropes to Close Ventilator

To close the ventilator, unhook the ropes and let the plastic unroll.

Finishing the Seedhouse

To strengthen, stabilize, and secure the seedhouse, use pieces of lumber such as 1 x 4's that are 48" to 60" long for cross braces. Nail cross braces to the posts, rafters, and stringers.

We recommend painting your seedhouse. Painting gives a finished appearance, preserves the wood, and increases the light factor in the greenhouse.

Build outside tables with flat, level tops 30" high so they are in full sun close to the seedhouse. Use the same construction procedures as you used to build the tables in the seedhouse. These tables are necessary for "hardening off" the seedlings before they are transplanted into the field or garden.

Plastic-covered greenhouses require some type of shading to lower the temperature and diffuse the bright sunlight during hot weather. Otherwise, the leaves on young seedlings will scorch from sunburn and the plants will die.

There are several types of synthetic materials available to use as shading. You can purchase these to fit nearly any size structure, and in various shading percentages. When temperatures are above 95 degrees Fahrenheit, you need 25 to 35 percent shade density.

This type of shading is quick and easy to use. Just pull the shade-cloth, called milar, over the greenhouse frame—plastic cover and all—in one sheet. The shade cloth provides uniform shade throughout the seedhouse and effectively lowers the temperature inside of the seedhouse.

During hot weather, you can stabilize the temperature in the greenhouse by opening the doors and the continuous ventilator and covering the greenhouse with shade cloth.

During short days and cooler weather, plants do best in full light. To accomplish this, just pull off the shade-cloth and store it properly until needed again.

Appendix E:

Learn More References

- Food for Everyone
- Gardening by the Foot
- Grow-Bed Gardening
- Let's Grow Tomatoes
- More Food From Your Garden aka Mittleider Grow-Box Gardens
- Six Steps to Successful Gardening
- The Garden Doctor (Books 1-3)

Food For Everyone

Offers a comprehensive treatment of the Mittleider Method with sixty-four chapters, 608 pages, and a thousand drawings, photographs, and color plates. Also provides a detailed discussion of all aspects of plant growth, soil and water, nutrients, disease and insect control, harvesting, and marketing. Large format, soft cover, $49.95. Also available on the Mittleidor Gardening Library CD.

Gardening by the Foot

Shows the Mittleider Method at work in grow-boxes. Contains numerous illustrations on how to plant and nurture food crops in limited space. Gives details and illustrations on bed construction, fertilization, harvesting. $12.95. Also available on the Mittleidor Gardening Library CD.

Grow-Bed Gardening

Describes how the Mittleider Method produces enormous increases in garden yields for both home gardeners and commercial growers in easy-to-prepare soil-beds. Includes precise, easy-to-follow methods for exact fertilization to avoid common nutritional deficiencies. Also provides valuable tips on weed control, easy care of plants, water conservation and simple greenhouse construction. Nearly 750 photographs illustrate every step. Only available as a digital download, $13.95, or on the Mittleider Gardening Library CD.

Let's Grow Tomatoes

Describes in detail the grow-box method to bountiful tomato harvests. Discusses all you need to know about growing tomatoes, from sprouting seed right through harvesting. Includes cultural methods, pruning, feeding, control of common diseases, how to grow strong seedlings, and how to overcome the problem of cracked fruit. Only available as a digital download, $10.95, or on the Mittleider Gardening Library CD.

More Food from Your Garden aka Mittleider Grow-Box Gardens

Gives simple, step-by-step instructions for setting up your own grow-box garden. Covers everything from planning and constructing grow-boxes to planting, watering and fertilizing the plants. Includes sections on building greenhouse-sheltered grow-boxes, making a simple greenhouse, and starting seedlings for transplanting. Only available as a digital download, $10.95, or on the Mittleider Gardening Library CD.

Six Steps to Successful Gardening

Describes how to apply the Mittleider Method in simple soil-bed gardens. Includes easy-to-use instructions on preparing soil-beds, transplanting and planting, watering, fertilizing, controlling weeds, and harvesting. Features a garden-planning and record-keeping guide, $10.95. Also available as a digital download, $8.95 or on the Mittleider Gardening Library CD.

The Garden Doctor (Books 1-3)

Illustrates plant deficiencies using more than 800 color photographs. Includes three volumes of detailed descriptions that teach what each nutrient does for plants and how to recognize the first and predominant symptoms of deficiency. Suggests appropriate dosages for your particular garden space, different methods of application, and the best time for treatment. Three-volume set, $49.95. Also available on the Mittleide Gardening Library CD.

You can order the books listed in this section and other valuable gardening materials by going to **www.growfood.com/shop** or by calling the following toll-free number:

888-548-4449

Appendix F:

Updates and Improvements-Too large to include on the page

P. 21 – Planting. Vegetable seeds need sustained temperatures above 60 degrees Fahrenheit to germinate and grow. Plant seedlings in your garden or use mini greenhouses to warm the soil.

P. 22 – A 16" rake is not recommended. It is too big to use comfortably in a soil-bed, and too heavy to be practi-cal for long-time use.

P. 28 – Soil in the aisle area only needs to be tilled 2-3" deep, so that soil can be moved into the bed area. Deeper tilling makes working more difficult, and brings weed seeds to the surface.

P.36 – If growing vertically using stakes plants should be planted on both sides of the soil-bed or Grow-Box. Space plants at twice the distance they would be if planted in one row using T-Frames. Each plant is tied to a stake. Example: Tomatoes planted 9" apart for T-Frames are planted 18" apart on both sides if using stakes. Spacing is alternating and stakes are placed at the top of the ridges.

P. 42 – Nitrogen – to be applied immediately after transplanting – can be (in order of preference) ammonium nitrate (34-0-0), urea for areas of high rainfall (46-0-0), ammonium sulfate for low rainfall areas (21-0-0), or calcium nitrate if others are not available.

P. 51 – (1) The Pre-Plant formula is lime (or gypsum), magnesium sulfate, and 20 Mule Team Borax in the of 80-4-1. However extensive experience gives evidence that good results can be achieved by simply applying calcium (1 oz/ft) and Weekly Feed (1/2 oz/ft) to the soil before planting, and thereafter including lime or gypsumin the Weekly Feed Mix (<= 10%). This represents a significant simplification of the fertilizing regimen while reducing the incidents of calcium deficiencies later in the year.

(2) "6 teaspoons equal one ounce" and " a pint is a pound the world around" refer to liquid measurements. Fertilizers are often significantly heavier than water, therefore most accurate feeding is done by weighing the needed amount and then marking the feeding container.

P.53 If you are mixing your own Weekly Feed, following are alternative materials. Because many states have outlawed the sale of ammonium nitrate, substitution of urea (46-0-0) or ammonium sulfate (21-0-0) may be necessary. If using ammonium sulfate, increase amounts by 50%. If using urea, use the same amount as recommended for ammonium nitrate.

Phosphorus may be available as diammonium phosphate (DAP – 18-46-0), in which case use 8# 4 oz N and 4# 8 oz DAP. If monoammonium phosphate (MAP – 11-53-0) is available use 9# 5 oz N and 3# 13 oz MAP.

Potassium may only be available as potassium sulfate (0-0-50). If so use 7# 3 oz.

P. 78 - **Reasons to eliminate weeds**: 1. Fertilizers are too costly to be used for growing weeds. 2. Insects and diseases are more difficult to control with weeds in the garden. 3. Weeds reduce crop yields by taking up space, air, food, and water.

Sprout and destroy surface weeds and remove them when no taller than one inch.

Do not cultivate to remove weeds, as cultivation can damage crop roots (root pruning). Cultivation also brings more weed seeds to the surface.

Crop increases of 100% - 600% have resulted from weed control in tropical climates.

P. 84 – Sand should be between 25% and 40%. Other materials that can be combined with sand include coconut husks, rice hulls, coffee hulls, and pine needles.

P. 92 – If growing vertically using stakes plants should be planted on both sides of the soil-bed or Grow-Box. Space plants at twice the distance they would be if planted in one row using T-Frames. Each plant is tied to a stake. Example: Tomatoes planted 9" apart for T-Frames are planted 18" apart on both sides if using stakes. Spacing is alternating and stakes are placed at the top of the ridges.

P. 94 - A useful rule of thumb for seed planting depth is 2 1/2 times the seed thickness. Tiny seeds can be planted 4 times the seed thickness. All seeds should be covered with sand or custom soil mix, rather than native soil.

P. 107 – (1) The Pre-Plant formula is lime (or gypsum), magnesium sulfate, and 20 Mule Team Borax in the ratio of 80-4-1. However extensive experience gives evidence that good results can be achieved by simply applying calcium (1 oz/ft) and Weekly Feed (1/2 oz/ft) to the soil before planting, and thereafter including lime or gypsum in the Weekly Feed Mix (<= 10%). This represents a significant simplification of the fertilizing regimen while assuring there are no calcium deficiencies later in the year.

(2) "6 teaspoons equal one ounce" and " a pint is a pound the world around" refer to liquid measurements. Fertilizers are often significantly heavier than water, therefore most accurate feeding is done by weighing the needed amount and then marking the feeding container.

P. 109 – The simplest solution for finding and mixing the Weekly Feed Mix is to purchase 25# of 16-16-16, then mix with 4# of Epsom Salt and a 10 oz packet of Micro-Nutrients (purchase @ www.growfood.com/shop).

If you are mixing your own Weekly Feed, following are alternative materials. Because many states have outlawed the sale of ammonium nitrate, substitution of urea (46-0-0) or ammonium sulfate (21-0-0) may be necessary. If using ammonium sulfate, increase amounts by 50%. If using urea, use the same amount as recommended for ammonium nitrate.

Phosphorus may be available as diammonium phosphate (DAP – 18-46-0), in which case use 8# 4 oz N and 4# 8 oz DAP. If monoammonium phosphate (MAP – 11-53-0) is available use 9# 5 oz N and 3# 13 oz MAP.

Potassium may only be available as potassium sulfate (0-0-50). If so use 7# 3 oz.

P. 119 – Pruning of sucker stems on tomatoes supported by stakes should still be done. To the extent that plants are further apart and more space is available, you can allow 2 or 3 vines per plant. Failure to prune sucker stems will leave you with a crowded, messy plant and garden, and reduce yields.

P. 155 – Amending clay soil is time consuming and costly. Consider this alternative: When preparing to plant, mix 1 part seeds with 100 parts sand, then spread thinly in a shallow furrow evenly throughout the intended planting distance. Cover only with sand. If cracks appear in the clay soil, cover cracks with sand, and water until cracks are filled in. Repeat as needed. Sand required per 30'-long soil-bed is 10-20#.

P. 178 – Greenhouse direction does not really matter. Just plant tall plants north or east of shorter plants, so that all plants receive maximum exposure to sunlight.

P. 270 – Illustration of In-The-Garden Greenhouse - Automated watering system to be placed 7" in from outside edges of box. 5 - 6" 2 X 4 supports for PVC pipe in 30' length. Stakes on exterior of box to be placed at 3" intervals. Arched PVC to be placed at 2' intervals and supported/tied together in the center by 1 X 2 strips of wood attached to pipe with plumbing strap and screws. 2 X 4 vertical support at each T-Frame supports the center of the arched roof.

Appendix G:

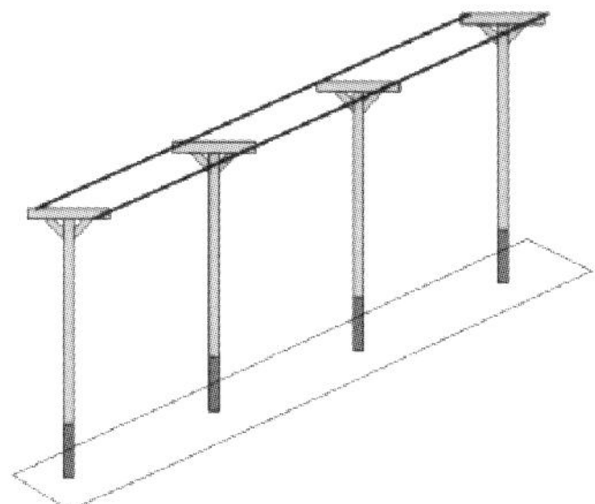

HOW TO BUILD & USE T-FRAMES

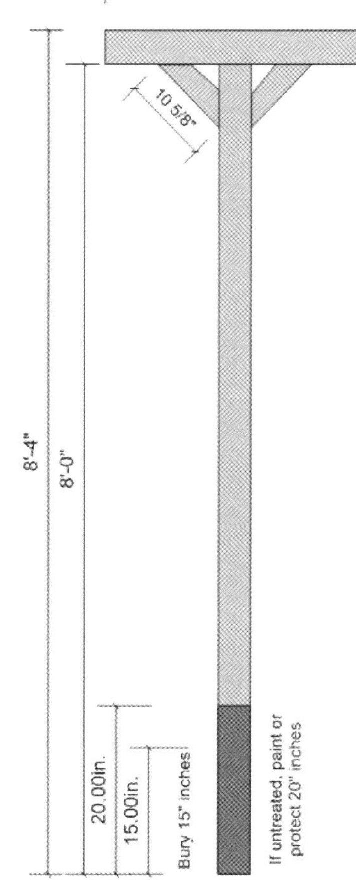

Author: Jim Kennard
Illustrations: James Gledhill

Supplies

The quantities below are required to build 4 T-Frames.
This is enough for one 30' foot-long grow bed

Quantity	Item / Description
6	**8' foot-long Treated 4x4** 4 of these will be used for the 4 post. The other two will be cut into sections for crossbars and support braces
8	**6" inch-long nails (spikes)** These are to attach the crossbar to the post
32	**Smaller nails or screws** These will be used to attach the support braces to the crossbar and the main post.

Construction

1. Set four of the 4x4's aside. They will be the main posts
2. Cut the other two 4x4's into equal lengths of 32" inches long.
   a. Four of these 32" inch pieces will be the top cross bar of the T-Frames
3. Mark two of the 32" inch long 4x4's as follows (see the diagram below for more detail)
   a. On the bottom of the 4x4, mark at the following locations — from left to right.
      i. 10 5/8", then 3 5/8", then 10 5/8", then 3 5/8"
   b. On the top of the 4x4, mark at the following locations — from left to right.
      i. 3 1/2", then 3 5/8", then 10 5/8", then 3 5/8"
   c. Draw lines between these marks, then, using a table saw, cut on the lines.
4. Pre-drill through the top center of the 32" tops, then use a 6" spike to nail into the 8' post.
5. Screw or nail the braces to the top and post.
6. If you feel like your wood could use more treatment where it will be placed in the ground, paint or cover the bottom 20" inches with exterior paint or roofing tar

Your T-Frame should look like the diagram above.

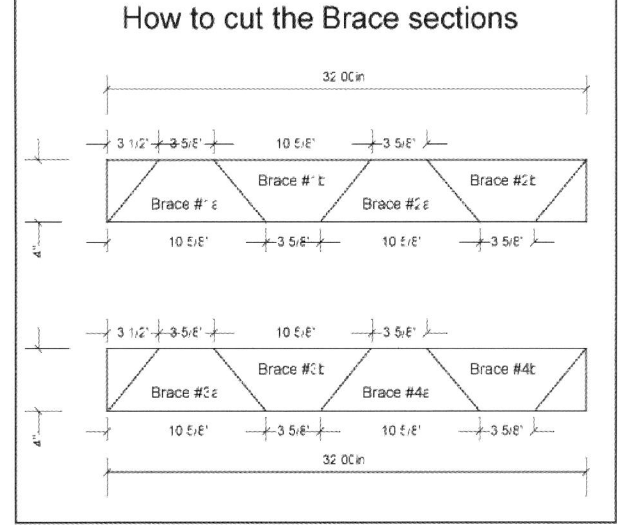

Put in the garden

1. Bury the T-Frame 15" in the ground at 10' foot (or shorter) intervals. T-Frames should be placed on the same side as your single-row ofplants. The outside edge of the post should be lined up with the top ofthe soil-bed ridge.
2. Install the wire/pipe between the "T"'s on the outside edges. Some options are:
   a. Use 1/2" galvanized pipe held in place by two nails (you may be able to find this at "junk/scrap" metal places), or
   b. Use 1/2" rebar, or
   c. Use 2 X 4's on edge (or other strong supports you can findfor a good price), or
   d. Use #8 gage wire and eyebolts between the T-Frames (this is very heavy gage wire — do not use smaller wire). Braces must be used on the outside "T"s to keep them from being pulled together by the weight of the fruit.
3. Attach a tie-wire to the outside edge of the "T"s at ground level — the tie-wire will follow the ridge. Nail 1 %" inch nails to the outside edge of the "T" and wrap tie-wire around the nail. Tightly stretch the tie-wire to the next "T" and wrap around that nail. Do this with each "T" until the end of the bed.

NOTE: *The weight on the support wire/pipe become very heavy as the plants grow. These supports need to be very strong to support that weight.*

How to use

1. Cut 9 %' feet lengths of bailing twine for each plant. Tie a knot on each end of the twine so they do not unravel. This way you can re-use them next year.
2. Tie the bailing twine with a slip knot to the wire/pipe at the top of the "T'. Alternate sides for each plant — left, right, left, right, etc. This creates an alternating "V" that allows the maximum sunlight in.
3. Attach bailing twine from both sides of the wire/pipe at the top of the "T" down to single tie-wire near the base of the plants.
4. As the plants grow, guide them up the bailing twine, alternating sides for each plant.
5. Remember to remove and prune suckers. (See Mittleider Gardening Course, Chapter 15 for details)

NOTE: *If you want to **extend the growing season**, use 2 X 4's on edge at the top of the "T", and make an arched canopy with 3/4" PVC and 45 degree Slip fittings every 2', then cover in early Spring and late Fall with 6 mil clear plastic. And for those in **hot climates** place 25-30% shade cloth on top of the arched canopy only sufficient to give partial shade during the hottest 3 hours of the day. This can help your tomatoes, etc. continue fruiting in the heat of summer.*

Cutting Details

The diagram to the right shows the major cuts used for the six 4x4 post.

Four posts kept un-cut at the full 8' feet.

Two posts are cut in three equal lengths of 32" inches. Four of these sections are used for the top crossbars.

The remaining two sections of 32" inches are cut for the supporting braces. (See diagram above)

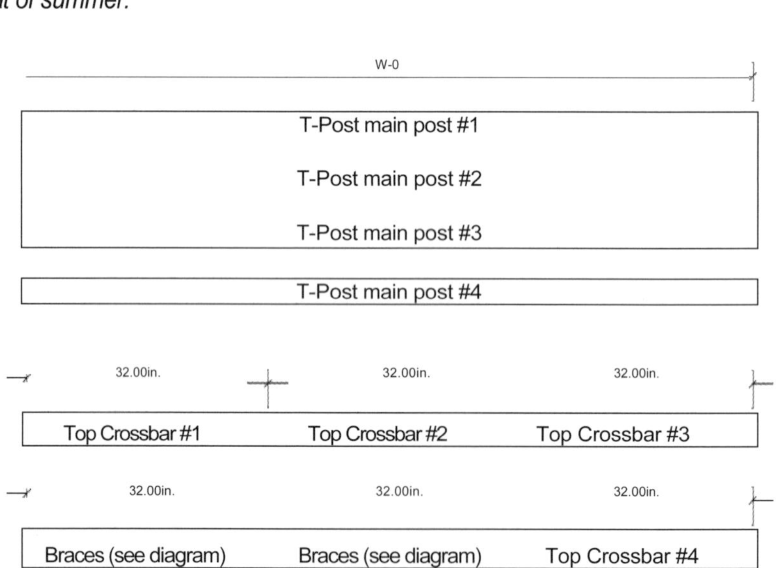

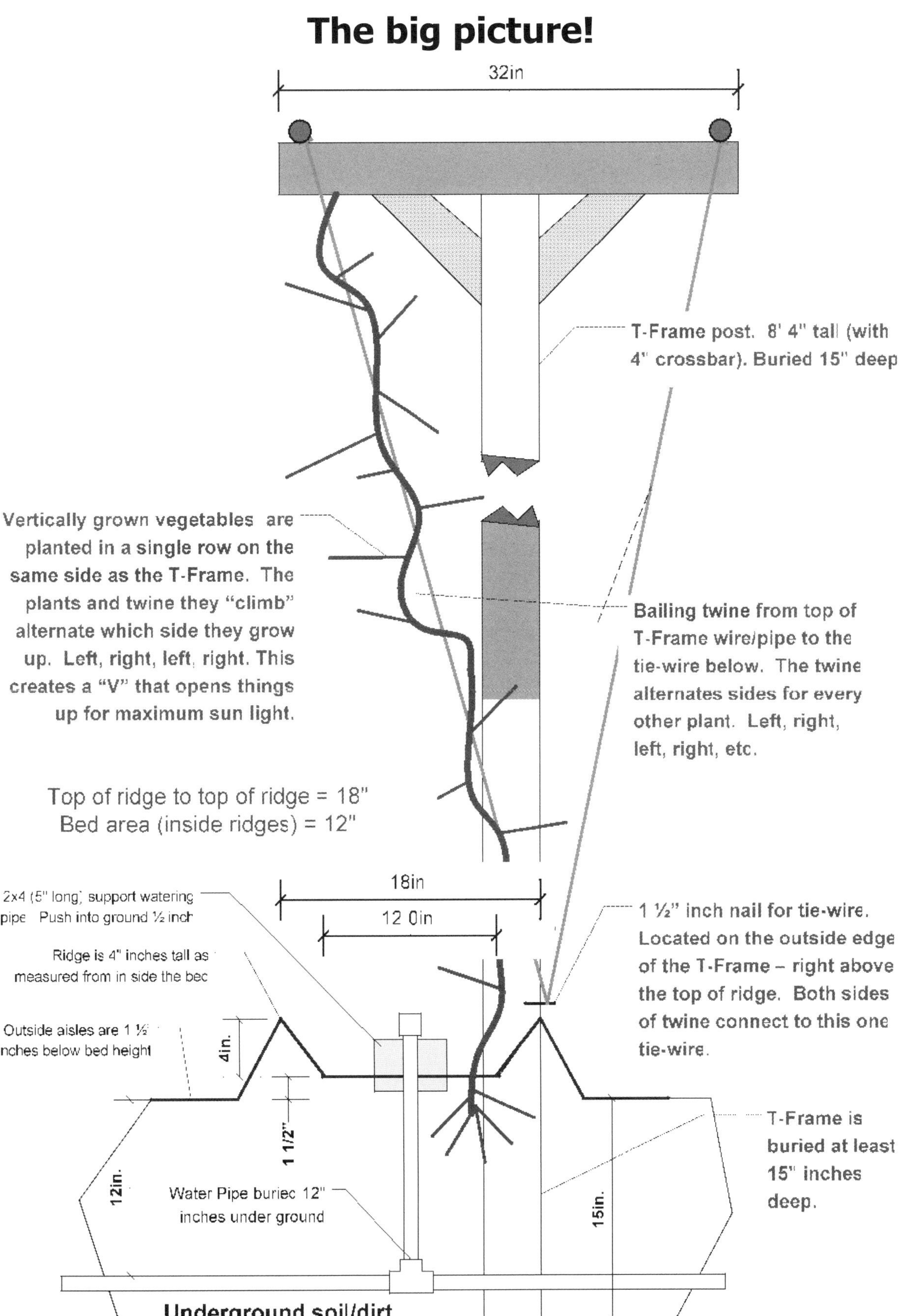
The big picture!
32in
T-Frame post. 8' 4" tall (with 4" crossbar). Buried 15" deep.
Vertically grown vegetables are planted in a single row on the same side as the T-Frame. The plants and twine they "climb" alternate which side they grow up. Left, right, left, right. This creates a "V" that opens things up for maximum sun light.
Bailing twine from top of T-Frame wire/pipe to the tie-wire below. The twine alternates sides for every other plant. Left, right, left, right, etc.
Top of ridge to top of ridge = 18"
Bed area (inside ridges) = 12"
18in
12 0in
2x4 (5" long) support watering pipe Push into ground ½ inch
Ridge is 4" inches tall as measured from in side the bed
Outside aisles are 1 ½ inches below bed height
4in.
1 1/2"
12in.
Water Pipe buried 12" inches under ground
15in.
1 ½" inch nail for tie-wire. Located on the outside edge of the T-Frame – right above the top of ridge. Both sides of twine connect to this one tie-wire.
T-Frame is buried at least 15" inches deep.
Underground soil/dirt

4’-Wide Grow-Box — In-The-Garden Greenhouse

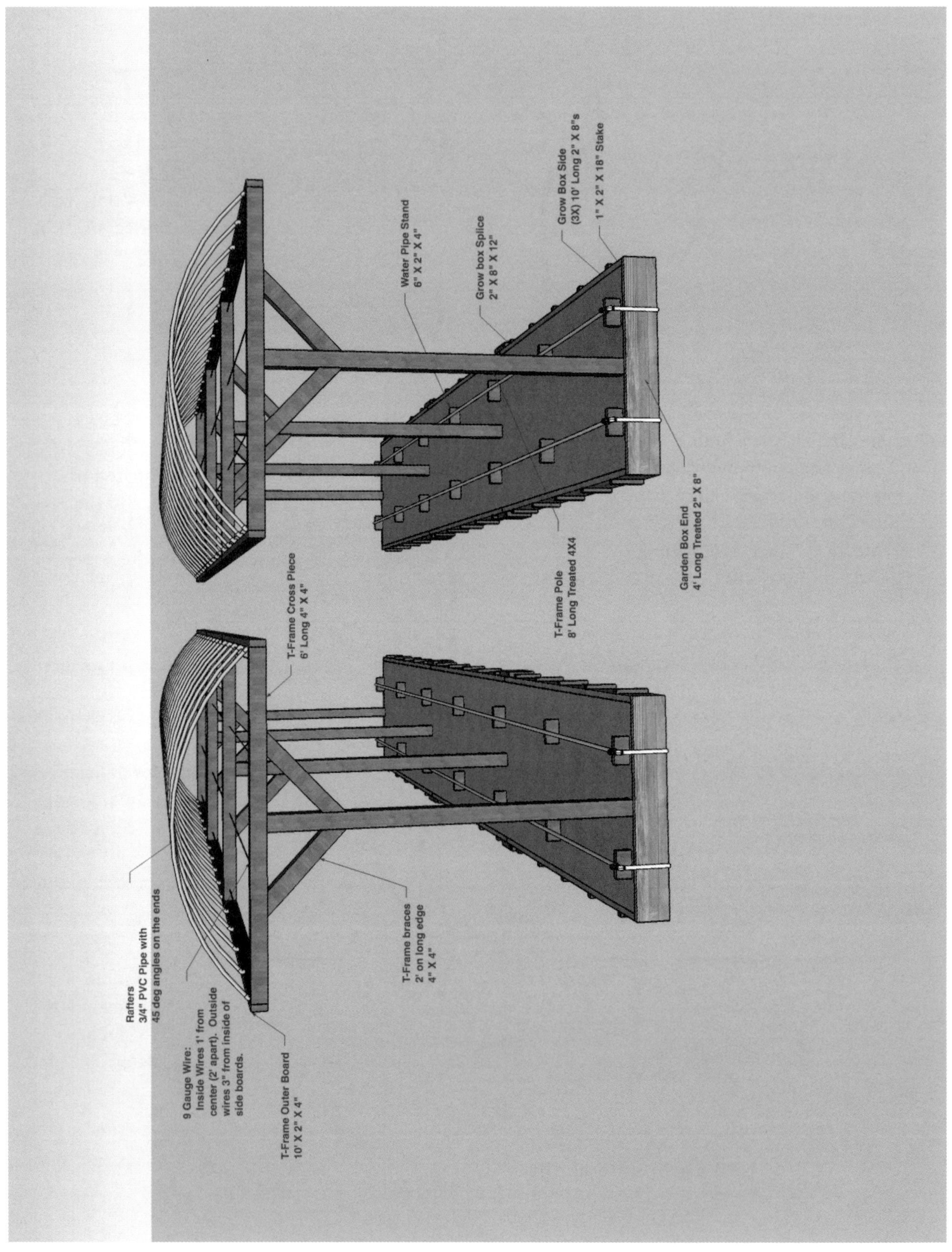

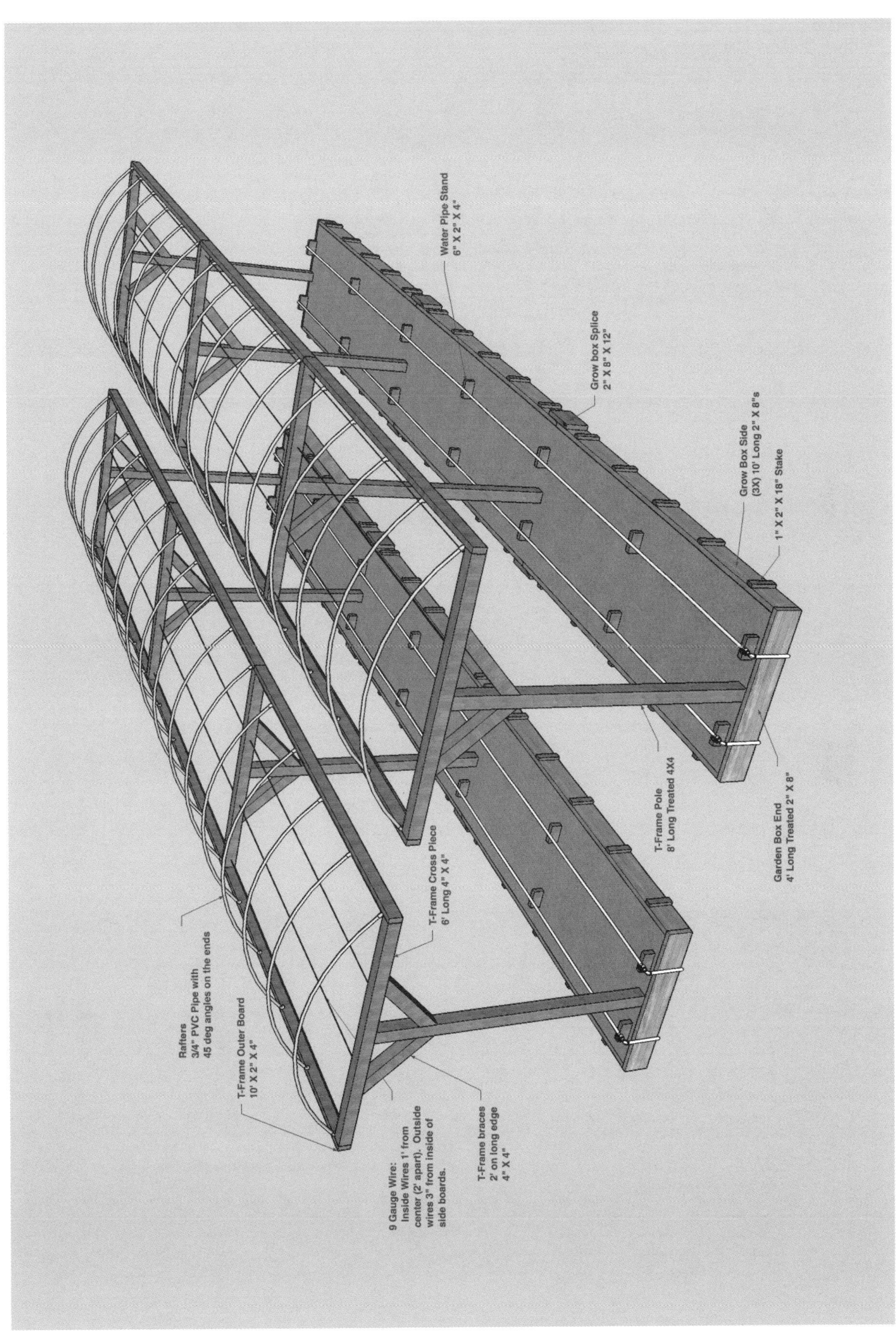
Rafters
3/4" PVC Pipe with
45 deg angles on the ends
T-Frame Outer Board
10' X 2" X 4"
9 Gauge Wire:
Inside Wires 1' from
center (2' apart). Outside
wires 3" from inside of
side boards.
T-Frame braces
2' on long edge
4" X 4"
T-Frame Cross Piece
6' Long 4" X 4"
T-Frame Pole
8' Long Treated 4X4
Garden Box End
4' Long Treated 2" X 8"
1" X 2" X 18" Stake
Grow Box Side
(3X) 10' Long 2" X 8"s
Grow box Splice
2" X 8" X 12"
Water Pipe Stand
6" X 2" X 4"

Index

R

S

Y

Z